OECD Economic Surveys

Euro Area

2009

OECD

ORGANISATION FOR ECONOMIC CO-OPERATION AND DEVELOPMENT

The OECD is a unique forum where the governments of 30 democracies work together to address the economic, social and environmental challenges of globalisation. The OECD is also at the forefront of efforts to understand and to help governments respond to new developments and concerns, such as corporate governance, the information economy and the challenges of an ageing population. The Organisation provides a setting where governments can compare policy experiences, seek answers to common problems, identify good practice and work to co-ordinate domestic and international policies.

The OECD member countries are: Australia, Austria, Belgium, Canada, the Czech Republic, Denmark, Finland, France, Germany, Greece, Hungary, Iceland, Ireland, Italy, Japan, Korea, Luxembourg, Mexico, the Netherlands, New Zealand, Norway, Poland, Portugal, the Slovak Republic, Spain, Sweden, Switzerland, Turkey, the United Kingdom and the United States. The Commission of the European Communities takes part in the work of the OECD.

OECD Publishing disseminates widely the results of the Organisation's statistics gathering and research on economic, social and environmental issues, as well as the conventions, guidelines and standards agreed by its members.

Also available in French

Corrigenda to OECD publications may be found on line at: *www.oecd.org/publishing/corrigenda*.

Table of contents

Boxes

Tables

Figures

OECD ECONOMIC SURVEYS: EURO AREA – ISBN 978-92-64-04824-9 – © OECD 20

This Survey *is published on the responsibility of the Economic and Development Review Committee of the OECD, which is charged with the examination of the economic situation of member countries.*

The economic situation and policies of the euro area were reviewed by the Committee on 15 October 2008. The draft report was then revised in the light of the discussions and given final approval as the agreed report of the whole Committee on 20 November 2008.

The Secretariat's draft report was prepared for the Committee by Nigel Pain, Jeremy Lawson, Marte Sollie and Sebastian Barnes under the supervision of Peter Hoeller. Research assistance was provided by Isabelle Duong.

The previous Survey of the euro area *was issued in January 2007.*

BASIC STATISTICS (2007)

	Euro area	United States	Japan
LAND AND PEOPLE			
Area (thousand km^2)	2 456	9 167	395
Population (million)	317.2	302.1	127.8
Number of inhabitants per km^2	129	33	323
Population growth (1997-2007, annual average % rate)	0.5	1.0	0.1
Labour force (million)	151.7	153.1	66.7
Unemployment rate (%)	7.4	4.6	3.9
ACTIVITY			
GDP (billion USD, current prices and exchange rates)	12 195.4	13 741.6	4 376.0
Per capita GDP (USD, current prices and PPPs)	32 372	45 489	32 006
In per cent of GDP:			
Gross fixed capital formation	21.8	18.8	23.2
Exports of goods and services	22.5	12.0	17.6
Imports of goods and services	21.3	17.2	15.9
PUBLIC FINANCE (per cent of GDP)			
General government:			
Revenue	45.1	34.3	32.2
Expenditure	46.1	37.4	35.8
Balance	–0.6	–2.9	–2.4
Gross public debt (end-year)	71.4	62.9	170.6
EXCHANGE RATE (national currency per euro)			
Average 2007		1.3705	161.3
October 2008		1.3322	133.5

EURO AREA – EXTERNAL TRADE IN GOODS (main partners, % of total flows, in 2007)

	Exports	Imports
Denmark, Sweden, United Kingdom	20.7	15.6
Other European Union member countries	15.4	12.2
Other Europe	17.0	17.1
OECD America	15.4	11.4
OECD Asia/Pacific	4.8	7.0
Non-OECD dynamic Asian[1] and China	7.8	16.1

1. Chinese Taipei; Hong Kong, China; Indonesia; Malaysia; Philippines; Singapore and Thailand.

SHARE IN EURO AREA GDP

Current market prices, 2007

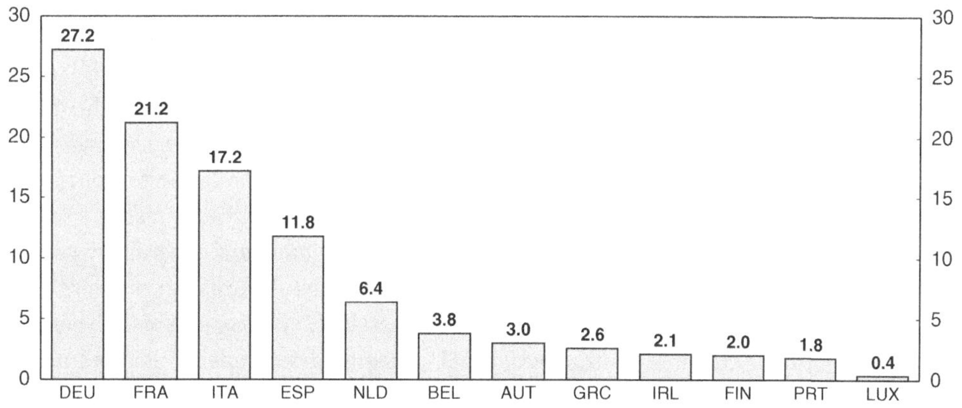

StatLink http://dx.doi.org/10.1787/518067783846

Executive summary

After a sustained period of good macroeconomic performance, new challenges have emerged for the euro area economy. Output growth moderated through 2007 and continued to lose momentum through 2008, with GDP declining in both the second and third quarters of the year. The slowdown has been compounded by the international financial market turmoil that began in August 2007 and intensified in September 2008. World economic activity has slowed markedly. Earlier increases in commodity prices drove inflation well above the European Central Bank's price stability objective, though it has subsequently fallen back.

Although the euro area initially weathered these shocks, output is now expected to contract in the second half of 2008 and the first half of 2009, with growth remaining below trend until mid-2010. Money market pressures had been contained by the central bank until recently but credit conditions for the private sector have tightened. However, a sharp contraction in bank credit has not yet occurred. Although upside risks to price stability have not completely disappeared, there is little evidence as yet of broad-based second-round effects and price expectations appear to have remained well anchored. There are, however, serious risks to the growth outlook. National and European authorities need to continue to assess and respond to developments in financial markets and the wider economy. This episode of financial instability has highlighted the need for adequate regulation of financial activity, which is a particular challenge in Europe's increasingly integrated capital market. It poses challenges for the authorities in the short term. In reacting to these developments, policy actions that would undermine longer term objectives should be avoided. There remain long-run challenges to achieve fiscal sustainability, improve macroeconomic resilience and raise living standards by enhancing structural reforms in European markets.

Financial innovation and integration have changed the landscape. *The European financial system has developed and become more integrated, although more could be done to enhance competition in retail banking. Credit growth has been buoyant, large complex cross-border banking groups have emerged and financial innovations have created possibilities for greater risk diversification, but have also increased risk-taking. This has increased the inter-linkages between national markets and is likely to have changed the transmission of monetary policy to economic activity.*

Strengthening the policy framework to deal with systemic risks in the financial system. *The on-going financial market turmoil associated with an unwinding of the credit cycle and the recent freezing in the interbank market has posed a major challenge to policy makers. Co-ordinated action by the European and national authorities has been taken to restore confidence in financial markets. Recent events also point to weaknesses in regulatory and supervisory frameworks which are being addressed at the European and international level. Although progress has been made, it is essential to reflect on how to align national supervisory systems to deal with cross-border risks by moving towards more centralised and EU integrated supervision. Policies need to be developed to deal with macro-prudential risks and ensure that regulation does not increase the pro-cyclicality of the financial system.*

The balance of risks to price stability has changed. *Headline inflation has reached very high levels but has recently decreased, and inflation expectations remain well anchored. With inflationary pressures diminishing, the ECB has cut its policy rate in concert with other central banks. The OECD projections suggest that substantial economic slack would develop over the next year, helping to bring down inflation further. Given these baseline projections, room for further easing of monetary policy could emerge. However, there is an unusual amount of uncertainty surrounding the economic outlook. If inflationary pressures turn out to be stronger than anticipated, room for manoeuvre will be constrained. Monetary policy should be ready to react should long-term inflation expectations become unanchored.*

Fiscal discipline should be improved further. *Fiscal performance in the euro area improved following the revision of the Stability and Growth Pact, helped by very favourable revenue growth, although in some member states sizeable deficits remained. The economic downturn and the costs of emergency actions taken by governments to stabilise financial markets will add to fiscal pressures. The long-run challenges due to the ageing of the population remain large and, in general, there is no strong case for discretionary fiscal expansion as the economy slows. Improving the quality of public finances, both on the spending and taxation side, would help to raise living standards.*

ISBN 978-92-64-04824-9
OECD Economic Surveys: Euro Area

Assessment and recommendations

The euro area achieved a high degree of macroeconomic stability over the first decade of economic and monetary union. The end of exchange rate turbulence and realignments within the euro area has proved to be a major asset. However, the financial market turmoil since the summer of 2007 and the intensification from mid-September 2008 is having a major adverse impact on the world economy. Although the immediate cause of the turmoil lay in the US subprime mortgage market, euro area financial institutions and markets were part of the prolonged credit cycle of recent years, and have been hit by heightened financial market stress. The current turmoil is the first financial crisis the euro area has had to face. It initially coincided with a very sharp increase in energy and food prices, as well as a substantial appreciation of the euro which mitigated the inflationary impact but reduced competitiveness. Today's priority for all member states is to find responses to the financial crisis and ensure their swift implementation. In reacting to these developments, policy actions that would undermine longer term objectives should be avoided. The necessary response to the possibility of financial instability touches many areas of policy making. It involves financial regulators, supervisors, central banks and finance ministries. This Survey reviews recent developments, looks at both monetary and fiscal policy and focuses on the nexus of issues related to financial markets. The macroeconomic analysis covers the euro area, while many aspects of financial regulation relate to national and European Union responsibilities within the European single market. Other structural issues related to growth will be dealt with in greater depth in the 2009 *Economic Survey of the European Union.*

The economic cycle has turned and growth has slowed

Economic activity began to slow in the early part of 2007 and has steadily lost momentum, with output declining in both the second and third quarters of 2008. The previous five years had seen a sustained upturn in activity, boosted by strong export and investment growth. Consumption had nevertheless remained relatively weak, accounted for by a high rate of household saving and muted growth of disposable income. With demand tending towards capacity, monetary policy was tightened from December 2005. The euro appreciated steadily and, by mid-2008, was 30% higher in nominal effective terms than in mid-2002. It remains at an elevated level despite recent declines. Since growth began to slow, the euro area has been hit by three major macroeconomic shocks: energy and food prices have risen sharply, the global credit cycle has turned, leading to prolonged and severe turmoil in international financial markets, and the housing cycle has peaked in several countries.

The turmoil was triggered by events in the US subprime mortgage market, which had a widespread impact on financial markets. These events marked the turning of a much broader and sustained credit cycle, in which long-term interest rates fell to well below their long-run average, risk-taking increased and asset prices rose. The credit cycle boosted housing markets in many countries: euro area house prices have increased by around 50% over the past five years. As the cycle has reversed, market participants have become more risk averse, the cost of capital has increased and financial asset prices have declined. The aggregate effect of these shocks has begun to be felt in the euro area, despite the cushioning impact of the euro appreciation on import prices, the lower oil intensity of output, the less pronounced housing cycle, the relatively strong household balance sheet position, and greater distance from the financial activities at the heart of the crisis. The latest OECD projections suggest that output will decline further in the fourth quarter of 2008 and the first half of 2009 before recovering gradually. Growth is not expected to move above trend rates until the latter half of 2010.

Monetary policy must ensure that price stability is maintained in the face of volatile rates of inflation and the impact of the ongoing financial turmoil

Monetary policy was tightened between late 2005 and July 2008, with the policy rate increasing from 2 to 4¼ per cent to address upside risks to price stability. Policy rates were reduced by 50 basis points in October 2008 in co-ordination with six other central banks, reflecting declining commodity prices, moderating inflationary pressures, and diminishing inflation expectations. An additional 50 basis point cut was made in early November. Furthermore, the intensification of the financial turmoil in the second half of September 2008 has augmented the downside risks to growth and diminished further the upside risks to price stability. *Ex ante* real rates now appear to be close to or below their long-run average. But credit spreads remain elevated due to the financial market turmoil and bank lending standards are tighter than before the turmoil, although the pace of credit expansion to the non-financial sector has slowed only gradually. The nominal exchange rate appreciated substantially, although it has fallen back somewhat since the spring of 2008. Despite the recent substantial cut in policy rates, financial conditions are not particularly accommodative.

Inflation rose substantially from the early part of 2007, reaching 4% in mid-2008. It had previously remained close to, but above the European Central Bank's definition of price stability. The sharp increase in inflation was largely due to an unanticipated surge in global energy and food prices, over which domestic monetary policy has little influence. Core inflation (excluding energy and food) has remained below 2% and services inflation has been steady at around 2½ per cent. This suggests that broad-based second-round effects have remained limited so far, although unit labour cost growth has risen, suggesting that underlying price pressures remain. Higher energy costs also dampen potential growth. Headline inflation has declined since July 2008 and if the recent weakening in commodity prices is sustained, it could drop well below 2% during the course of 2009 according to the OECD projections. With weak output growth, sizeable economic slack may develop, provided potential growth does not slow excessively, moderating underlying wage and price pressures. Given these baseline projections, room for further easing of monetary policy would emerge. However, there is an unusual amount of uncertainty surrounding this baseline scenario. If financial conditions were to be more severe than anticipated, or activity to drop particularly rapidly, deeper interest rate reductions could prove necessary. On the other hand, if inflationary pressures are stronger than anticipated, room for manoeuvre will be constrained. Monetary policy should be ready to react should long-term inflation expectations become unanchored.

The ECB has established a sound policy framework, but the communications framework could be refined

The euro has successfully established itself as a stable currency and the ECB has developed a sophisticated framework for setting monetary policy. Over the first ten years of monetary union, inflation has been close to, but just above, 2% on average and has been relatively stable around that level both compared with past experience and the performance of other developed economies. This achievement has been underpinned by the ECB's two-pillar strategy. Clear communication is an important part of this success, although further enhancements should be introduced. It is recommended that the ECB publishes forecasts showing to the public quarterly profiles sufficiently far into the future for first-round effects from shocks and policy changes to be completely absorbed, as they may help shape expectations about future inflation. However, any enhancement of the current projections should be done in full accord with the ECB's two-pillar strategy which already links medium-term inflation expectations to monetary developments. In this context, more detailed and regular explanation of analysis under the monetary pillar of the ECB's framework could provide more information to the public about the implications of current monetary growth for future inflation and the basis on which policy rates are set. The decision of the Governing Council of the ECB from 2007 to further enhance its monetary analysis along a number of well-defined avenues should help to address the need for further information.

Liquidity management has contained the immediate impact of the financial turmoil on money markets

The current episode of financial instability has seen marked turmoil in the money markets. The difficulty of assessing the value of exposures related to the US subprime mortgage market made banks reluctant to lend to each other. As a result, money market interest rates rose sharply. The ECB and other central banks provided liquidity to the banking system through various types of refinancing operations. Although greater liquidity provision contained the increase in spreads on money market lending during the first phase of the financial turmoil, the intensification of financial stress in September and early October of 2008 caused spreads to increase dramatically. This in turn has brought about further co-ordinated liquidity injections from the ECB and other central banks. The ECB has needed to make relatively few changes to its operational framework as a wide range of collateral was already accepted, many institutions had access to its monetary operations, and banks are required to hold relatively high levels of reserves, which are remunerated. The ECB has used the flexibility of its framework to enhance market liquidity, particularly since the intensification of financial turmoil in mid-September 2008. For example, the ECB introduced a fixed rate tender with full allotment for its main refinancing operations and widened its list of eligible collateral. Action and communication by the ECB helped to contain the increase in market interest rates, although these remain higher than before the turmoil began. Consideration should be given to the lessons that can be learnt from this episode for collateral pricing and risk control.

European financial markets have become deeper and more integrated, transforming the financial landscape

Considerable progress has been made in integrating and deepening European financial markets during the first decade of monetary union, including the cross-border consolidation of financial companies and infrastructures. The introduction of the euro has created broader and deeper capital markets for debt securities and equity financing, and new policies have helped to bring down barriers to the provision of financial services across borders and create new common payments infrastructures. Financial innovation and enhanced market integration have increased competitive pressures and facilitated financial deepening. The assets and liabilities of households, businesses and financial institutions have risen markedly relative to incomes and output, and the geographical distribution of assets has become more dispersed. But, impediments to cross-border provision of financial services remain, especially in mortgage markets, and policy should do more to foster integration, for instance, by improving the access of foreign institutions to national credit and land registries and harmonising the cost and duration of foreclosure procedures. Supervisory and regulatory practices will have to keep pace with deeper cross-border integration.

Financial market growth and financial innovation have widened the range of financing and investment opportunities available to households and companies. Ultimately, such changes should be beneficial for growth prospects. The changes will also affect the speed and extent to which monetary policy decisions are transmitted to the euro area economy. Some channels of policy transmission have strengthened over the past decade and new channels have appeared, while others may have become weaker. Greater opportunities for risk-taking are likely to exacerbate potential non-linearities in the transmission of policy, with policy-induced changes in asset and collateral values also affecting risk perceptions and risk tolerance. The overall balance of such changes is difficult to evaluate, given the comparatively short time period for which data are available, but the analytical work of the Eurosystem Monetary Transmission Network should be revisited and updated.

Sound financial regulation is needed to manage risks to financial stability

More integrated and developed financial markets in Europe have contributed to economic growth and fostered resilience as larger and more diversified financial systems are better placed to absorb economic shocks. However, it may also open up additional channels for the transmission of financial shocks, including across borders. Moreover, several new financial products have contributed to more risk taking. The appropriate design of regulation is a complex issue, which requires the balancing of stability, innovation and growth considerations. It is unlikely that future episodes of instability can be avoided altogether. It will always be challenging for regulators and supervisors to stay informed, because of information asymmetries, about the institutions they supervise and to keep pace with innovations and their potential impact on the stability of financial markets. The European single capital market continues to be heavily reliant on co-operation between national regulators working within differing supervisory structures, having different responsibilities, instruments and powers. Against this background, it is necessary to continue efforts to ensure a level playing field, to enhance the sharing of information between regulators and supervisors and to align the incentives of national authorities with the cross-border impact of their institutions.

The on-going global financial market turmoil has raised a number of issues about how institutions should be regulated and supervised. European authorities are participating in a number of international initiatives to respond to the weaknesses revealed by the financial instability. In October 2007, the Economic and Financial Affairs Council (ECOFIN) agreed a specific roadmap of policy actions in the wake of the onset of financial turmoil, consistent with recommendations made at the international level, *i.e.* notably the Financial Stability Forum and the G7. The Council agreed on a work programme, aimed at reviewing, along with the EU's international partners, how to further improve transparency, valuation processes, risk management and market functioning. EU authorities should continue to follow international initiatives closely. The main policy priorities are:

- Improving transparency through enhanced disclosure of risk, improved valuation methods and a more comprehensive picture of off-balance sheet entities.
- Changing the role of credit rating agencies and improving their functioning.
- Strengthening risk management standards and procedures, and providing better incentives to hold appropriate levels of capital. Liquidity risk management should be improved.
- Regulators and supervisors should become more responsive to risks. This requires: better information about financial developments; a well-defined framework for liquidity provision in conjunction with the monetary authorities; enhanced mechanisms for identifying and dealing with failing banks at an early stage; more effective and specific bankruptcy procedures for banks; and better cross-border supervisory arrangements.
- Ensuring that adequate deposit-insurance schemes are in place and that payouts are swift and predictable.
- Developing policies to reduce the pro-cyclicality of financial regulations and policies that can be used to "lean against the wind" such as smoothing capital and provisioning requirements.

Concrete steps have been taken by the EU authorities in these areas. The European Commission has already put forward a revision of EU rules on deposit guarantee schemes.

In response to the intensification of the financial turmoil in September and early October 2008, individual countries initially pursed a wide variety of responses, including comprehensive packages to recapitalise the banking system, *ad hoc* measures to recapitalise or provide emergency funding to individual financial institutions, providing blanket guarantees of all retail deposits, and guaranteeing that no financial institutions would be allowed to fail. These initiatives were followed by a co-ordinated rescue plan for the EU banking system adopted by the European Council in mid-October. This committed governments to:

- Ensuring appropriate liquidity conditions for financial institutions.
- Providing financial institutions with additional capital resources and allow for efficient recapitalisation of banks.
- Adopting changes to accounting standards to mitigate the consequences of the exceptional recent turbulence in financial markets.
- Enhancing co-operation procedures among European countries.

Moreover the Council also decided to establish a financial crisis unit to ensure a rapid EU response to crisis situations and improve the co-ordination of measures taken by individual member states. The European Commission is playing its part in ensuring that national rescue plans are implemented quickly by providing rapid decisions on their compatibility with state aid rules. Member governments have since announced the details of how these guidelines would be translated into actions in their respective countries. While indicators for the financial sector have started to show some improvement since mid-October, indicators for non-financial companies and emerging markets have been deteriorating further, reflecting concerns about the weakness of the global economy.

Policy interventions in financial markets need to be designed carefully. For instance, allowing institutions to deviate from strict application of marking their assets to market may give them some breathing room during the current crisis, but it may also undermine price discovery. It is also unclear whether guarantees to prevent banking failures are appropriate when some institutions, which are not systemically important, may prove insolvent. However, in real time it can be difficult to distinguish between insolvency and illiquidity. As agreed by the European authorities, interventions should be timely and temporary, mindful of tax payers' interests, and ensure that existing shareholders bear the consequences of the intervention and that management does not receive undue benefit. Detailed consideration will also have to be given to how countries exit from the commitments they have made when the turmoil eventually dissipates. Finally, while differences in liquidity and solvency concerns mean that it is appropriate for countries' responses to the crisis to differ, countries should keep externalities for other European countries to a minimum, and competition should not be distorted.

Financial regulation and supervision need to reflect Europe's integrated capital market and cross-border risks

The main challenge is to manage systemic and cross-border risks in order to ensure financial stability in an integrated financial market. The Capital Requirements Directive establishes the key standards for banking solvency. Banking supervision, however, has primarily remained the responsibility of national supervisors. The single EU banking passport sets out many areas where home country supervisors are responsible for branches of cross-border banks, while subsidiaries are supervised by host country supervisors. The Lamfalussy structure provides a framework for updating EU financial regulations as well as converging supervisory practices. Co-ordination between national supervisory authorities is encouraged both through the Lamfalussy level 3 committees (covering banking, insurance and securities markets) and the Banking Supervision Committee.

This current regulatory regime in the EU has a number of advantages. It aligns regulatory and legal responsibility for firms with political and fiscal responsibility, should things go wrong, and with the operation of national insolvency law and the operation of national deposit guarantee schemes. However, the EU's current regime and the patchwork of different instruments, institutions and responsibilities does carry some disadvantages, especially as large complex financial institutions have extensive cross-border activities and the potential to have a significant impact on the wider economy. There is a risk that differences in regulation between countries lead to regulatory arbitrage, undermining the objectives of the regulation and distorting the operation of the European single market in capital services. The existing system relies heavily on close co-ordination and information sharing between different regulators with a variety of responsibilities and approaches. It also imposes a considerable burden on cross-border firms that have to report to an array of different authorities. National supervisors are closer to the institutions they supervise, but a more centralised and uniform system for supervising large complex financial institutions would also have advantages by pooling information, regulating in a consistent way, enhancing preparedness for a crisis and reducing regulatory costs. Although the ECB carries out macro-prudential supervision in the euro area, there is a need for better linkages between macro and micro-prudential supervision. The envisaged co-operation between the Committee of European Banking Supervisors and the ESCB Banking Supervision Committee regarding a semi-annual risk assessment in the EU is a useful step in this direction. Moreover, further convergence of regulatory and supervisory practices would be desirable.

Progress is being made to improve EU regulation: ECOFIN adopted a roadmap on improving the Lamfalussy framework in December 2007. This improves and streamlines the processes for developing financial regulations and enhances the role of the level 3 committees. The Commission is working on a revision of the Commission Decisions establishing these Committees. By the end of 2008, they will be assigned specific tasks, such as mediation, drafting recommendations and guidelines and having an explicit role to strengthen the analysis and responsiveness to risks to the stability of the EU financial system. In October 2007, the Council adopted conclusions setting out further steps at both EU and national levels for the development of financial stability arrangements. The conclusions included common principles, a new Memorandum of Understanding for crisis management, and a roadmap for the enhancement of co-operation and preparedness and for reviews of the tools available for crisis prevention, management and resolution.

Proposals are being formulated or considered to deal with a number of issues, including the cross-border transfer for assets and other questions within the review of the Winding Up Directive and amendments to the EU regulations relating to Deposit Guarantee Schemes. Moreover, in October 2008, the Commission adopted a proposal for a revision of the Capital Requirements Directive. Elements of this proposal relate to the establishment of Colleges of Supervisors to enhance cross-border co-operation between supervisors, the mandatory exchange of information between supervisors to help detect signs of financial stress, reducing banks' exposure to interbank lending markets, and requiring firms issuing asset-backed securities to hold a portion of the securities on their balance sheets. In this context, a coherent group-wide supervision could be supported by strengthening the role of the "consolidating supervisor". In the meantime, guidelines concerning the public support for banks have been issued.

Achieving a coherent system of financial supervision as well as managing cross-border risks calls for a more centralised and integrated approach. Possible options might include the establishment of a single EU financial supervisor or a European system of supervisors, with a central agency working in tandem with national supervisors. Either option has the potential to improve the monitoring and containment of systemic risks within the rapidly growing and increasingly integrated European financial market. A European system would probably be easier to integrate with the existing framework and might be able to ensure cultural and geographic proximity of supervision. In principle it should be possible to balance the interests of both home and host countries. However, if such a system was unable to overcome national biases and the externalities that arise from them, a single supervisor should be considered. As a matter of urgency the principles and procedures for burden sharing should be specified in greater detail, a European dimension should be added to the mandates of national supervisors to align their incentives, regulations should be more closely harmonised to limit compliance costs and EU-wide reporting forms introduced. Colleges of supervisors should also have enhanced powers to foster effective supervision, and the role of level 3 committees should be expanded to ensure that the colleges work effectively. Recent events have made it clear that it is essential to reflect on how to elaborate a longer term and shared vision of the EU supervisory architecture, combining the need to safeguard EU financial stability with legitimate national interests.

The public finances have improved, but the downturn will test the Stability and Growth Pact

Fiscal performance improved in recent years. The overall euro area fiscal deficit shrank from 2.5% of GDP in 2005 to 0.6% in 2007 and the cyclically-adjusted fiscal deficit declined as well. Some countries achieved impressive fiscal positions but some high-debt countries made little effort to improve their fiscal position. The last economic expansion was particularly rich in revenue and generated strong growth in receipts from corporation tax and taxes related to capital gains and property, so that the measured improvement in the underlying fiscal position is likely to be overstated. The economic downturn, unfavourable developments in tax elasticities, and the actions being taken by governments to stabilise financial markets will add to fiscal pressures. The euro area actual fiscal deficit is expected to increase by 0.8% of GDP in both 2008 and 2009, reversing much of the decline in 2006-07. Government debt had fallen as a share of GDP, but is now set to rise again. The major challenge for long-run fiscal sustainability remains ageing and healthcare costs: the most recent estimate from the European Commission suggests an increase in the share of age-related spending of 4.4% of GDP between 2010 and 2050, bringing this share to about 28% of GDP but the actual costs could be much higher. Consideration should be given to how this challenge will be addressed through structural reforms and pre-funding.

The revised Stability and Growth Pact (SGP) agreed in 2005 has been successful up until recently, but has yet to be tested in an economic downturn, or a financial crisis. Euro area countries had emerged from Excessive Deficit Procedures under the "dissuasive arm" of the Pact in recent years. The greater discretion under the revised Pact has hardly been used so far and should be used only sparingly. In fact this is exactly what has happened since the 2005 reform of the Pact. The SGP's "preventive arm" has continued to develop, with greater focus on the achievement of long-run fiscal sustainability. Nevertheless, the existing range of the country-specific medium-term budgetary objectives (MTOs) does not fully reflect the fiscal sustainability challenges facing different countries: the current proposals to take implicit liabilities into account when setting MTOs should be implemented. The objective of attaining the MTOs by improving the structural balance by 0.5% of GDP or more in "good times" has had mixed results. The definition of good and bad times and the calculation of their impact on budgetary balances could be refined further. There should be greater emphasis on asset prices and a disaggregated analysis of revenues in assessing structural balances.

Fiscal policy in some euro area member states tightened as the economy expanded in recent years, but policy has remained pro-cyclical in others and a few were forced to tighten policy under adverse cyclical circumstances. In the context of the current economic slowdown and the exceptional measures being taken to support the financial system, discretionary fiscal policy may be appropriate where room for manoeuvre exists. Any discretionary easing should be timely, targeted and temporary and take into account specific challenges of the country concerned. The reformed Stability and Growth Pact provides sufficient flexibility to allow for fiscal policy to play its normal stabilisation function. The relatively large automatic stabilisers in Europe will help cushion the slowdown. The priority should remain improving long-run fiscal sustainability, given the challenges stemming from ageing. This is in line with the conclusions of the October 2008 ECOFIN Council. In addition, fiscal incentives to invest in housing exacerbate the housing cycle and should be phased out in the long run. Moreover, in some cases there is opportunity for property taxation to be designed more efficiently, allowing it to function as a built-in stabiliser. However, due account would need to be taken of the timing of these changes, especially with regard to the risk of exacerbating further the present difficulties in the housing market.

he quality of public finances should be aised further

The efficiency of government intervention is an important way in which fiscal policy can contribute to raising living standards, with key factors including the ways in which money is spent and the design of the tax system. This is a key issue for the euro area because public spending accounts for around 45% of GDP on average. Infrastructure investment can help to raise living standards, although it should be well-designed and policies such as user charges can contribute to its efficient use. The efficiency of public spending is hard to assess. But, there is some evidence that euro area countries could benefit from improving value for money: educational attainment could be raised by following international best practice or raising the efficiency within national systems towards those of the best performing schools; and health spending could be better used to improve outcomes. The design of the tax system should be improved by increasing the use and efficiency of consumption taxes, which would be less distorting than the current degree of reliance on personal income taxes, although in seeking such reform it is important to consider the effect on the distribution of real incomes. Moreover, strong fiscal governance frameworks can help to ensure sound budgetary positions and improve the efficiency of public spending.

ISBN 978-92-64-04824-9
OECD Economic Surveys: Euro area

Chapter 1

Key challenges

Economic growth in the euro area economy began to moderate in early 2007 and has steadily lost momentum, with the area-wide economy now having slipped into recession. Consumption is expanding sluggishly, investment is now declining, and net exports are being weakened by the slowing world economy. Past increases in food and energy prices had pushed headline inflation well above the rate consistent with price stability, although it has now begun to decline sharply as global prices have dropped and the economy has slipped into recession. Since August 2007, the euro area and other developed economies have experienced a period of turmoil in international financial markets following a prolonged global credit cycle. This intensified after mid-September 2008 and is now placing considerable downward pressure on activity, adding to the drag on output from declines in residential investment. The immediate challenges stemming from the liquidity squeeze have been addressed by the European Central Bank through its monetary operations and by the emergency support measures taken by European governments to restore confidence in financial markets, but there continues to be considerable stress in financial markets. The policy rate has been reduced sharply already as downside risks to activity have emerged and inflationary risks have receded, and there could well be scope for further monetary easing in the coming months as economic slack develops. For the longer term, the financial market turmoil highlights the considerable challenges facing the European policy framework, as well as underlining the importance of appropriate measures to deal with the possibility of relatively rare, but severe, systemic events in financial markets that have the power to harm the wider economy.

The euro economy enjoyed a sustained period of growth from mid-2003 until the first quarter of 2008. GDP growth was above trend during this period and the output gap closed. Investment was strong and export performance supportive. Employment expanded at a fast pace during the recovery phase and the unemployment rate fell to 7.1%, the lowest in three decades. At the same time, the year-on-year GDP growth rate peaked at only just over 3% and averaged just 2¼ per cent over the five years up to 2008 Q1. This is somewhat weaker than for the OECD as a whole, reflecting in part a relatively low estimated potential growth rate. One notable feature of the expansion was that the recovery in consumption was muted, with only modest gains in real disposable incomes and households being unwilling to reduce saving.

The cyclical upturn began to moderate in early 2007. The stance of monetary policy tightened as nominal interest rates were raised towards more neutral levels from December 2005 onwards, and the real effective exchange rate moved above its longer term average level. Since the slowdown began, the euro area has been hit by three substantial negative macroeconomic shocks. Firstly, since August 2007, the economy has been impacted by the turmoil in international financial markets and the end of an extended global credit cycle. This turmoil has intensified since mid-September 2008, following the bankruptcy of Lehman Brothers. Secondly, the economy is still experiencing the after-effects of the sharp rise in the world price of many commodities until mid-2008. However, these should fade quickly given the sharp decline in commodity prices since that time. Thirdly, the housing cycle in a number of economies has peaked and gone into reverse.

The achievements of EMU have been considerable over the first decade (Box 1.1). But, recent developments pose a difficult challenge because of the need to balance the response to short-term pressures with continued pursuit of medium-term objectives. The economy has slipped into recession, reflecting a combination of tighter financial market conditions, weakening domestic and external demand and, in some member states, declining levels of housing construction. Business and consumer confidence have fallen to their lowest levels since the start of EMU. Output declined in the second quarter of 2008, but headline inflation did not begin to turn down until well into the third quarter, although it has subsequently fallen sharply. The on-going financial market turmoil creates further downside risks. For the long term, however, challenges remain to consolidate the success of the first decade. The credibility of the monetary policy regime needs to be maintained and further efforts are required to ensure that fiscal policy, despite progress in recent years, is put on a sustainable path as revenue growth eases and the support offered to financial markets adds to actual and contingent government liabilities. This cycle has shown that there are still substantial differences in economic performance between different euro area economies. Considerable structural challenges remain for the euro area economy to raise living standards and macroeconomic resilience. Financial market regulation needs to continue to promote financial integration and development within the single market, while adapting to the transformation of the European capital markets that has led to cross-border loans of monetary financial institutions rising from a quarter of total lending

Box 1.1. **A decade of monetary union**

European monetary union is ten years old: stage 3 of Economic and Monetary Union (EMU) began on 1 January 1999 with euro notes and coins circulating from 2002. The euro area has a population of over 300 million and is the second largest economy in the world, after the United States. Four countries have joined the original eleven members of the monetary union with Slovakia set to join on 1 January 2009. Others are likely to follow.

After a decade of experience, it starts to become meaningful to try to assess this historic policy action, despite the inherent difficulties of separating the effects of EMU from other factors and knowing what would have happened otherwise. A recent assessment by the European Commission concludes that EMU has been a "resounding success" even though it notes that it has fallen short of some initial expectations in terms of output and productivity growth (EC, 2008). It is an achievement to have replaced successfully historic national currencies with a single currency. The end of nominal exchange rate turbulence and realignments within the euro area has made a major contribution to economic stability. The euro has established itself as a sound currency: inflation has averaged around 2%, long-term interest rates are around 4¼ per cent and the currency has appreciated significantly against most major global currencies over the past six years. The euro area as a whole has not experienced substantial external imbalances. The euro has established itself as a world currency with a five-fold increase in holdings of Euros since 1999, although its share of international currency reserves remains far below that of the US dollar.* The ECB has achieved an impressive reputation for maintaining price stability. Inflation expectations have been well-anchored around the ECB's definition of price stability (ECB, 2008a).

Several likely benefits of EMU were identified before its creation. Have these hopes been realised? EMU was expected to boost output by increasing competition and scale in the single market. But, growth in GDP per capita has averaged only around 1¾ per cent over the past decade, slightly slower than in the previous decade and in the United States; the growth of output per hour worked, a measure of productivity, has slowed more sharply. A recent study suggests that GDP may eventually rise by 2% in five "core" member countries as a result of EMU, perhaps more when taking into account lower output volatility (Barrell *et al.*, 2008), but these effects only arise very gradually and have not been sufficient to offset weak productivity growth rates due to other factors such as the relatively slow increase in human capital. By contrast, employment growth has been vigorous and unemployment rates have fallen towards the lowest level in several decades.

A "consensus estimate" suggests that the initial effects on trade were to boost intra-euro area commerce by 5 to 10% (Baldwin, 2006). Capital market integration has increased, with the convergence of yields in many markets and a shift towards holding asset portfolios that are more diversified across countries, especially for bonds (Chapter 2). Greater integration within both product and capital markets increases competitive pressures and should raise welfare.

The main risk with EMU was that macroeconomic adjustment might be painful for individual economies without national monetary policy or adjustment of the nominal exchange rate. Such adjustment would be needed if there were asymmetric economic shocks hitting some parts of the euro area economy or for countries that were experiencing a different rate of structural growth such as Ireland. In fact, until recently, the main economic development over the past decade was a period of relative economic stability both among euro area countries and across the developed world. Within the euro area, differences have remained but inflation differentials across countries, for example, have been only slightly greater than across states in the United States or Australia. One notable divergence has been the housing booms experienced in some countries, particularly Ireland and Spain, which were not shared elsewhere.

Box 1.1. **A decade of monetary union** *(cont.)*

It was argued that EMU itself would moderate the risk of painful adjustment by increasing flexibility and by making economies more similar, even if greater specialisation would tend to increase structural differences. The currency area would therefore become optimal through this endogenous process (Frankel and Rose, 1998). There is little evidence that this has happened despite the increase in trade. Macroeconomic resilience continues to be held back partly by ineffective regulation of labour and product markets (Duval *et al.*, 2007), although progress has been made in some areas to reform product and labour markets (Leiner-Killinger *et al.*, 2007).

* Allocated reserves in the IMF Currency Composition of *Official Foreign Exchange Reserves* (COFER) *database.*

in 1998 to almost 45% today. This chapter examines recent macroeconomic developments, the impact of the financial market turmoil and the monetary policy response. Chapter 2 explores the changing financial landscape in Europe, together with its implications for monetary policy. Chapter 3 sets out the challenges for financial stability and regulation. Chapter 4 discusses fiscal policy.

A slowing economy, receding inflationary pressures and financial market turmoil

The euro area economy has slipped into recession

The expansion in euro area activity from 2003 began to moderate in early 2007. The economy has steadily lost momentum since then and output declined in both the second and third quarters of 2008. The period of sustained above-trend growth was largely accounted for by rising domestic demand with net exports, unusually, initially acting as a drag on GDP growth before making a small positive contribution (Figure 1.1). Investment increased rapidly with business surveys indicating high levels of confidence and, beginning in 2006, high capacity utilisation. Capital expenditure was supported by low interest rates and favourable financing conditions until recently. The slowdown in the euro area economy since the peak in growth rates has been broadly based across the different components of demand.

Figure 1.1. **Contributions to GDP growth**

Change relative to the same period of the previous year

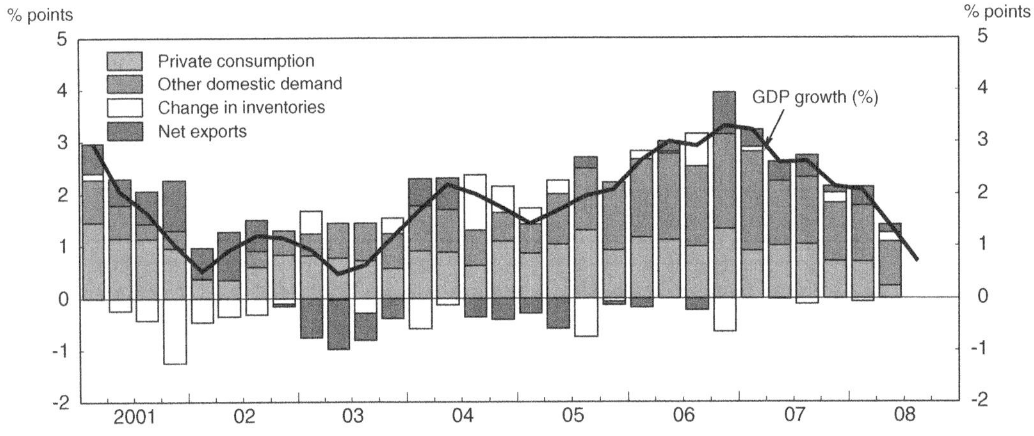

Source: Eurostat.

StatLink http://dx.doi.org/10.1787/518104257737

Housing investment cycles in some euro area countries led to rapidly rising house prices and a surge in construction, particularly in Ireland and Spain but also to a lesser extent in Belgium, France and Finland. The share of housing investment in GDP was similar to that of the United States at the peak of the cycle, but the increase in housing construction was more muted in the euro area. Many economies did not experience a significant housing boom. Euro area housing investment is estimated to have declined by around 6% since its peak in 2007 Q1, compared with a fall of around one-third in the United States since the end of 2005. With the exception of Ireland, Spain and Greece, where house building has already fallen very sharply, the limited contraction to date is partly due to the cycle having turned only recently in several of the countries that experienced booms. Housing market activity and house prices are also slowing in many euro area countries after several years of rapid growth. Euro area nominal house prices rose by around 50% over five years up to the end of 2007, almost as much as in the United States over the same period. The increase was around 75% if the inert Austrian and German markets are excluded. But, the vulnerability of the euro area housing market is generally less than in the United States as no substantial subprime mortgage market developed and active home equity withdrawal is difficult in most countries. Nevertheless, housing markets on both sides of the Atlantic have decelerated since around 2005, although less rapidly in the euro area than in the United States. Prices in the euro area as a whole have now begun to fall. In Spain and Ireland, house prices are now more than 10% below their peak in nominal terms.

Consumption growth was relatively weak during the last expansion, with household expenditure rising at an annual rate of only 1½ per cent over the five years up to 2008 Q1, well below the overall growth rate of activity. This can be accounted for by two factors (Figure 1.2). Firstly, the growth of real disposable incomes has been sluggish. Despite the rapid increase in employment and falling unemployment, household incomes failed to keep pace due to pressures on post-tax real wages and slow productivity gains. Real compensation per employee (in terms of the consumption deflator) was 1.9% lower in 2007 than when the cycle began. More recently, sharply rising prices have lowered real incomes further. Secondly, household consumption has been weak in relation to income during this cycle, with the saving ratio falling only modestly relative to past cycles. Savings rates have

Figure 1.2. **Consumption and income**

Year-on-year growth rates

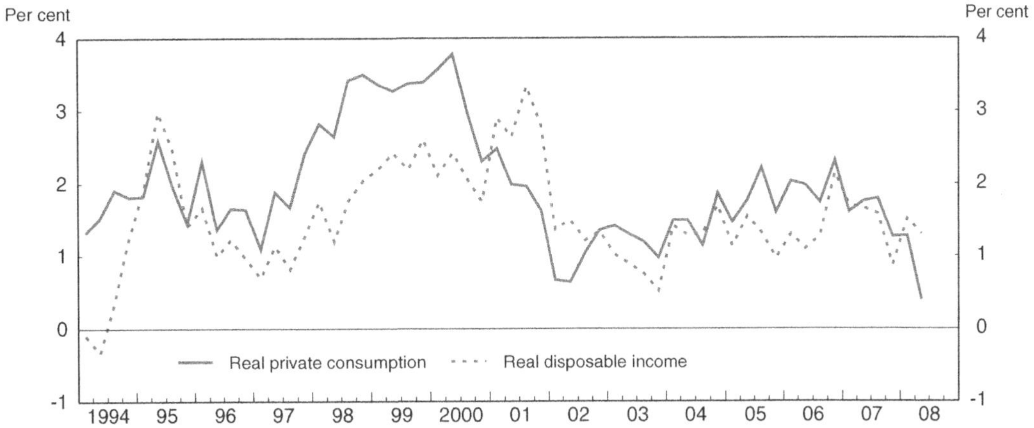

Source: OECD, *OECD Economic Outlook database*.

StatLink http://dx.doi.org/10.1787/518117138743

remained well above those in the United States and United Kingdom. This is surprising given that real interest rates were initially low and that asset prices, including house prices in many countries, rose substantially over much of the period. There is substantial evidence that euro area consumption has been boosted in the past by wealth effects from rising financial worth, perhaps to a similar degree as in other major economies (Chapter 2). Increasing housing wealth also tends to boost consumption in some member states, particularly in Finland, Ireland, the Netherlands and Spain, although the effects are small in the largest euro area countries (Catte *et al.*, 2004).[1] The limited possibilities for refinancing mortgages or extracting home equity through further lending have tended to dampen the overall impact of house prices on consumption. Survey measures of area-wide consumer confidence did reach relatively high levels in recent years, but remained somewhat lower than at the peak of the previous cycle. The sluggish growth of consumption poses a challenge for the outlook to the extent that more solid growth would help counterbalance rapidly slowing external and investment demand and support overall economic growth.

With the expansion already beginning to slow, the euro area has been hit by three substantial negative macroeconomic shocks in 2007 and 2008. Firstly, the exceptionally sharp rise in energy and food prices has reduced real incomes and lowered the supply capacity of the economy. Secondly, the international financial market turmoil marks the end of a period of historically favourable financing conditions for firms and households, raising the cost of financing and posing marked risks for growth prospects, especially if the recent intensification of the turmoil were to persist. Thirdly, the housing cycle has peaked in a number of euro area countries leading to large falls in construction activity in those economies. This has led to a modest short-run drag on euro area GDP growth, which may well persist for some time. The sharp falls in global energy and food prices since mid-2008 will help to alleviate these shocks, but cannot do so completely. The three shocks are common across many developed countries and strong international financial and trade linkages have helped spread the economic effects widely. Their overall impact on the euro area economy will be substantial. Historically, growth in Europe has been highly correlated with the US economy with a lag of a few quarters on average (Figure 1.3). Against the

Figure 1.3. **Euro area and US GDP growth**

Annualised two-year growth rate, per cent

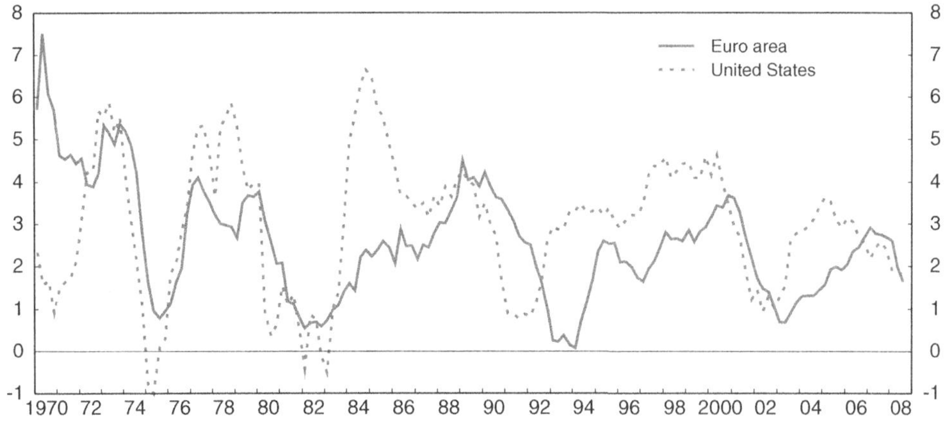

Source: OECD, *OECD Economic Outlook database.*

StatLink http://dx.doi.org/10.1787/518127766787

background of sharply weakening economic indicators, GDP growth in the euro area is presently expected to decline further until the middle of 2009, and thereafter turn up only gradually, with growth remaining below trend rates until the latter half of 2010.

The period of high oil prices will have had some negative impact on supply potential, with the real oil price having been around 2½ times its average over the past two decades. All else equal, a sustained change of this magnitude could have reduced steady-state output by around 2 per cent in the euro area, implying a small negative impact on growth in the short to medium term.[2] However, the recent declines in global oil prices, although dampened by the depreciation of the euro, will ensure that the adverse impact on supply is smaller than this. The supply effect in the euro area is about half of that estimated for the United States, partly because of the effect of the appreciation of the euro during the period of rising oil prices and because the oil and gas share of output is around one-third lower in the euro area. The impact of this shock on activity in the euro area is also tempered by the orientation of oil producers' imports to euro area goods and services: around two-thirds of the revenue accruing to oil producers from additional imports of oil by euro area countries is re-spent on additional exports from the euro area.

Rising energy and food prices have created inflationary pressures

Year-on-year harmonised CPI inflation (HICP) reached 4.0% in July 2008, the fastest rate of inflation since the creation of the euro and a pace not experienced in the euro area since the early 1990s. It has subsequently declined sharply, falling to 2.1% in November. Headline inflation had generally been close to, although slightly above, the ECB's price stability objective of inflation "below but close to 2.0%" for most of the past four years until the surge in late 2007. The increase in inflation up to July 2008 can be accounted for by food and energy prices (Figure 1.4). Input and producer price inflation increased markedly from late 2007, although they have recently begun to ease somewhat. Year-on-year inflation is likely to fall substantially, reflecting lower oil and food prices as well as the anticipated slowdown in demand. Both headline and underlying inflation are projected to average less than 2% in 2009 and 2010.

Figure 1.4. **Contributions to harmonised CPI inflation**

Annual growth rates

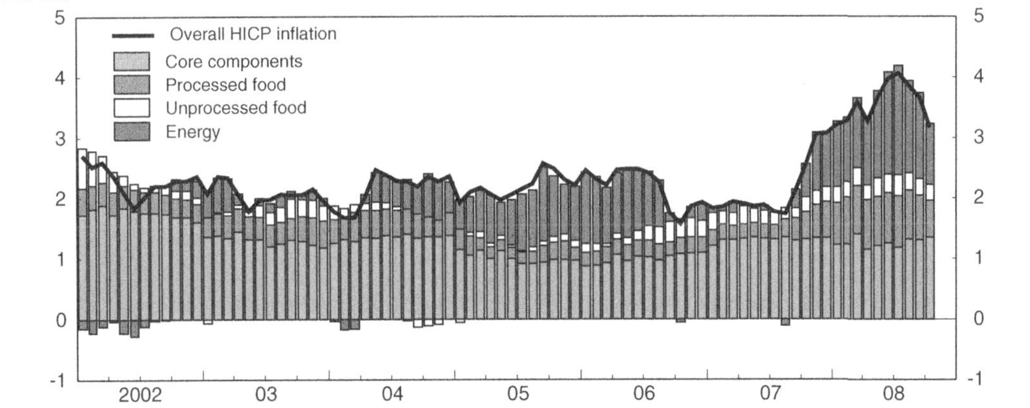

Source: Eurostat.

StatLink http://dx.doi.org/10.1787/518150568457

The unanticipated surge in world energy and food prices up to mid-2008 and the subsequent collapse imply that headline inflation in the euro area may provide a misleading picture of the underlying pressure of total demand on domestic supply. Statistical measures of core inflation exclude or reweight various components of inflation to try to give a clearer picture of this underlying pressure (Catte and Sløk, 2005). Many of these measures of inflation move in line with headline inflation. For instance, weighted median inflation rose from late 2007 to reach around 3% by mid-2008. Statistical measures may, however, provide a misleading signal about underlying price developments given the combination of energy and food price shocks: these goods together account for around one third of the total basket and so have some influence on most of the statistical measures. Excluding all energy and food components, as in the OECD's measure of underlying inflation, abstracts from these two main drivers of the recent strength in headline inflation. Core year-on-year inflation on this measure has remained below 2% throughout 2008 and is close to its average level over the past five years.

The distribution of inflation in the individual subcomponents has also been relatively stable, other than the big change in inflation for items connected to energy and food; these switched from increasing at an annual rate of around 1% in July 2007 to rising at exceptionally high rates a year later (Figure 1.5). Services inflation may provide some indication of the pressure of demand on domestic supply and this has remained flat at around 2½ per cent since the beginning of 2007, close to its average of the past five years and lower than services inflation in a number of other major OECD economies. This has been offset to some extent by declines in the prices of some goods. The annual rate of increase of non-energy industrial goods has been a little below 1% on average since early 2007. Taken together, all these indicators suggest that second-round effects on inflation from the rise in energy and food prices have been largely contained. Total hourly wages rose by 2.8% in the year up to 2008 Q2, less than consumer prices, but raising nominal unit labour costs by around 3%.

Econometric analysis reported in the previous *Survey* suggests that headline inflation feeds through to core inflation (excluding food and energy) but in a limited way, with core inflation rising in a range of around 0.025 to 0.25 percentage points three quarters after a

Figure 1.5. **Components of the euro area HICP**[1]

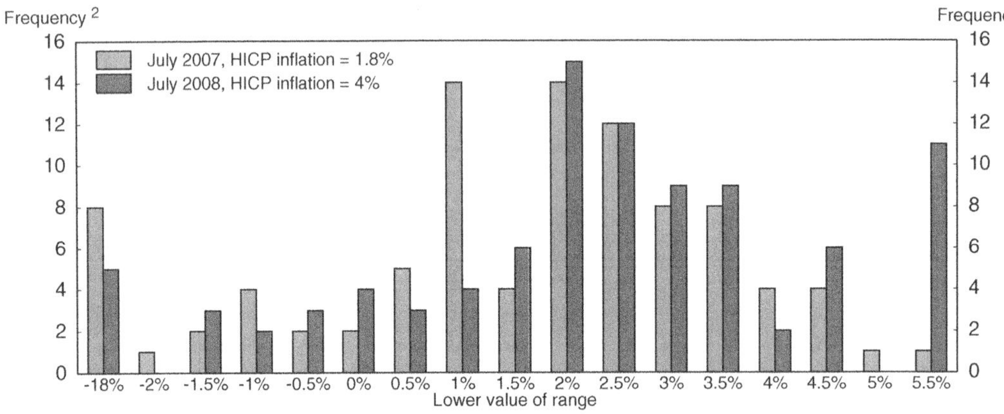

1. Year-on-year growth rates of the HICP components.
2. Unweighted.

Source: Eurostat.

StatLink http://dx.doi.org/10.1787/518162084334

one percentage point increase in the headline rate (OECD, 2007a). During the sharp increase in oil prices in 2004-05, the spill-over effects to core inflation were particularly muted. This appeared to result from a long period of low and stable inflation, which probably helped to contain private sector inflation expectations, together with lower energy intensity than in the past and the remaining slack in the economy (van den Noord and André, 2007). In the episode in 2007 and the first half of 2008, the economy started closer to capacity but was slowing. The concurrent increase in food and energy prices also raised additional challenges, both because the increase in the price level was greater but also as the response of households and wage setters to higher food prices may not be the same as for energy prices. Some possibility of second-round effects on wages and prices remains, but the rapid decline in international commodity prices since mid-2008 should ensure that headline inflation moderates rapidly as base effects drop from the annual comparison and the economy slows further. The annual rate of headline inflation had already fallen back to 2.1% by November 2008 and further declines appear likely.

Divergences in economic performance remain

Differences in inflation and growth performance are inevitable in any monetary union due to differences in economic structures and institutions. National differences in performance in the euro area tend to increase during expansions as output picks up more in some countries than others. Despite considerable co-variation of cycles between countries since the beginning of monetary union, there remains heterogeneity in the timing, amplitude and nature of developments in different countries (Table 1.1). For example, the orientation of German exports of goods and services towards both oil producing economies in OPEC and dynamic Asian countries is much higher than for most other euro area countries. Demand growth in these economies remains stronger than in most OECD economies, although it is set to moderate significantly with the ongoing global economic downturn. At least a tenth of exports in Germany, Greece and Ireland go to the weak US economy, while the share is less than half of that in Austria, Portugal and Spain.

Table 1.1. **Economic performance in euro area countries**

Average of annual rates 2003 to 2007

	GDP growth	HICP inflation	Output gap	Real unit labour cost growth	Unemployment rate	Current account (% of GDP)	Housing investment (% of GDP)
Austria	2.6	1.8	–0.7	0.7	5.7	1.4	4.5
Belgium	2.3	2.0	0.1	0.5	8.2	2.9	5.3
Finland	3.6	1.0	0.2	2.3	8.2	4.8	5.5
France	1.9	2.0	0.1	1.0	8.6	–0.2	5.6
Germany	1.4	1.8	–0.6	–0.2	9.5	5.1	5.5
Greece	4.3	3.3	1.1	2.7	9.1	–9.0	7.6
Ireland	5.5	2.8	1.4	3.2	4.5	–2.6	12.0
Italy	1.1	2.3	–0.5	0.2	7.5	–1.8	4.9
Luxembourg	4.6	3.0	–0.3	–0.6	4.3	10.2	n.a.
Netherlands	2.3	1.7	–0.9	0.9	4.2	7.4	6.1
Portugal	1.0	2.7	–0.9	–0.1	7.3	–8.6	n.a.
Spain	3.5	3.2	–0.4	–1.0	9.5	–7.0	8.7
Euro area	**2.0**	**2.1**	**–0.3**	**0.1**	**8.4**	**0.6**	**5.8**

Source: OECD (2008), *OECD Economic Outlook 84 database.*

One notable feature of the recovery in euro area growth since 2003 is that some countries continued to perform poorly, experiencing comparatively weak recoveries. Output growth in Italy and Portugal was slow and output was persistently below trend without the necessary substantial falls in real unit labour costs. Although growth performance was stronger in Greece and Spain, these economies had high inflation and large current account deficits, with growth supported in part by strong housing construction. Taken together, weak performance and poor resilience to economic shocks appear to be related to structural policy settings. In Spain, for example, there is a need to improve the functioning of the labour market (OECD, 2008d).

The varied experiences of euro area countries in terms of growth and labour market performance during the recent upswing may be indicative of differences in structural policy settings. Negative shocks in countries with more rigid labour and product markets tend to have less initial impact but to have more persistent effects that ultimately lead to a greater loss of output (Duval *et al.*, 2007). The evidence from the period 1983 to 2003 suggests that Austria, Belgium, France, Italy, Spain and, to a lesser extent, Germany suffered these effects. By contrast, social partnership in the Netherlands allowed for a swift recovery from the slump of 2002/03 as wages were frozen to restore competitiveness. As well as improving resilience, structural reforms before or during the recovery in some countries may have had an immediate one-off positive impact on output or the labour market in some cases. It is important to ensure that policy settings become more favourable because growth and inflation differentials are relatively persistent, compared for example with the US states, partly reflecting a lower degree of integration. This implies that the potential for long drawn-out booms or slow growth is high and that great effort can be required from some countries to recoup competitiveness.

The crisis in international financial markets

International financial markets experienced severe distress from August 2007, reaching crisis point in mid-September 2008. Triggered by significantly higher-than-expected default rates on US subprime residential mortgages, the initial period of stress was marked by illiquidity and unusually high funding costs in term interbank lending markets, falls in equity prices and a generalised increase in risk premia and uncertainty across many markets (OECD, 2008a). Credit conditions began to tighten considerably for firms and households, although the flow of bank loans to the non-financial private sector remained strong. From mid-September 2008, the turmoil intensified following the failure of Lehman Brothers; term interbank lending rates soared, credit default swap rates on bank debt increased sharply and equity prices plunged, alongside a wider tightening of credit conditions for both market and bank finance. Many of the initial pressures on interbank lending were contained by the ECB's existing framework for monetary operations, but wider policy action has been necessary as the crisis intensified. The measures undertaken by the ECB, as well as the wide range of guarantees and recapitalisations announced by European governments (Chapter 3) have helped to ensure the immediate stability of the financial system.

The origins of the turmoil

This sharp deterioration in financial conditions followed a prolonged global credit cycle during which low risk-aversion helped to reduce the cost of borrowing to historically low levels and credit increased substantially (Figure 1.6). The OECD synthetic indicator of

Figure 1.6. **Developments during the credit cycle**

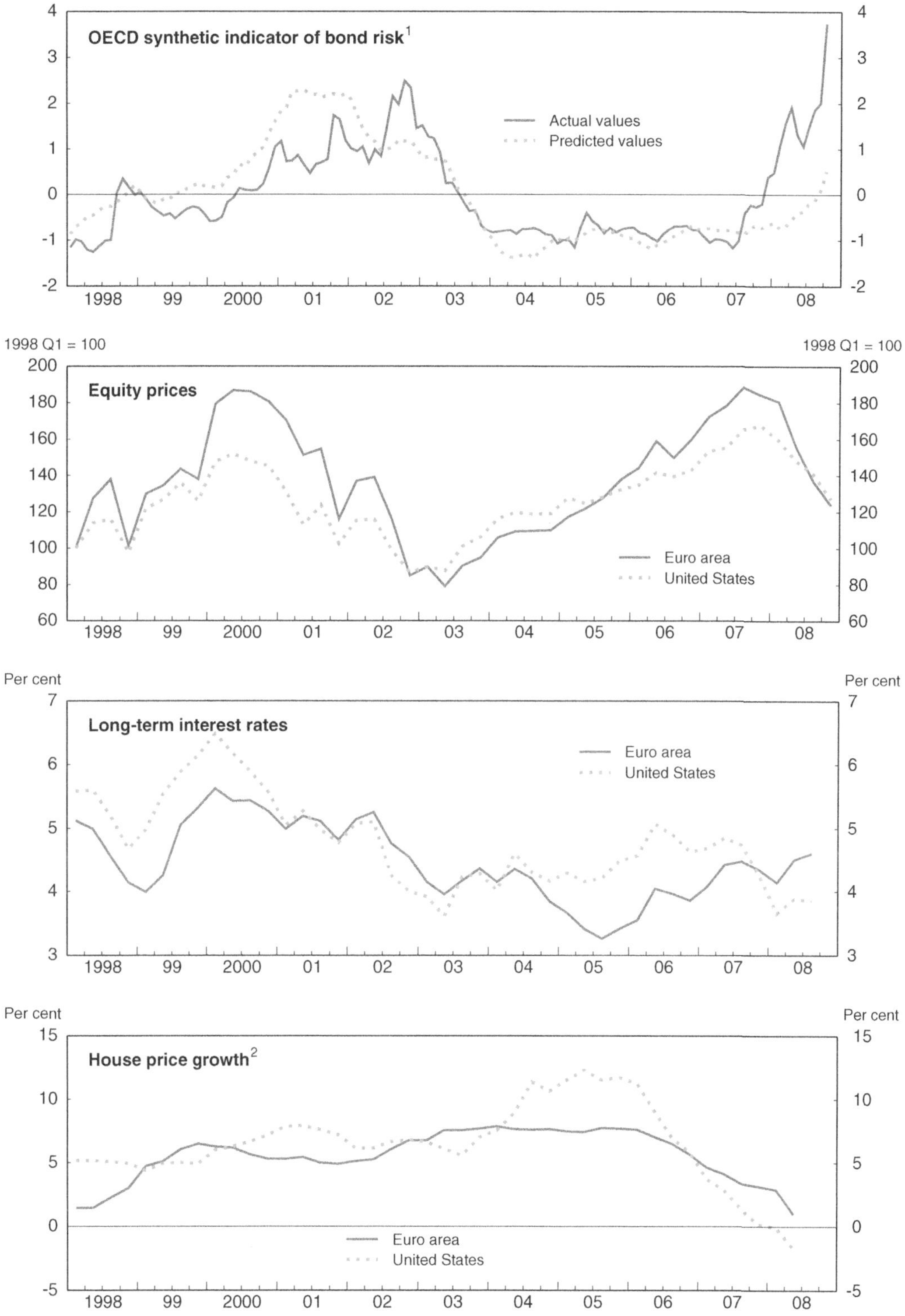

1. Deviation from average, in terms of standard deviations of the synthetic indicator discussed in OECD (2006).
2. Year-on-year percentage change. US house price measured by Office of Federal Housing Enterprise Oversight (OFHEO) all homes index.

Source: OFHEO, Datastream and OECD, *OECD Economic Outlook database.*

StatLink http://dx.doi.org/10.1787/518201445424

risk suggests that risk perceptions were substantially below their long-run average from 2004 to 2007. Long-term interest rates on government debt also fell in 2005 to their lowest level in recent decades. This led to a rapid increase in credit, with the total assets of euro area monetary financial institutions (MFIs) having risen by around 50% in real terms over the past five years. Asset prices rose sharply. Equity prices recovered from 2003 onwards, although they did not reach the same peak in real terms as in 2000, partly because investors may have been deterred by the recent memory of substantial losses in 2001 and 2002. Similar developments were seen in many markets, such as corporate and emerging market bonds. However, the intensity of the housing cycle was perhaps the main feature of the credit expansion.

The origins of this credit cycle lie in a combination of cyclical and structural factors. Evidence suggests that a combination of rapid financial market innovation and accommodating monetary policy at the global level over the period 2002-05 is likely to explain much of the swift expansion in credit and the run up in asset prices (Ahrend *et al.*, 2008), although the deviation of policy interest rates from those implied by an estimated Taylor rule suggests that monetary policy in the euro area was much less accommodative than in the United States. Within the euro area, there is a clear relationship across countries over this period between the housing cycle and the extent to which the euro area monetary policy stance differed from the national stance that might otherwise have been expected given the output gap and inflation (Figure 1.7). Loose monetary conditions in Ireland and Spain were associated with particularly intense cycles in residential investment activity.

Figure 1.7. **Deviations from a Taylor rule and housing activity**

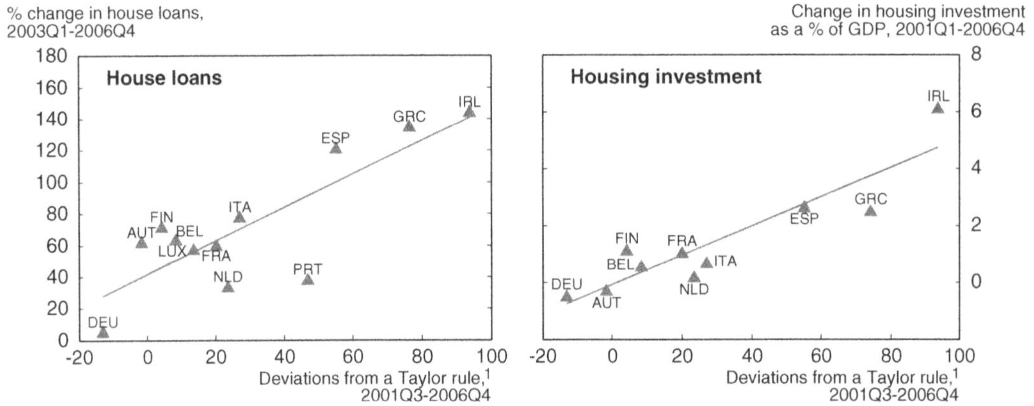

1. Sum of differences between actual short-term interest rates and those implied by a Taylor rule.

Source: Ahrend, R. *et al.* (2008), "Monetary Policy, Market Excesses and Financial Turmoil", *OECD Economics Department Working Papers*, No. 597, OECD, Paris.

StatLink http://dx.doi.org/10.1787/518216743375

The credit and asset-price cycle peaked in August 2007, with the difficulties in the US subprime mortgage market leading to a prolonged period of turmoil in financial markets as banks became reluctant to lend to each other except at very short maturities and a wider re-pricing of risk took hold. Equity prices fell, many market interest rates rose sharply and the implied volatility of many financial instruments increased substantially. There was a modest recovery following the Federal Reserve's intervention to resolve the difficulties at Bear Stearns investment bank, but in June 2008 pressures returned to a similar position as in March. Difficulties in financial markets reached crisis point in mid-September 2008 following the failure of Lehman Brothers. The reaction to this event and uncertainty about the resulting losses was compounded by ongoing suspicions about the health of the banking system in the face of accumulating losses and the fear of a severe downturn in the world economy. The cost of term interbank lending soared, equity prices fell sharply and risk spreads increased on non-financial debt.

The emerging financial crisis called forward emergency measures in many countries to ensure the stability of the financial system, including changes to the conduct of ECB market operations and an intensification of those operations and a concerted action plan for euro area countries. These actions have helped to stabilise the financial system and risk spreads in the interbank market have subsequently narrowed, although they remain above the level observed during the initial phase of financial market turmoil.

The liquidity of many financial markets has been impaired since August 2007

A key feature of this episode has been illiquidity in term money markets and to a lesser extent the overnight funding markets. In the initial turmoil, widespread uncertainty about the size and distribution of exposures to the subprime market arose from the range of relatively new and complex financial instruments used to develop this market, including structured residential mortgage-backed securities, collateralised debt obligations (CDOs) and credit derivatives written on them. There were difficulties in valuing these financial instruments without deep markets that made banks reluctant to lend to each other even at very short horizons, or to expose themselves to counterparty risk through the normal sources of short-term funding. Subsequently, ongoing suspicions about the health of the financial sector and the failure of some institutions led to a near-panic in financial markets in autumn 2008 that made banks very reluctant to lend each other, especially outside the overnight market. As a result, the cost of cash and short-term funding surged and interbank rates were well above the ECB minimum bid rate, both in the initial turmoil and even more so as the crisis intensified after mid-September 2008. There has been some subsequent moderation, but spreads remain elevated (Figure 1.8).

During the initial phase of market turmoil, the ECB was able to contain pressures in interbank markets using its existing operating procedures (Box 1.2), although term interbank lending rates did increase. The ECB announced on 9 August 2007 that it stood ready to ensure orderly conditions in the euro money market. It subsequently responded with a combination of more frequent fine-tuning operations, changing the pattern of the allocated amount in the main refinancing operations throughout the reserve maintenance period (and sometimes announcing operations without a defined size),[3] supplementary longer term refinancing operations for three and then six months, and operations under the USD Term Auction Facility to provide dollar liquidity to European markets. At all times, the ECB has made frequent communications to the market to explain its actions. During this phase of the turmoil, pressures in the interbank market varied, intensifying for instance at the end of each quarter with the settling of many contracts in other markets. The ECB both anticipated and responded to these developments with further operations.

The ECB made few changes to its operating procedures and did not materially expand the size of its balance sheet during this period compared with other major central banks.[4] The existing framework already allowed for a wide range of eligible counterparties and had a broad definition of acceptable collateral, so euro area financial institutions had access to

Figure 1.8. **Short-term interest rates**

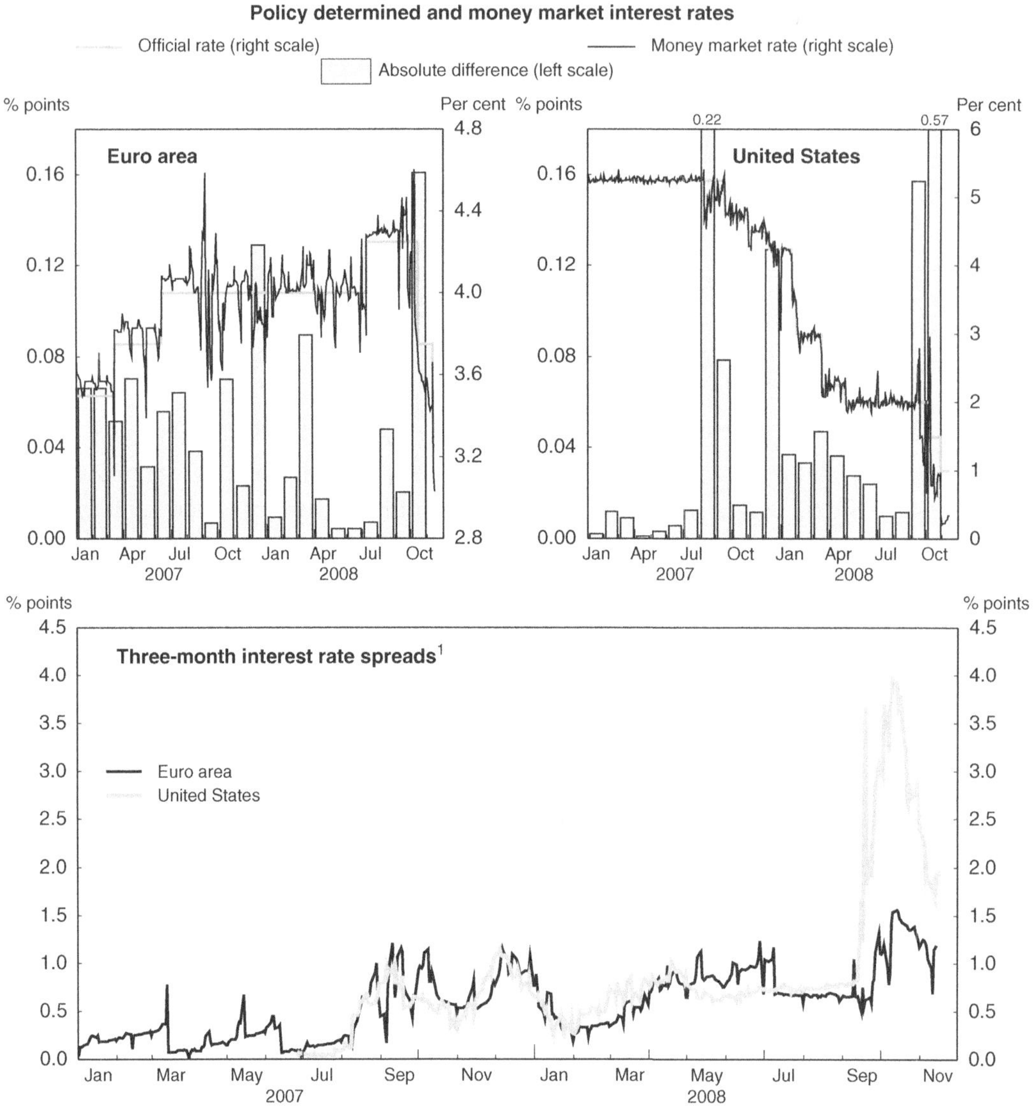

1. Spread defined as Euribor 3-month rate over Euro Overnight Index Average rate for the euro area and 3-month certificate of deposit rate over overnight indexed swap rate for the United States.

Source: Bloomberg; Datastream; and European Central Bank.

StatLink http://dx.doi.org/10.1787/518217167086

ECB liquidity when it was needed. Furthermore, there was no particular stigma for institutions that borrowed from the ECB. The ECB requires banks to meet relatively high minimum reserve requirements, which is facilitated by the remuneration of reserves.[5] More generally, the structure of the Eurosystem balance sheet implies a large liquidity deficit. For example, the stock of euro bank notes is 7½ per cent of GDP compared with 5½ per cent in the United States and 3% in the United Kingdom. As a result, banks are required to have a large volume of central bank money on average and the ECB's refinancing operations are very large; the stock of refinancing in the recent past has been more than twice what it was in the United States. In the context of financial turmoil, this framework made it easier for banks to absorb shocks to euro liquidity with very few changes to the ECB's operating procedures. The main difference during this period was that

Box 1.2. **Implementation of ECB monetary policy**

The monetary policy decisions of the Governing Council of the ECB with respect to the minimum bid rate in the main refinancing operations are implemented by the Executive Board of the ECB, with the assistance of the euro area national central banks through three principal types of operation:

- Regular main refinancing operations for one week.
- Longer term financing operations with maturities of one month (maintenance period operations), three and six months.
- *Ad hoc* fine-tuning operations.

So far, monetary operations by the ECB have taken the form of reverse transactions, whereby counterparties exchange assets as collateral in return for cash. Any "credit institution" under the EU definition is eligible to be a counterparty subject to fulfilling certain conditions. There are around 2 000 eligible counterparties for the main open-market operations.

Collateral must meet high standards. Since January 2007, there has been a "Single List" of eligible assets. This includes both marketable assets and non-marketable assets, which covers loans to the public sector, non-financial corporations, international and supranational institutions, and retail mortgage-backed securities (RMBS). Risks to the ECB's capital from these transactions are managed through the Eurosystem Credit Assessment Framework (ECAF). Credit assessment information is based either on ratings agencies, national central banks' in-house credit assessment systems, counterparties' internal ratings-based systems or third-party ratings tools (ECB, 2006). The collateral framework has been renewed and tighter conditions will be imposed in some areas from February 2009, while the range of eligible collateral was increased in October 2008.

"Valuation haircuts" are applied so that the collateral is valued at a fraction of the market (or other) valuation of the asset. For marketable assets, these discounts depend on residual maturity and the type of asset: government debt, public debt, corporate debt, credit institution debt and asset-backed securities. The discounts range from 0.5% to 20% for fixed and zero coupon instruments. Discounts on non-marketable assets range from 7% to 41% for eligible credit claims and 20% or more for retail-mortgage backed debt instruments. Uniform haircuts of 12% will be applied to all asset-backed securities from February 2009. A further haircut in the form of a valuation markdown of 5% will be applied to asset-backed securities that are given a theoretical value from February 2009. Conditions on the acceptance of asset-backed securities were tightened in 2006. Margin calls are applied if the value of the underlying assets deteriorates while the collateral is held. The ECB also has the power to set initial margins; set limits to exposure to issuers, debtors or guarantors; and require additional guarantees or exclude certain assets.

longer term refinancing operations were lengthened and came to account for a somewhat larger share of the balance sheet, reflecting the greater need for liquidity outside the overnight market. Although the ECB was generally successful at controlling overnight interbank rates, spreads remained at a historically elevated level in other connected markets such as three-month interbank rates. The ability of the ECB's existing operating procedures to contain the stress contrasts with the Federal Reserve and the Bank of England that both substantially increased lending to private financial institutions over the initial phase of the turmoil.

As the crisis intensified from mid-September, the ECB made a series of changes to its framework for implementing monetary policy. Firstly, measures were taken to change and ultimately broaden the range of eligible collateral and related conditions. On 15 October 2008, the list of eligible collateral was extended to include some syndicated loans, some instruments such as Certificates of Deposit not traded in regulated markets, and subordinated debt with appropriate guarantees. Furthermore, the credit threshold was lowered from A- to BBB- (except for asset-backed securities) with an additional valuation margin of 5% on the lower-rated assets. Secondly, on 9 October changes were made to interest rates in ECB monetary operations. The interest rate in the main refinancing operation is now fixed with unlimited allotment of liquidity at that rate, in contrast to the previous system of variable rate tenders.[6] The standing facilities corridor around the interest rate at the main refinancing operation was narrowed, so that the rate on the marginal lending facility is 50 basis points higher than the interest rate of the main refinancing operation and the deposit facility rate is 50 basis points lower, compared with the previous spreads of 100 basis points. As a result of these measures and the pressures in the interbank money market, the overall size of the ECB's balance sheet increased by around 40% between the last week of September and mid-November. Combined with other measures to support the European banking system, this action appears to have narrowed the spreads on short-term money market rates but they remain well above their levels prior to the onset of the turmoil in August 2007.

Given the objectives of maintaining the overnight interest rate at a level close to the minimum bid rate in the Eurosystem's main refinancing operations and of keeping money markets functioning, the actions undertaken by the ECB were clearly necessary. There are, however, risks to this strategy and some issues that need to be addressed, both in the current situation and for future cycles. Firstly, if the risk control measures do not reflect market and credit risk conditions appropriately, the ECB would be excessively exposed to the risk that credit institutions do not honour the repurchase agreements and that the collateral is subsequently worth less than the ECB's claim. In addition, there would be an incentive for financial institutions to post collateral with the ECB that is relatively illiquid. The ECB has already refined its risk management through its biennial review of risk control measures. This will result in some larger valuation margins (Box 1.2), tighter conditions on the assessment of risk for asset-backed securities and stricter conditions on the distance between the issuer of the debt and the entity posting it as collateral. Secondly, there is a risk in the long run of moral hazard if credit institutions were encouraged by changes in how liquidity is provided from the central bank to make inadequate provision for uncertainty about future liquidity needs, because of an expectation of being able to access funds at the central bank. This applies also to the type of assets held by banks, since the possibility of obtaining liquidity from the central bank in this way may reduce the perceived cost of holding more illiquid assets. At a minimum, this underlines the importance of banking regulation to ensure that institutions manage liquidity appropriately. Thirdly, it is not normally the role of the central bank to be the main provider of liquidity in the market but, if the current situation is sustained, there is a danger that institutions become used to avoiding other private counterparties, particularly if the terms offered by the central bank are relatively favourable. With high international capital mobility, there is a risk that the central bank offering the best terms will find itself implicitly providing liquidity to other markets, given that institutions are able to swap funds obtained in one currency into other currencies. Valuation margins are also important in this context to ensure that interest rates on ECB lending do not imply a subsidy on a risk-adjusted basis, given the collateral against which the lending is secured.

Overall, the operational framework of the ECB has provided essential support to its objectives during the financial market turmoil, even if money-market interest rates have risen. Consideration should be given to the lessons that can be learnt from this episode in terms of risk management and liquidity. The ECB could consider providing more timely and detailed information, along the lines of the Reserve Bank of Australia, about the assets it has accepted as collateral if this would help to reduce uncertainty in financial markets.

The economic impact of financial market conditions

The increase in the cost of borrowing for banks, as well as the broader turning of the credit cycle and the intensified financial market turmoil, is likely to have an effect on the real economy through the credit channel of monetary policy transmission. Prominent within this process, the banking channel has two key mechanisms (Bernanke and Gilchrist, 1995): the balance sheet channel, whereby falls in the value of collateral or reduced cash flow make it harder to borrow, and the bank lending channel, whereby the supply of loans from banks is reduced. As banking disintermediation has progressed, other financial intermediaries have become more important and made the risk-taking channel more salient: the incentives of investment managers heighten market risk due to herding behaviour and risk-taking can become excessive because rare tail risks are not appropriately taken into account (Rajan, 2005). These channels are interconnected and may feed back on each other, such as when asset prices fall in response to a reduced supply of credit, as well as other economic developments (Chapter 2).

Credit conditions for households and non-financial corporations have tightened as the credit cycle turned. The cost of bank finance has increased as a result of the increase in interbank lending rates relative to the official intervention rate as well the increasing difficulties in obtaining funds through securitisations. The spread on 3-month borrowing has been elevated since the turmoil began, compared with early 2007, and large by historical standards. In addition, the profitability and financial position of euro area banks has weakened, partly related to losses stemming from the US subprime mortgage market (Chapter 3). A number of institutions in European countries have required public support to avoid failure and a co-ordinated rescue plan for the EU banking system was adopted by the European Council in mid-October 2008, including significant government guarantees for parts of the banking system. Lower confidence, the slowing economy and housing market weakness in some euro area countries may also be weighing on the willingness to lend, as well as the reduced intensity of competition among lenders.

The ECB's quarterly Bank Lending Surveys (BLS) have shown that lending standards have been tightened consistently since mid-2007, both for enterprises and for households. This reflects growing concerns about the deteriorating economic and sectoral outlook, as well as increasing difficulties in obtaining funds from wholesale markets and balance sheet constraints. The reported effects of the financial turmoil have risen over the past year, with a marked jump in the most recent survey in October 2008. Between 20-30% of responding banks in the October survey indicated that a hampered access to wholesale funding from money markets or debt securities was having a considerable adverse impact on the quantity and price of their loans, with a further 60% indicating that it was having some impact. MFI interest rates on new long-term loans to companies and households increased between January and September 2008 by around 25 basis points. The prevalence of long-term fixed-rate loans in the euro area implies that the change in the marginal cost of finance has had a much smaller impact on the average effective interest rate on existing loans. Between January and September the latter rose by around 15 basis points on loans for house purchase and around 25 basis points on long-term loans to non-financial corporations. Although there has been an increase over time in the extent to which non-price factors have contributed to the tightening of terms and conditions for approving loans, the October 2008 BLS indicates that the tightening of non-price conditions has not been widespread so far and that banks are generally continuing to lend in the normal way but requiring a higher rate of return.

The cost of non-bank sources of finance has also tightened, which will also push up the cost of raising new capital for firms. Spreads on corporate bonds have increased, notably for higher risk debt, and equity values have declined sharply so that the overall cost of external finance has risen, even if internal funds remain available from the historically high share of profits in GDP.

Despite the tightening of bank lending conditions and the higher cost of borrowing, bank credit has continued to expand, although the annual growth rate has turned down. In the year to September 2008, credit growth to non-financial corporations increased by 12%, but credit growth to households has slowed to less than 4%. In part, this increase in bank on-balance sheet lending reflects "involuntary" lending, with banks taking securitised lending back on to their own balance sheets and borrowers drawing down pre-arranged credit lines. But, the strength of bank lending is also partly the result of substitution away from other sources of funding as issuance of securities by non-financial corporations has slowed. Re-intermediation implied by the need to finance off-balance sheet activities may explain the rapid growth in lending to other financial intermediaries.[7] Credit growth is likely to slow further, both due to the reduced supply of credit and as demand for borrowing is depressed by reduced confidence about the prospects for the economy.

Monetary policy must ensure that price stability is maintained

Although inflation remains above the ECB's definition of price stability, the balance of risks to price stability has changed sharply in recent months as the financial crisis has intensified and global commodity prices have tumbled. The economy has slipped into recession and housing and financial markets are likely to continue to weigh on demand for some time to come, suggesting that substantial economic slack will develop over the coming year. This should help to moderate underlying wage and price pressures, reinforcing the downward impetus to inflation from declining commodity prices. In this event, room for further easing of monetary policy should be available. The OECD projections show scope for the ECB minimum bid rate to be reduced to 2% during 2009. However, there is an unusual amount of uncertainty around the economic outlook at present; if inflationary pressures turn out to be stronger than now anticipated, room for manoeuvre will be constrained. Monetary policy should remain ready to react should long-term inflation expectations become unanchored.

Monetary policy stance

The 25 basis points increase in key ECB interest rates in July 2008 was the first change in interest rates in over a year. Subsequently, as inflationary pressures declined markedly, the financial turmoil intensified and the prospects for global economic growth turned down, the refinancing rate was lowered by 50 basis points in both October and November.

The monetary stance, however, evolved more than this suggests. Real interest rates, measured as the *ex post* annual rate and deflated by the consumption deflator, rose as the policy rate was increased beginning in December 2005 and remained close to 2% throughout 2007, well above the near-zero rates of previous years. But, rising inflation and inflation expectations pushed down real interest rates in the latter part of 2007 and *ex post* real rates fell to close to zero. They have remained close to that level since July 2008, with the reductions in the refinancing rate being mirrored by a similar decline in the headline inflation rate. *Ex ante* real interest rates provide a more relevant measure of the cost of additional borrowing or returns to saving at the margin for forward-looking economic agents. There is considerable uncertainty about inflation over the next year or two but, even if inflation is expected to return fairly swiftly to levels at or below 2%, *ex ante* real interest rates would appear to be below their average of the past decade suggesting that the stance of monetary policy is becoming accommodative provided that the financial turmoil is not unduly impeding the transmission mechanisms of monetary policy.

Beyond the level of real interest rates, however, other indicators point to tighter monetary conditions. The euro has appreciated against the dollar from around 0.85 dollars in 2002 to around 1.40 dollars in the latter part of 2008, down a little from a high close to 1.60 dollars in July 2008. The impact of the global adjustment of the US dollar on the euro has been accentuated by the absence or limited movement of other important currencies against the dollar. Since 2002, the euro nominal effective exchange rate has appreciated by around 30%. This reflects relatively stable euro exchange rates against major trading partners such as Sweden and Switzerland, stability against sterling until the latter part of 2007, and depreciation against Central and Eastern European currencies. The appreciation increases the relative price of domestic currency with a dampening effect on net exports. The exchange rate is likely to be above the long-run equilibrium as the exchange rate against the dollar is above its average level since 1970.[8] Furthermore, as discussed in the previous section, market interest rates have increased relative to the main refinancing rate, reflecting both tighter liquidity conditions and heightened concerns about credit risk.

Inflation has been somewhat higher than would be consistent with the ECB's definition of price stability for most of the past five years and in the first half of 2008 overshot 2% by a considerable margin. Past energy and food price increases have raised headline inflation, but this will be offset in the coming months by the impact of the sharp declines in global commodity prices since mid-2008. The immediate impact of monetary policy on headline inflation is limited and an attempt to engender large short-term changes in inflation would be de-stabilising. Nonetheless, the past increases in oil prices will have had some adverse impact on medium-term supply and, if nominal demand were not to adjust to lower potential output and incomes, supply pressures would gradually increase, maintaining upward pressure on domestic inflation. However, it appears more likely that the slowdown in demand, strengthened by the intensification of the financial crisis and the turning of the housing cycle, will push demand below potential supply. The risks of broad-based second-round effects on wages and prices have not materialised, but have yet to fade completely. Nonetheless, the likely emergence of sizeable economic slack should lead to a marked reduction of inflationary pressures.

Output growth in the euro area contracted in the second and third quarters of 2008, pushing the economy into recession (Table 1.2). The most likely outcome at present is for further contractions in the fourth quarter of 2008 and the first half of 2009. The downturn in external demand, the financial turmoil and the contraction in the housing market in

Table 1.2. **Short-term outlook**[1]

Percentage change

	2005	2006	2007	Projections[1]		
				2008	2009	2010
Private consumption	1.8	2.0	1.6	0.4	0.2	1.2
Government consumption	1.5	1.9	2.3	1.8	1.2	1.2
Gross fixed investment	3.4	5.8	4.1	0.4	–4.4	1.0
Total domestic demand	2.0	2.9	2.3	0.8	–0.5	1.1
Net exports[2]	–0.2	0.2	0.4	0.2	0.0	–1.8
Real gross domestic product (GDP)	**1.8**	**3.0**	**2.6**	**1.0**	**–0.6**	**1.2**
Output gap	–0.9	0.2	0.8	–0.1	–2.4	–3.1
Inflation: harmonised CPI	2.2	2.2	2.1	3.4	1.4	1.3
Inflation: harmonised underlying	1.4	1.4	1.9	1.8	1.6	1.3
Employment	1.9	2.0	2.0	1.0	–0.7	–0.1
Unemployment rate (% of labour force)	8.8	8.2	7.4	7.4	8.6	9.0
Current account balance (% of GDP)	0.5	0.4	0.3	–0.4	–0.1	0.0
Government net lending (% of GDP)	–2.5	–1.3	–0.6	–1.4	–2.2	–2.5
Government debt (% of GDP)	70.4	68.6	66.5	67.4	69.4	71.1

1. Projections are based on *OECD Economic Outlook*, No. 84.
2. Contribution to GDP growth.
Source: OECD, *OECD Economic Outlook 84 database.*

member states will moderate over time, but the subsequent pick-up in activity is projected to be only gradual. A decline in headline inflation through 2009, along with a gradual easing in financial market turmoil and the effects of policy stimulus will all help to support an eventual expansion. By the latter half of 2010 activity is projected to begin to rise more rapidly than potential output, starting to reduce the sizeable amount of economic slack that opens up through 2009. The size and duration of the downturn could be alleviated somewhat if the fiscal support measures discussed in the European Recovery Plan presented by the European Commission in November 2008 are implemented by member states. However, this would require that any measures are timely, well-targeted and only temporary, supported by a clear and credible framework for medium-term fiscal sustainability. Substantial risks remain around this scenario. Simulations based on the new OECD Global Model (Hervé *et al.*, 2007) suggest that the sensitivity of the euro area economy to a worsening of the US housing market or lower emerging market demand is relatively modest. But, factors such as intensified financial market turmoil, a reversal of recent oil price declines and renewed depreciation of the US dollar could all have a non-negligible effect on output. Some of these risks could be correlated.

The broad-based risks to price stability that were thought possible in the first half of 2008 have not materialised, but have not disappeared completely. Some delayed second-round effects from high headline inflation onto wages and prices could still emerge, and longer term inflation expectations could become decoupled from the ECB's price stability objective, although they are not at present. Moreover, although currently moderating, some risks to price stability also stem from the continued underlying strength of monetary and credit growth seen since late 2004. Core inflation, excluding energy and food, has risen only modestly over the past eighteen months, and should now slip back, but needs to be monitored very closely. Across countries there will be differences in the speed at which headline inflation recedes, in part because of the existence of widespread wage indexation to prices in countries such as Belgium, Finland, Luxembourg and Spain (Du Caju *et al.*, 2008).

If inflation expectations were to become de-anchored, with changes in actual inflation generating corresponding changes in expected inflation, monetary conditions would need to change to generate sufficient pressures to achieve price stability. Until recently, there was some concern that high headline inflation was helping to push statistical measures of medium-term inflation expectations up and away from levels consistent with the ECB's definition of price stability. Now that headline inflation has begun to recede, and with sizeable economic slack projected to develop over the next two years, there is a possibility that expectations of medium-term inflation below the levels consistent with price stability could develop. Nonetheless, surveys and financial market data indicate that, at least in the past, long-run inflation expectations have remained well-anchored in the euro area, more so than in the United States (Beechey *et al.*, 2008).

The communication strategy is important in shaping expectations. The monthly press conferences of the President of the ECB provide an important forum for explaining the Governing Council's thinking both on their current decision and looking ahead, although the ECB never pre-commits to future interest rates. Furthermore, frequent speeches by members of the ECB Governing Council and Executive Board allow the ECB to explain its current thinking, give messages to other policy makers and economic agents, and signal its commitment to price stability. A recent review of theory and evidence suggested that central bank communications can play an important role in enhancing the predictability of policy and potentially helping to achieve policy objectives, but that a consensus on the optimal strategy had yet to be reached (Blinder *et al.*, 2008). As argued in the previous *Survey* (OECD, 2007a), the ECB could improve its communication of its economic analysis, particularly with a view to emphasising how price stability will be maintained in the medium run:

- It may be useful to extend the forecast horizon of the published staff forecast to at least eight quarters ahead of the current date at all times, rather than under the existing practice whereby the December staff forecast has only a horizon of 12 months. Recent developments, where the short-term outlook for inflation is dominated by shifts in the price of energy and food, underline the importance of providing forecasts that look beyond these near-term events to a horizon over which these shocks and the effects of policy changes would be completely absorbed. Publishing a quarterly path alongside the calendar year numbers would give a clearer picture of underlying developments, as annual averages can mask important within-year movements in growth and inflation rates. In addition, it would be helpful to publish more detailed forecasts of output and other measures including, for example, a measure of inflation excluding the full impact of oil prices and food, or capacity utilisation, so that the assessment of the underlying balance of demand and supply was clearer. Taken together, this additional information about the staff forecast may help shape expectations about future inflation. However, it is important that any enhancement of the information in the current projections should be presented in a manner that ensures consistency with the two-pillar strategy under which monetary analysis also plays an important role in explaining medium-term developments.
- Presentation of the risks around the forecast could be improved further. The methodology of presenting ranges has been refined with the recent adoption of a model using Bayesian techniques to provide stable real-time estimates of uncertainty (ECB, 2008c). This has somewhat narrowed the range of uncertainty for inflation one-year ahead. It may be useful to show more information about the forecast distribution than a simple range, particularly if the distribution is skewed. This could be particularly important at a time of high instability.

In each case, it would be important to make it clear that any additional information relates to the staff forecasts and not those of the Governing Council.

Monetary developments

The ECB's monetary policy strategy is distinctive in the prominent role given to monetary analysis and has an ambitious agenda to develop the underlying analysis (Stark, 2008). The monetary analysis is used to cross-check the economic analysis of cyclical dynamics and shocks. The growth rate of the M3 aggregate has begun to slow but, as of September 2008, remains close to 8½ per cent, almost twice the reference rate of 4.5%, although this may overstate the underlying pace of monetary expansion because of the current attractiveness of M3 assets relative to those outside the measure and, to a lesser extent, because of re-intermediation by the banking system. The expansion of narrow money has slowed consistently since the end of 2005 with the annual growth rate of M1 now around 1%.

Information from monetary analysis played an important role in signalling the need for and communicating the tightening of the policy stance that began in 2005, at a time when real economy developments alone may not have supported such action in themselves. The current financial turmoil provides another natural test of one of the benefits of the special emphasis on monetary developments as well as indicators of real economic activity: the closer link between monetary conditions and financial developments. Strong money growth is associated with asset price inflation and wealth is one determinant of the growth of M3 (Boone *et al.*, 2004). The monetary analysis has helped to identify the extent of credit supply distortions during the turmoil, although the financial dislocation also makes it harder to interpret signals coming from the monetary data. As suggested in the previous *Survey* (OECD, 2007a), it would be helpful if the ECB published on a regular basis further details of its quantified, money-based analysis of the outlook for inflation and more detailed information on the signals about inflation obtained from its framework for monetary analysis. This could help the public to understand how information from the monetary pillar is incorporated in policy decisions. The ECB does publish such analysis on an *ad hoc* basis in its *Monthly Bulletins* but with intervals of more than a year.[9] These provide a great deal of information about the factors shaping money supply and demand, but have less information about the link between monetary indicators and inflation. The Governing Council decided in 2007 to undertake a programme of work to further enhance its monetary analysis. This should help to provide further information.

Monetary policy over the medium term

The performance of the ECB over the first ten years of its existence has been impressive (Box 1.3), but recent macroeconomic developments underline the importance of relatively rare but high impact events which the central bank is now confronting for the first time. For example, the increase in real oil prices up to mid-2008 was almost unprecedented since the beginning of the modern oil industry (Figure 1.9). Credit cycles also build up over long periods of time but can correct very rapidly in a way and with a timing that is hard to predict. As recent events show, these developments pose the risk that inflation may be blown far off course in the short run. What is the appropriate response to such tail risks?

Rare events are hard to predict and their distribution is hard to evaluate, precisely because historical experience is by definition limited. It has been suggested that policy

Figure 1.9. **The US dollar price of oil**

In real terms[1]

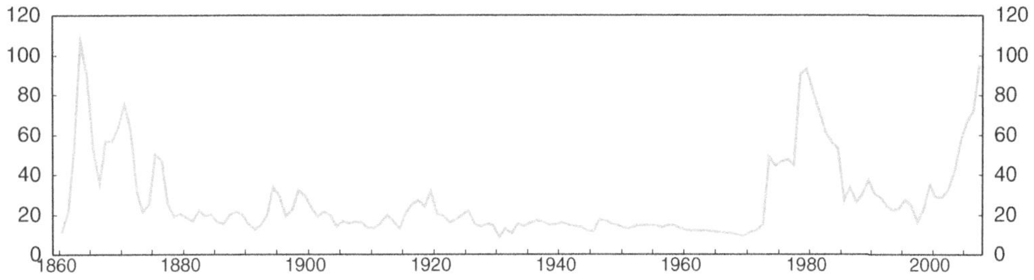

1. 2007 prices.

Source: BP (2008), *BP Statistical Review of World Energy*, June and OECD calculations.

StatLink http://dx.doi.org/10.1787/518232808406

should be set on average to take these possibilities into account by way of insurance, but this is difficult. There are strong arguments against taking insurance against rare events given that this implies that the price stability objective may potentially not be met for the vast majority of the time. It is also difficult to anticipate the likely impact, frequency and nature of rare events, and there is a risk that policies that aim to provide insurance create moral hazard and therefore increase the probability of such events (BIS, 2008). Such a policy would also change economic behaviour and expectations of how monetary policy operates, thereby possibly undermining some of the achievements of monetary stability.

Such extreme events pose some difficulties for the design of monetary policy. By defining a numerical objective for price stability to be maintained over the "medium term", there is little guidance within the framework about the expected margin of variation in the

Box 1.3. **The performance of the ECB**

The performance of any central bank is difficult to assess as it is hard to benchmark institutions with different mandates, where each faces different economic structures and shocks. The unconditional performance of the ECB in terms of its price-stability mandate over the first ten years of monetary union has been extremely good with inflation of just above 2% on average, albeit somewhat lower in the early years and then mostly above the reference level of 2% more recently. This is similar to other countries such as Australia, Canada, Korea and the United States, and much better than others such as Sweden and Norway, which experienced inflation well below their own targets (Table 1.3). This picture is confirmed by the low average deviations from target, measured by the Root Mean Square Error (RMSE), and the low standard deviation of inflation. Furthermore, both the level and volatility of the change in the national accounts private consumption deflator, a broader measure of the price of consumption, have been relatively low in the euro area. This is consistent with price stability being achieved, although there is little variation in the change in the price level over the past decade for many other countries. Forward-looking measures such as surveys of inflation expectations or yields on index-linked bonds further suggest that inflation is well-anchored at longer horizons around the ECB's objective, as it is in many other countries. The ECB Survey of Professional Forecasters shows that the dispersion of inflation forecasts for 2012 is extremely narrow with a standard deviation of just 0.1% compared with 0.51% for the average of inflation over the next ten years for the United States in the Federal Reserve Bank of Philadelphia's Survey of Professional Forecasters.

Box 1.3. The performance of the ECB *(cont.)*

Table 1.3. Alternative measures of inflation performance 1999 to 2007

	Target measure				Consumption deflator	
	Objective[1]	Average	RMSE	St. dev.	Average	St. dev.
EURO	1.90	2.06	0.44	0.42	1.99	0.51
AUS	2.50	2.76	1.16	1.14	2.26	1.10
CAN	2.00	1.84	0.48	0.46	1.73	0.51
CHE	2.00	0.91	1.16	0.44	0.78	0.40
CZE	3.00	2.69	1.45	1.35	1.92	1.41
DNK	2.00	1.72	0.66	0.61	1.95	0.68
GBR[2]	2.5/2.0	1.55	1.05	0.57	1.96	0.53
HUN	3.50	6.77	4.14	2.58	6.20	2.98
ISL	2.50	4.54	2.99	2.02	4.27	2.68
KOR	2.50	2.36	0.98	0.99	3.29	1.09
NOR	2.50	1.89	1.46	1.17	1.75	1.05
NZL	1.50	2.28	1.33	1.09	1.63	0.89
SWE	2.00	1.33	1.07	0.85	1.49	0.55
USA	2.00	2.28	0.65	0.60	2.28	0.60

1. Objectives based on Mishkin and Schmidt-Hebbel (2001), updated using central bank websites. The mid-point of stated ranges is used where necessary. The objective of the ECB follows the interpretation of the price stability objective given in Fischer *et al.* (2006). Objectives that are specified in terms of a "core" measure of inflation are assessed against the OECD's measure of core inflation rather than the specific national target series.
2. It is assumed that the change in objective is immediate at the point it occurred in 2004.

A credible monetary regime and judicious policy measures should achieve price stability with a minimal degree of disruption to output. Euro area GDP growth has been relatively stable at the same time as inflation has been very steady (Figure 1.10). However, OECD estimates of the output gap suggest that output has been relatively far from potential compared with other economies over this period and hence on this basis the performance of the ECB seems broadly in line with most other OECD central banks. In any case, experience supports the view that the ECB's focus on price stability has not come at the expense of output volatility, underlining the fact that a single mandate achieves the desired outcomes.

Ten years is a short period over which to draw conclusions about the performance of any central bank. While the ECB has established itself successfully and its performance compares well to that of other central banks and of European countries in previous decades, economic volatility has been relatively low during the past decade in many countries. There is considerable debate about the nature and causes of the "great moderation" and to what extent it reflects structural changes in the economy, better monetary policy institutions or simply good luck. Recent shocks suggest that the inflation performance achieved during the first ten years of monetary union may have partly been due to the absence of relatively rare but high impact shocks.

Box 1.3. **The performance of the ECB** *(cont.)*

Figure 1.10. **Inflation and output volatility**[1]

Standard deviation of year-on-year percentage growth since 1999:Q1

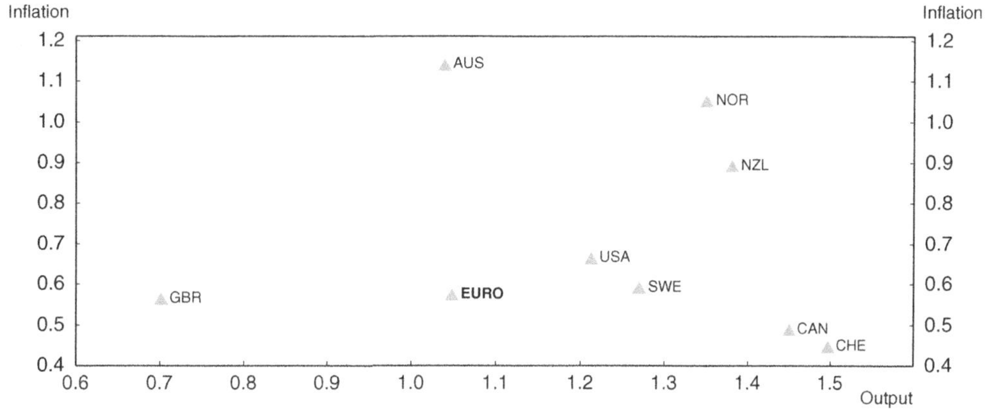

1. Inflation represented by the private consumption deflator and output by GDP volume.

Source: OECD, *OECD Economic Outlook database*.

StatLink http://dx.doi.org/10.1787/518237288336

short term or the period in which inflation is expected to be close to 2%, although this can be communicated by the Governing Council in other ways as the conjuncture evolves. This approach does, however, give the ECB sufficient flexibility to find the appropriate reaction to rare events without endangering its credibility. The objective of keeping HICP inflation "below, but close to, 2%" is judged to be sufficient to hedge against the risks of both very low inflation and deflation. In general, all central banks face the challenge that greater efforts need to be made to predict and understand rare events. For instance, although technical assumptions may be a reasonable approach to forecasting commodity prices in normal times, the increases experienced in recent years have, to a great extent, been driven by the economic expansion of emerging economies. An important lesson from the previous increases in oil prices in the 1970s is that while an increase in inflation is likely in the short run, it is important that inflation is not allowed to persist at such levels long enough to trigger changes in behaviour. For instance, CPI inflation in Germany peaked at 7% in the early 1970s but this was brought down within a couple of years to rates similar to those seen before the energy crisis, thereby avoiding the much longer experience of higher inflation in many other developed economies.

Corrections of asset price bubbles or credit cycles are a particular case of rare events, in the sense that they are more closely related to monetary conditions. While asset prices should not normally be granted a special role in monetary policy-making, due account has to be taken of their behaviour and there is a case for trying to "lean against the wind" in the expansionary phase so as to minimise the size of the effect when events reverse. Evidently, this requires that policy makers should be able to identify bubbles and act against them effectively, as discussed in the previous *Survey*.[10] In this sense the monetary analysis performed at the ECB seems to be well suited to cope with challenges brought about by asset price developments. The identification of asset price misalignments in real time is difficult and subject to uncertainty, but a substantial departure from historical experience may provide a signal of misalignment in many cases. However, it is difficult for monetary policy to temper rising asset prices as the required tightening would likely to be very considerable and would compromise the stability of prices in the near term; there would therefore be a trade-off with other objectives (Mishkin, 2008). Monetary policy may not be the appropriate instrument for addressing these issues *ex ante*, particularly those related to credit, but this raises the question of what other policy instruments would be more appropriate, which is discussed in the next section.

Challenges to build more effective markets and better institutions

Alongside sound macroeconomic policies, effective structural policies are important both to raising living standards in the long run and because of their impact on macroeconomic developments and risks. The euro area faces a number of long-standing challenges to improve the performance of its labour, product and capital markets. Financial innovation, increasing competition and integration have improved long-run economic growth prospects. These trends have also transformed the financial landscape in Europe and made the capital markets of euro area countries more tightly interwoven with each other. The functioning of the European financial system has evolved enormously over past decades as the capital market has become more integrated, changing the way in which the European economy works and introducing new risks (Chapter 2). These developments, as well as the recent financial market turmoil, have underlined the importance of an adequate framework for financial regulation and supervision (Chapter 3). In addition, there will be strong future pressures on fiscal policy and performance from population ageing (Chapter 4). This section sets out the key challenges relating to the financial stability of the euro area and policies to raise long-term economic performance.

Challenges to financial stability

The recent financial market turmoil underlines the risk that developments in the financial system pose for the wider economy, even if such events are relatively rare. The proximate cause of the turnaround in financial markets was in the United States but the impact was widespread. Although an improvised policy response has been able to contain the crisis, the costs so far around the world have been large and could rise by considerably more.

A question that cuts across a number of structural policies is how far policy can be used to "lean against the wind" when credit cycles build up either at the euro area or national level. In the case of asset-price bubbles at the euro area level, monetary policy should play a role. However, as argued above, monetary policy can and should only play a limited role in the case of country-specific bubbles. Alternative macro-prudential instruments may therefore be considered, although there is no comprehensive experience of applying such policies. This is particularly important in the context of the euro area where monetary policy cannot address country-specific asset-price bubbles either *ex ante* or *ex post* (Ahrend *et al.*, 2008). Furthermore, while monetary policy may not be the most appropriate instrument for dealing with asset price bubbles and not all bubbles should be pricked, there is a case for considering what policies can be used to dampen credit cycles (Mishkin, 2008). These policies can be divided into "automatic" financial stabilisers, regulatory frameworks that tend to dampen credit cycles, such as counter-cyclical capital requirements and dynamic provisioning, and discretionary policy actions such as imposing *ad hoc* restrictions on banks' activities in order to reduce lending at a point when the strength of the credit cycle is a concern. The policy response to financial turmoil touches a number of different policy instruments, particularly financial regulation and fiscal policy.

A key challenge facing the euro area, as discussed in Chapter 3, is the regulatory response to cross-border risks in the financial system. The implications of this, however, reach far beyond financial regulation: cross-border banking assets are large relative to GDP in many countries. Banking exposures of EU countries to each other are on average 27% of GDP for foreign branches and 34% for subsidiaries (ECB, 2007). There is a wide dispersion in the scale of foreign banking exposures by country (Figure 1.11). The extent of cross-border banking activity implies that serious problems for an institution in one country could have a substantial impact on the financial system elsewhere, while the potential exposures of a home country government to liabilities associated with branches in another country may be large. Unlike other areas of European integration where inaction presents an opportunity cost in terms of a failure to reap the rewards of creating a larger and more effective market, failure to create an adequate regulatory architecture is both a hindrance to a more effective capital market and also leaves a tail risk of very substantial fiscal and economic costs.

Figure 1.11. **Foreign exposures of domestically headquartered banks**

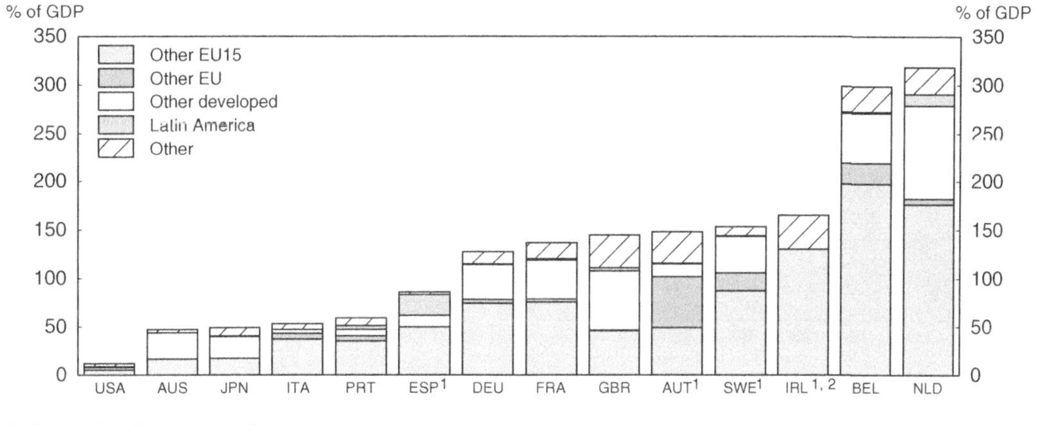

1. Immediate borrower basis.
2. Incomplete breakdown.

Source: BIS (2008), *Consolidated Banking Statistics*, August, *www.bis.org/statistics/consstats.htm.*

StatLink http://dx.doi.org/10.1787/518240185035

Policies to raise living standards and sustainability

The key long-term challenge the euro area faces is to raise living standards (Figure 1.12): GDP per capita is on average almost one-third lower than in the United States with relatively low labour utilisation in many countries and weak productivity in others. Furthermore, the rate of growth in income per person in most countries implies a very slow rate of convergence, or even divergence, with the leading OECD economies. Employment rates as a share of the working-age population have continued to rise, particularly for women and older workers, and the unemployment rate has fallen. Although the employment rate of those aged 55-64 remains low by international standards and compared to prime-aged workers, there has been a sharp rise in the employment of older workers, partly due to pension reforms that have reduced high implicit taxes on continued

Figure 1.12. **Key structural indicators**

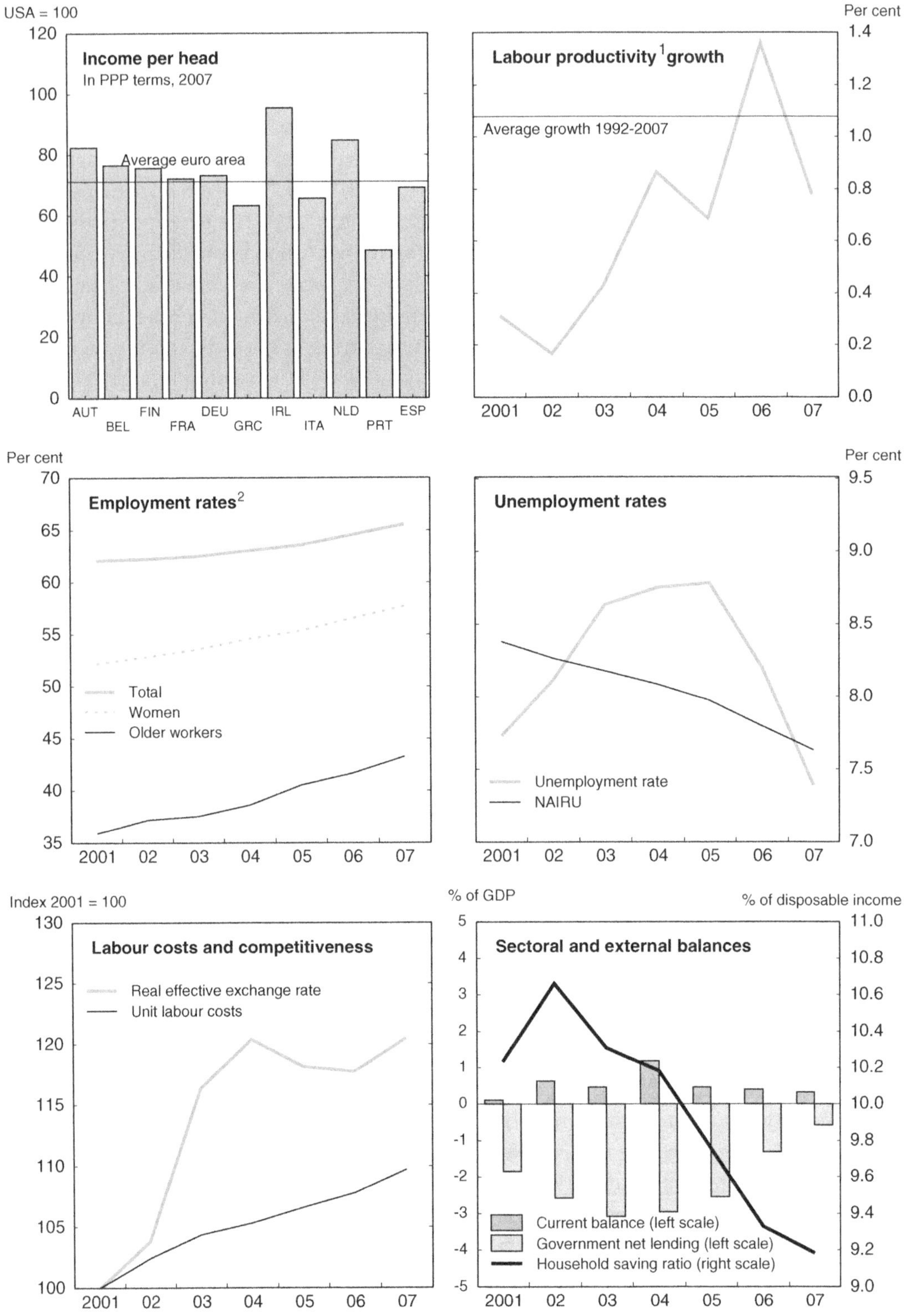

1. Gross domestic product per employee.
2. As a percentage of population aged 15-64, except for older workers, defined as those aged 55-64.

Source: OECD (2008), *OECD Economic Outlook 84 database* and *Productivity database*.

StatLink http://dx.doi.org/10.1787/518240507254

work and removed pathways into early retirement. Productivity growth has picked up since the early 2000s, but has remained below its long-run average. It has been argued that rising employment, particularly by relatively low-skilled groups, may have depressed measured productivity growth. However, the total effect of population structure on the level of labour productivity may be fairly modest (Boulhol and Turner, 2008) so that the magnitude of these effects would probably be fairly small. This suggests that the slow rate of labour productivity growth is likely to have its origins in other factors.

The euro area faces major challenges to raising living standards. Easing of restrictive product market regulations and employment protection would help to boost living standards in many countries. The Lisbon Strategy for Growth and Jobs, which was re-launched in 2005, provides a framework for such policies where National Reform Programmes identify the action to be taken by each member state. The main challenges identified in the *Survey* of the European Union (OECD, 2007b) and *Going for Growth* (OECD, 2008c) include raising competition in network industries, encouraging greater competition in the services sector, enhancing the functioning of the internal market and making regional cohesion policy more effective. Removing barriers to labour mobility by increasing the portability of pensions and social welfare rates, as well as facilitating the recognition of qualifications, would help to enhance the functioning of labour markets. Productivity could also be improved by raising the efficiency of public spending and the tax system (Chapter 4).

Notes

1. As discussed in Chapter 2, it is likely that these effects are shifting as a result of financial market deepening, integration and innovation, although the overall direction of such changes is hard to evaluate.
2. Based on Table 3.1 of *OECD Economic Outlook 83* (OECD, 2008b).
3. This front loading means that larger operations are carried out towards the beginning of each reserve maintenance period, thereby ensuring that banks are closer to achieving the targeted average level of reserves at an earlier point in time and do not face pressures to increase reserves as the reserve period draws to an end.
4. The response by the authorities in the United States is discussed in the forthcoming *Economic Survey* of the United States (OECD, 2008e).
5. See Keister *et al.* (2008) for a discussion of this issue.
6. The ECB also currently conducts its longer-term refinancing operations and its US dollar operations as fixed rate tenders with full allotment. The ECB also conducts Swiss franc liquidity providing operations and has created euro swap or repo lines with some EU national banks.
7. Excluding insurance corporations and pension funds.
8. Measured using quarterly observations of an index of the euro and its predecessor currencies.
9. The most recent update was in July 2007. The previous update was in October 2005.
10. See Box 2.3 "Should central banks respond to asset price booms?" (OECD, 2007a).

Bibliography

Ahrend, R., B. Cournède and R. Price (2008), "Monetary Policy, Market Excesses and Financial Turmoil", *OECD Economics Department Working Papers*, No. 597, OECD, Paris.

Baldwin, R. (2006), "The Euro's Trade Effects", *ECB Working Paper*, No. 594, March, ECB, Frankfurt.

Barrell, R. *et al.* (2008), "The Impact of EMU on Growth and Employment", *Economic Papers* 318, April.

Beechey, M.J., B.K. Johannsen and A.T. Levin (2008), "Are Long-Run Inflation Expectations Anchored More Firmly in the Euro Area than in the United States?", *Federal Reserve Board Finance and Economics Working Paper*, No. 2008-23.

Bernanke, B. and M. Gilchrist (1995), "Inside the Black Box: The Credit Channel of Monetary Policy Transmission", *Journal of Economic Perspectives*, Vol. 9 (Fall), pp. 27-48.

BIS (Bank of International Settlements) (2008), *BIS 78th Annual Report*, BIS, Basel.

Blinder, A. *et al.* (2008), "Central Bank Communication and Monetary Policy: A Survey of Theory and Evidence", *NBER Working Paper Series*, WP 13932.

Boone, L., F. Mikol and P. van den Noord (2004), "Wealth Effects on Money Demand in EMU: Econometric Evidence", *OECD Economics Department Working Papers*, No. 411, OECD, Paris.

Boulhol, H and L. Turner (2008), "Recent Trends and Structural Breaks in US and EU15 Labour Productivity Growth", *OECD Economics Department Working Papers*, No. 628, OECD, Paris.

Catte, P. *et al.* (2004), "Housing Markets, Wealth and the Business Cycle", *OECD Economics Department Working Papers*, No. 394, OECD, Paris.

Catte, P. and T. Sløk (2005), "Assessing the Value of Indicators of Underlying Inflation for Monetary Policy", *OECD Economics Department Working Papers*, No. 461, OECD, Paris.

Du Caju, P. *et al.* (2008), "Institutional Features of Wage Bargaining in 22 EU countries, the US and Japan", *mimeo.*

Duval, R., J. Elmeskov and L. Vogel (2007), "Structural Policies and Economic Resilience to Shocks", *OECD Economics Department Working Papers*, No. 567, OECD, Paris.

EC (2008), *EMU@10 – Successes and Challenges After 10 Years of Economic and Monetary Union*, European Commission, Brussels.

ECB (2006), *The Implementation of Monetary Policy in the Euro Area: General Documentation on Eurosystem Monetary Policy Instruments and Procedures*, September.

ECB (2007), *EU Banking Structures*, ECB, Frankfurt.

ECB (2008a), 10th Anniversary of the ECB, *Monthly Bulletin.*

ECB (2008b), "The Eurosystem's Open Market Operations During the Recent Periods of Financial Market Volatility", *Monthly Bulletin*, May.

ECB (2008c), "New Procedure for Constructing ECB Staff Projection Ranges", Mimeo, Frankurt, 4 September.

Fischer, B. *et al.* (2006), "Money and Monetary Policy: The ECB Experience 1999-2006", Paper presented at the 4th ECB central banking conference, 9-10 November, Frankfurt.

Frankel, J. and A. Rose (1998), "The Endogeneity of the Optimum Currency Area Criteria", *Economic Journal*, Vol. 108, Issue 449 (July).

Geraats, P. (2008), "ECB Credibility and Transparency", European Economy, Economic Papers, 330, June 2008.

Hervé, K. *et al.* (2007), "Globalisation and the Macroeconomic Policy Environment", *OECD Economics Department Working Papers*, No. 552, OECD, Paris.

Keister, T., A. Martin and J. McAndrews (2008), "Divorcing Money from Monetary Policy", *Federal Reserve Bank of New York Policy Review*, forthcoming, New York.

Leiner-Killinger, N. *et al.* (2007), "Structural Reforms in EMU and the Role of Monetary Policy: a Survey of the Literature", *ECB Occasional Paper Series*, No. 66, July.

Mishkin, F. (2008), "How Should We Respond to Asset Price Bubbles?", speech given on 15 May 2008 at the Wharton Financial Institutions Center and Oliver Wyman Institute's Annual Financial Risk Roundtable, Philadelphia, Pennsylvania, 15 May.

Mishkin, F. and K. Schmidt-Hebbel (2001), "One Decade of Inflation Targeting in the World: What Do We Know and What Do We Need to Know?", *NBER Working Paper*, No. W8397, July.

van den Noord, P. and C. André (2007), "Why has Core Inflation Remained so Muted in the Face of the Oil Shock?", *OECD Economics Department Working Papers*, No. 551, OECD, Paris

OECD (2006), "The OECD Synthetic Indicator of Risk Premiums", Appendix I.2 in *OECD Economic Outlook*, No. 80, OECD, Paris.

OECD (2007a), *OECD Economic Surveys: Euro Area*, Vol. 2006/16, OECD, Paris.

OECD (2007b), *OECD Economic Surveys: European Union*, OECD, Paris.

OECD (2008a), *Financial Market Trends*, No. 94, Vol. 2008/1, OECD, Paris.

OECD (2008b), *OECD Economic Outlook*, No. 83, June, OECD, Paris.

OECD (2008c), *Going for Growth*, OECD, Paris.

OECD (2008d), *OECD Economic Surveys: Spain*, OECD, Paris.

OECD (2008e), *OECD Economic Surveys: The United States*, OECD, Paris.

Rajan, R. (2005), "Has Financial Development Made the World Riskier?", *NBER Working Paper*, No. W11728, November.

Stark, J. (2008), "A Strategic Vision for Statistics – Challenges for the Next 10 Years", statement delivered at the 4th ECB Conference on Statistics, Frankfurt am Main, 24 April.

ISBN 978-92-64-04824-9
OECD Economic Surveys: Euro Area

Chapter 2

Financial integration, innovation and the monetary policy transmission mechanism

Over the past decade, considerable progress has been made in integrating Europe's financial markets, facilitated by policies to ensure the free flow of capital and provision of financial services across borders and the adoption of the euro. Financial innovation and enhanced market integration have changed the face of the European financial system, enhancing competitive pressures, although impediments still remain. New financial products have led to the unbundling of risks and large banking groups have emerged, operating across national borders and in multiple market segments. These have increased the inter-linkages between markets and institutions across the euro area, raising questions about whether the speed and the channels of monetary policy transmission in the euro area have changed.

The first decade of monetary union has witnessed marked changes in the size and structure of European financial markets. The assets and liabilities of households, businesses and financial institutions have risen markedly relative to incomes and output, and the geographical distribution of assets has become more dispersed. Financial innovations worldwide have led to the increasing use of new products and techniques for diversifying and monitoring financial and economic risks, although the pace of change has undoubtedly slowed during the present financial market turmoil. The introduction of the euro, EU-wide measures to eliminate obstacles to the supply of financial services, and the development of new common payment infrastructures have all helped to foster integration. But much more remains to be done, especially in retail financial services. Taken together, financial market deepening and innovation are likely to be having important effects on the euro area economy. Provided that there is efficient supervision, enhanced competition will be beneficial for output growth, and deeper markets will offer new opportunities for smoothing fluctuations in incomes and consumption. Changes in financial structure will also affect the workings of different channels of monetary policy transmission, and possibly also the overall speed and impact of policy changes.

Financial market deepening

Euro area household financial assets and liabilities have risen relative to household disposable income over the last decade (Figure 2.1). Net financial wealth at the end of 2007 was between 2 to 2¼ times the level of disposable income, comparable to Canada, but lower than in Japan, the United States and the United Kingdom (OECD [2008], Annex Table 58). Tangible non-financial assets have also risen relative to income in the largest euro area economies and are large relative to net financial assets. As of the end of 2006,

Figure 2.1. **Household financial balance sheet**

In per cent of net disposable income

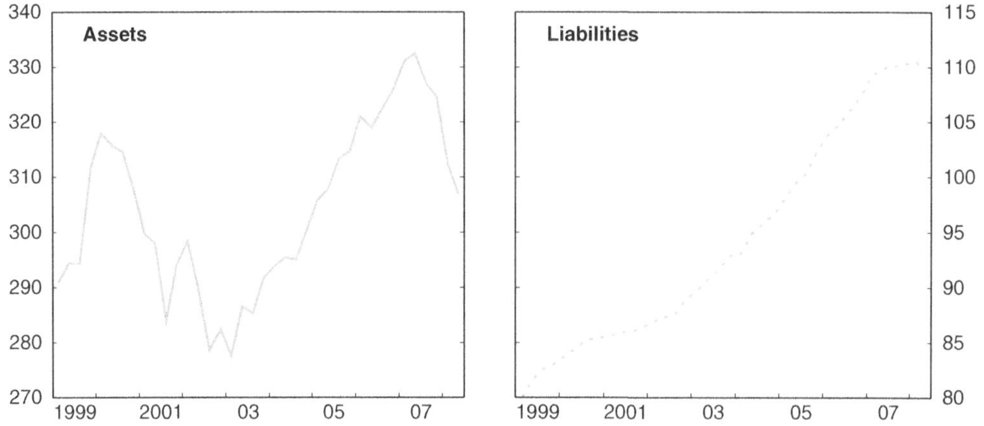

Source: European Central Bank and OECD, *OECD Economic Outlook database.*

StatLink http://dx.doi.org/10.1787/518257165355

non-financial assets were between 4 to 6 times the size of disposable income in Germany, France and Italy. ECB estimates for the euro area suggest that the share of housing wealth in total wealth was around 60% in 2007 (ECB, 2008c). As elsewhere, rising housing wealth in the euro area has been accompanied by rapid growth in household financial liabilities, especially since 2002, although debt-income levels remain below those in many other major economies.

The balance sheets of euro area monetary and financial institutions (MFIs) have also expanded sharply in recent years (Figure 2.2) and total assets are now almost 2½ times the level of euro area GDP. Bank loans continue to be the dominant financial asset, although their share in MFIs on-balance sheet financial assets has gradually declined. The balance sheet data may understate the overall growth of banking activities, as regulatory provisions (Basel I capital requirements) have induced banks, at least until recently, to move some activities off their balance sheets, a trend reinforced by financial innovations.

Figure 2.2. **MFI assets and loans**

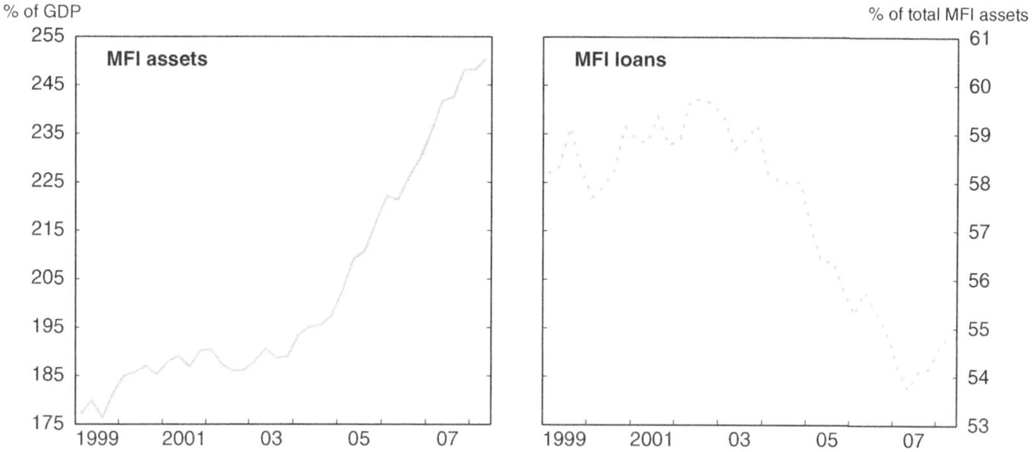

Source: European Central Bank.

StatLink http://dx.doi.org/10.1787/518267672016

Balance sheet expansion has been accompanied by consolidation in the euro area banking sector, with the number of credit institutions declining by 3% per annum on average between end-2002 and end-2006 (ECB, 2007b). The extent of consolidation has been especially marked in France, the Netherlands and Germany. Measures of market concentration, such as the share of the largest five banking groups, have edged up in the euro area (and the EU) over the past five years (ECB, 2007b). This offers opportunities for efficiency gains from economies of scale, but also points to a need for active monitoring of the banking market by competition authorities.[1]

Euro area financial markets have also become increasingly subject to global influences over the past decade, with international investment assets and liabilities having risen rapidly relative to GDP (Figure 2.3). Euro area investors have thus become more exposed to fluctuations in international asset prices and exchange rates. But equally, euro area-specific "shocks" may have less direct effect on the euro area economy than before, since stronger linkages outside the euro area ensure that a larger proportion of such "shocks" will have to be absorbed by foreign investors (Hervé *et al.*, 2008). This has implications for the workings of the monetary transmission mechanism, discussed further below.

Figure 2.3. **Euro area international investment position**

In per cent of GDP

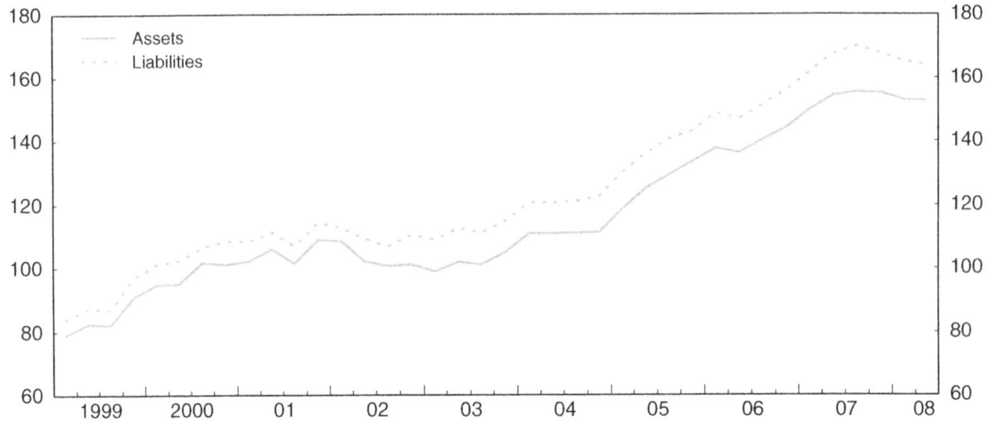

Source: European Central Bank.

StatLink http://dx.doi.org/10.1787/518286813056

Although extra-area investments have expanded, they still remain small relative to cross-border investment within the euro area (Figure 2.4). For euro area monetary and financial institutions (MFIs), the proportion of their assets held outside the euro area and the proportion of their liabilities held by extra-area investors are closely matched, possibly reflecting a continued desire to reduce exchange rate risks. In total, the share of cross-border assets in MFI portfolios is greater than the share of cross-border liabilities, but this is almost entirely accounted for by intra-area investments.

The rapid growth in financial markets in the euro area has yet to change the principal differences between financial development in the euro area and the United States. Over the two-year period 2005-06, aggregate capital market size in the euro area, measured as the ratio of the total value of stock, bond and loan markets to GDP, averaged 256% of GDP, broadly comparable to that in Japan, but well below the United States, where total capital market size was over 350% of GDP (Trichet, 2007; Hartmann *et al.*, 2007 and ECB, 2008a). This suggests there may be further scope for financial deepening in the euro area.

Stock and bond market capitalisation in the euro area remain well below that in the United States; in contrast, the banking sector in the euro area is considerably larger than that in the United States. Such differences in financial structures are also present inside the euro area and the European Union (Figure 2.5; Bartiloro *et al.*, 2007; ECB, 2008a). The share of deposits in total household financial assets has declined over time in almost all of the euro area economies but, with the exception of the Netherlands, remains higher than the share in either the United States, or the United Kingdom. Bank deposits account for almost half of household assets in Austria and Greece. These persistent cross-country differences in financial structures have implications for monetary policy transmission, since countries that have a higher proportion of assets held in deposits are less likely to be exposed directly to wealth effects from fluctuations in asset prices, all else being equal.

OECD ECONOMIC SURVEYS: EURO AREA – ISBN 978-92-64-04824-9 – © OECD 20

Figure 2.4. **Cross-border assets and deposits of euro area MFIs**

Per cent of total aggregate MFI assets/liabilities

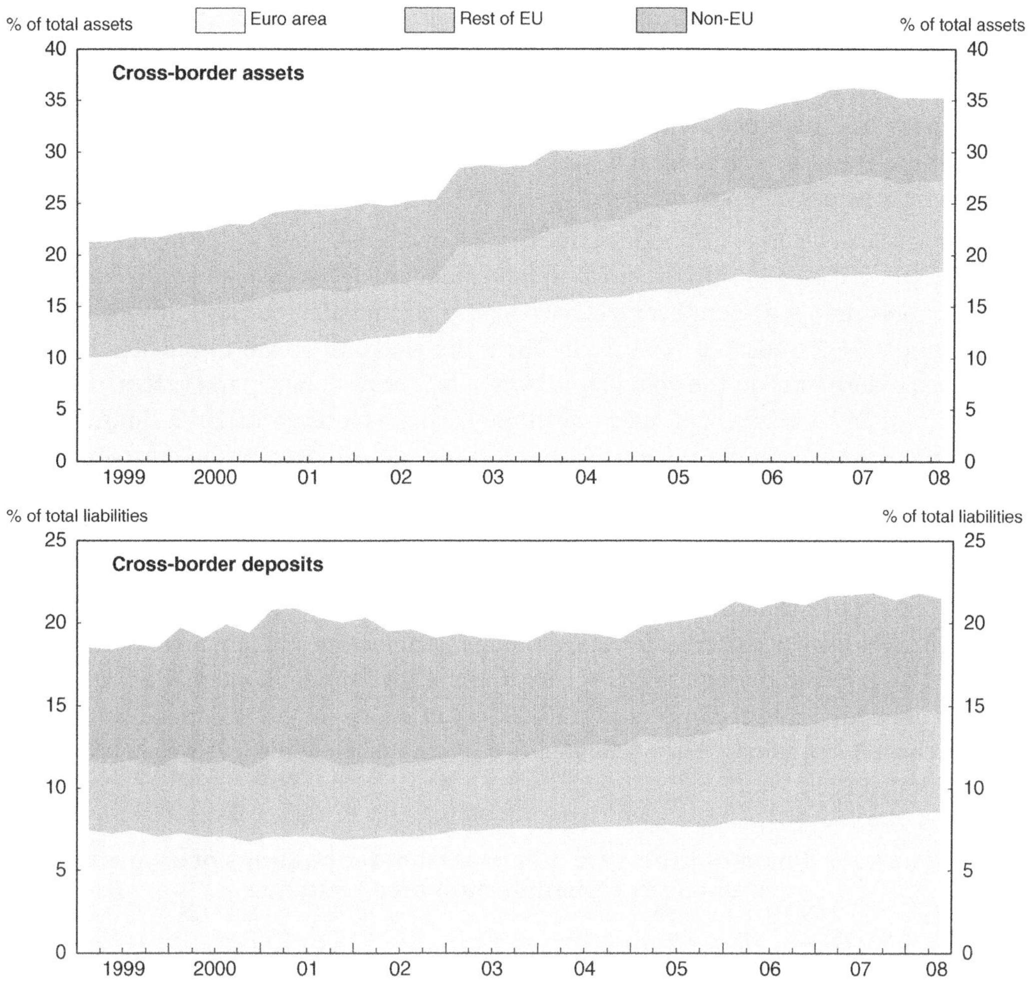

Source: European Central Bank.

StatLink http://dx.doi.org/10.1787/518417358427

Figure 2.5. **Share of currency and deposits in household financial assets**

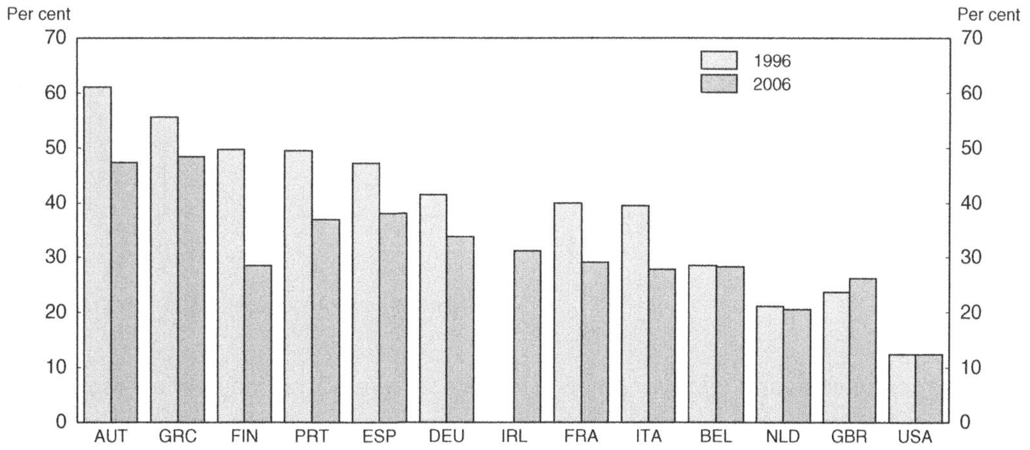

Source: OECD, *National Accounts – Financial Balance Sheets 1995-2006*, Volume IIIb.

StatLink http://dx.doi.org/10.1787/518428050304

Financial integration in Europe

Financial market integration has progressed alongside market expansion in Europe. Increasingly, market participants are becoming subject to a single set of rules and can access or sell financial instruments and services regardless of their geographical location. Cross-border activity may also be hampered by factors such as cultural and linguistic differences and distance, which may dampen the potential extent of cross-border integration. Even so, available indicators suggest that the extent of integration varies considerably across different market segments (OECD, 2007; EC, 2007a; ECB, 2008a).

The euro area short-term money market has in effect been a single market since the introduction of the euro, with the cross-country standard deviation of unsecured interbank lending rates dropping from over 100 basis points in mid-1998 to close to zero from the beginning of 1999 until mid-2007. Since then, the global financial turbulence has been accompanied by a rise in the volatility of very short-term money market rates. It is likely that these changes reflect continued uncertainty about counterparty risk, as indicated by a widening of spreads between overnight and three-month rates in the euro area and a continued need, by at least some financial institutions, to adjust liquidity positions for reporting purposes at quarter-ends.

Euro area markets for securities have also become more integrated since 1999 (Figure 2.6). ECB estimates suggest that cross-country yields and returns have become increasingly driven by common factors, although local factors still remain important (ECB, 2008a). The most rapid progress has occurred in the government bond market, which was almost perfectly integrated up until mid-2007 (Christiansen, 2007). Cross-country yield spreads have subsequently risen (Chapter 4), but remain below the levels seen prior to the advent of EMU.

Figure 2.6. **Share of intra euro area cross-border holdings of securities and equity issued by euro area residents**

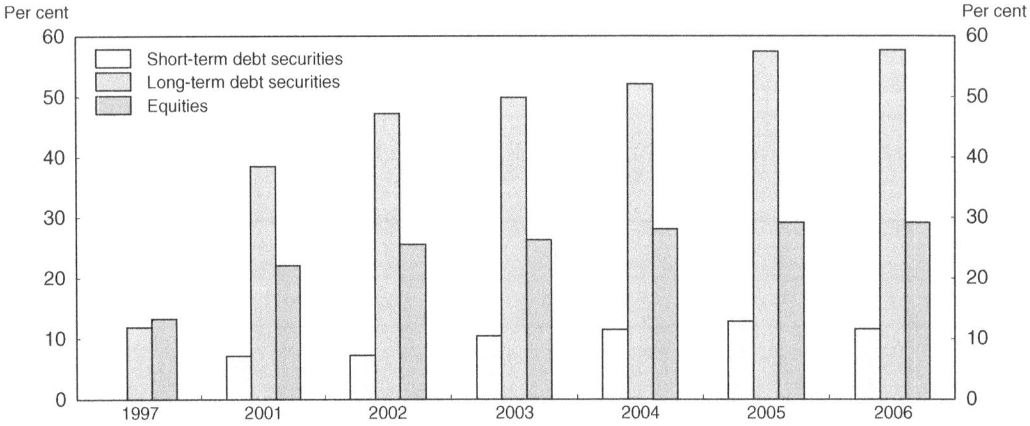

Source: ECB (2008), *Financial Integration in Europe.*

StatLink http://dx.doi.org/10.1787/518448741315

Corporate bond and equity markets have also integrated, although to a lesser extent. At the end of 2006, over half of all long-term (above 1 year) bonds issued by euro area residents were held by other euro area residents outside the country of issuance, as were almost 30% of the equities issued by euro area residents. To some extent, it might be expected that there would be less convergence in private bond and equity returns than in government bonds, since the former are more likely to reflect different, and time-varying, cross-country premia for the probability of corporate default (Demyanyk *et al.*, 2008).

Cross-border lending into the EU by euro area MFIs has increased steadily over the past decade, although integration continues to be primarily in wholesale rather than retail banking (Figure 2.7). Retail markets remain much more segmented and there continue to be marked differences across euro area member states in MFI loan rates on comparable products, particularly for consumer credit and mortgages. This is indicative of the comparatively low extent of cross-border competition in retail banking markets, reflecting continued barriers to market entry as well as differences in national consumer preferences, languages, and investor and consumer protection. The existence of such obstacles highlights the need to look beyond market share indicators when considering the need for measures to further enhance market contestability. However, considerable convergence in MFI loan rates across countries is occurring, with the cross-country standard deviation of MFI interest rates on both household and corporate loans having declined since 2003 (Vajanne, 2007). The greatest convergence has been in rates charged for large loans to non-financial corporations, possibly because such corporations have a greater ability to access loan offers from different suppliers.

Figure 2.7. **Cross-border loans by euro area MFIs**

Loans in EU as a percentage of total loans

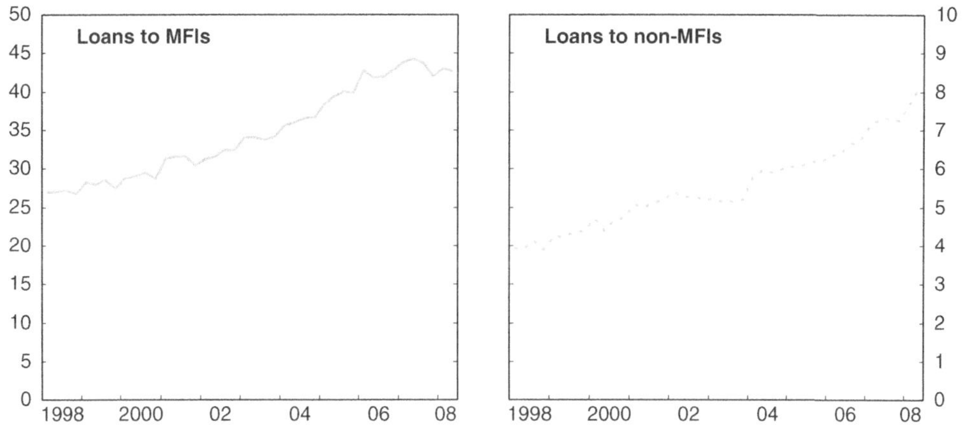

Source: European Central Bank.

StatLink http://dx.doi.org/10.1787/518544131834

The euro area banking market has gradually become more internationalised over the past few years, with foreign-owned subsidiaries and branches accounting for a rising share of total banking assets. At the end of 2006, cross-border subsidiaries and branches of banks from all other EU countries controlled 16% of euro area banking assets, up from 12½ per cent in 2002. The majority of these assets continued to be controlled by subsidiaries, rather than branches, despite the apparent incentives for banks to convert subsidiaries to branches to benefit from a unified (home country) supervisory regime.

The euro area is also continuing to become a more important centre for international banking over time. Estimates by McGuire and Tarashev (2008) show that just over a quarter of the total international liabilities of all BIS-reporting banks were held by euro area banks as of the end of 2006, compared to around one-sixth in 1990.[2] Banks resident in the UK accounted for a similar proportion of total international liabilities, reflecting the importance of London as an international banking hub. A marked difference between international banking in London and the euro area, is that the majority of international banking activity in the latter is carried out by euro area banks. In contrast, foreign-owned banks are responsible for the majority of activity in London. Banks from the euro area account for just over a third of international banking activity in London.

European banks and other financial institutions are also able to enter EU markets through the cross-border provision of financial services. One indicator of the increasing extent of cross-border provision and the progress of financial market integration is the average annual growth rate of 23% in intra-EU exports of financial services in the period 2004-07 (Eurostat, 2008), around three times the rate of growth of total intra-EU service exports.

An important factor behind market integration in the euro area has been the introduction of new payment and settlement infrastructures. Prior to 1999 each member state used different infrastructures, adding to the cost of undertaking cross-border financial transactions. The TARGET system was set up by the Eurosystem as of January 1999 to provide a common area-wide settlement facility for all euro-denominated payments. As a decentralised structure, the system kept in place the existing national architecture of real-time gross settlement systems.[3] These were replaced in full only as of May 2008, with the completion of the single shared platform system for large-value euro payments, called TARGET2. Moreover, in view of the current fragmented post-trading infrastructure for securities, work has just begun on the TARGET2-Securities project, with the objective of providing a single platform for the settlement in central bank money of securities transactions in Europe. However, much remains to be done to remove all the barriers to the provision of cross-border trading services (Giovannini, 2008). In addition to TARGET2-Securities, other ongoing initiatives related to post trading activities include the Code of conduct and the removal of the other barriers identified by the Giovannini Group in 2001. All these efforts together should reduce the costs associated with cross-border settlements, and strengthen integration in securities settlements systems across the EU.

Related steps have also occurred in the area of cross-border retail banking payments in the euro area. Until recently there had been little integration, resulting in costly cross-border banking transactions for consumers. The Single European Payments Area (SEPA) was launched in January 2008 and will be supported by the legal framework set out in the Payment Services Directive adopted in 2007. All member states have to implement this by November 2009. Ultimately, the SEPA is intended to ensure that economic agents can make any payments in euro by credit transfer, direct debit and payment cards throughout the euro area using a single payment account.

Financial services regulation in Europe

Regulatory reforms introduced by the European Commission in the Financial Services Action Plan (FSAP) from 1999 to 2005, and the follow-up White Paper on Financial Services 2005-10 have played an important role in fostering financial market integration and competition in the EU. The principal aims of the FSAP have been to ensure a single market for wholesale financial services, open and secure retail markets and state-of-the-art prudential rules and supervision within Europe (Table 2.1).

Table 2.1. **The Financial Services Action Plan: Main actions**

Measure	Deadline	Objective
Strategic Objective 1: A single EU wholesale market		
1.1. Raising capital on an EU-wide basis		
Prospectus Directive	2005	Create a single passport for issuers of equity and debt securities on the basis of the prospectus approved by the regulatory authority of the issuer's country.
Transparency Directive	2007	Establish disclosure requirements for securities issuers.
1.2. Establishing a common legal framework for integrated securities and derivatives markets		
Market Abuse Directive	2004	Harmonise rules on the prevention of insider dealing and market manipulation on regulated and unregulated markets.
Markets in Financial Instruments Directive (MiFID)	2007	Regulate the authorisation, behaviour and conduct of business of securities firms and exchanges. Provide securities firms with an updated EU "passport".
1.3. Towards a single set of financial statements for listed companies		
International Accounting Standards (IAS) Regulation and 4th and 7th Company Law Directives	2004-05	Implement accounting standards according to International Financial Reporting Standards (IFRS) (*e.g.* on fair value reporting).
Commission Recommendation on EU auditing practices		Clarify the duties and responsibilities of statutory auditors, their independence and ethics, criteria for national public oversight of the audit profession.
1.4. Containing systemic risk in securities settlement		
Settlement Finality Directive and Commission Communication on Clearing and Settlement (originally the Communication was not part of the FSAP)	1999-2004	Reduce systemic risk in payment and securities settlement systems.
Financial Collateral Directive	2003	Promote the integration and cost-efficiency of financial markets by increasing the legal certainty regarding the validity and enforceability of collateral arrangements backing cross-border transactions.
1.5. Towards a secure and transparent environment for cross-border restructuring		
Takeover Bid Directive	2006	Improves rules for cross-border restructuring by setting minimum guidelines for the conduct of takeover bids; provisions to protect minority shareholders.
Other measures		Set out the grounds on which a company can become a European Company (SE). 10th Company Law Directive that facilitates cross-border mergers.
1.6. Single market which works for investors		
Undertaking for Collective Investment in Transferable Securities directives (UCITS III)	2003	Two directives: *First* – harmonise national rules on depositors' assets in UCITS and secure the convergence of prudential requirements (*e.g.* single authorisation); *second* – widen the scope for financial instruments in which UCITS can invest.
Institutions for Occupational Retirement Provision (IORP) Directive and Commission Communication on Funded Pension Schemes	2005	Optimise the conditions in which pension investors operate, create common approach to registration and authorisation and prudential supervision (mutual recognition).
Strategic Objective 2: Open and secure retail markets		
Several measures		*e.g.* Insurance Mediation Directive, measures enhancing information disclosures for consumers and the Communication on the framework for a single market for payments.
Strategic Objective 3: State-of-the-art prudential rules and supervision		
Winding up Directives	2003-04	Set out measures for the winding-up of insurance undertakings and credit institutions. Entitle the authorities in the home country to decide on reorganisation measures, including for branches in other countries.
E-money Directive	2002	Establish a new prudential supervisory regime for electronic money institutions (ELMIs).
Money Laundering Directive	2003	Prevent the financial system being used for money laundering (*e.g.* identification requirements on transactions).
Commission Recommendation on disclosure of financial instruments		Complements already existing directive on the accounts of banks and other financial institutions.
Capital Requirement Directive (CRD)	2007	Lays down the capital adequacy requirements applying to investment firms and credit institutions; rules for their calculation and prudential supervision (Basel II).
Amended Solvency I	2002	A limited reform was agreed by the European Parliament and the Council in 2002. It became clear during the Solvency I process that a more fundamental and wider ranging review of the overall financial position of an insurance undertaking was required. This resulted in the Solvency II proposal.
Financial Conglomerates Directive (FCD)	2004	Identifies "significant financial groups" and designates a supervisory co-ordinator for each conglomerate (transpose adoption by G10).
General Objective (Objective 4): Wider conditions for an optimal single financial market		
Several measures		*e.g.* Taxation and corporate governance.

Source: Communication of the Commission (1999), "Financial Services: Implementing the Framework for Financial Markets: Action Plan".

Additional measures have been added in response to market developments. A detailed overview of the work undertaken on financial market prudential regulation is provided in Chapter 3. The main emphasis of the White Paper 2005-10 was on monitoring, implementing and enforcing the changes introduced by the FSAP. However, further attention has been given to issues such as the single payments area, retail banking and consumer credit.

In many areas, the EU legal framework has set out minimum standards that must be met, while allowing individual countries to liberalise further or pursue tighter regulations if they wish. As of the end of 2007, 26 separate legislative measures had been introduced in this programme, with the aim of bringing about common rules and standards across member states (OECD, 2007). A number of implementing measures have also been introduced for particular framework directives, based on the Lamfalussy process (Chapter 3). The rate of transposition, as of mid-2008, has been good, with comparatively few instances of non-compliance.

Securities market integration has been enhanced by the implementation of the Markets in Financial Instrument Directive (MiFID) as of November 2007. This introduced a comprehensive regulatory regime to govern financial trading and intermediation in the EU. The principal steps were to strengthen the single passport for investment firms, allowing them to operate anywhere within the EU on the basis of a single national authorisation, to strengthen investor protection and to stimulate greater competition between trading exchanges. There have been delays in transcribing the directive into national laws in some countries, which the Commission has followed up on actively. It is too early to judge the full impact of MiFID, but it should help to lower costs and create a deeper European capital market. During the past few months there has been an increase in the number of Multilateral Trade Facilities (MTFs) operating on a pan-European basis.[4] These MTFs operate at lower fees in the markets, putting competitive pressures on national stock exchanges.

Another aspect of current financial services policies is linked to the wider Better Regulation Agenda, with the Commission undertaking checks both for possible simplifications to existing regulation, and for possible inconsistencies in regulations for different financial sectors. New measures have recently been proposed to reduce the number of separate EU regulations covering investment funds. Such proposals should help to reduce transactions costs somewhat and improve market efficiency in European financial markets.

Retail banking and residential mortgage markets remain almost entirely national in Europe, in part because of differences in regulatory regimes and institutional structures (Box 2.1). Competitive pressures in retail banking could be enhanced through measures to reduce the costs of switching bank accounts, including the possibility of portable account numbers, although this measure would bring costs as well as benefits (OECD, 2006). The European Banking Industry Committee produced proposals this year to facilitate bank account switching, but it remains to be seen whether these will improve cross-border account mobility (Deutsche Bank, 2008).

The Commission unveiled a White Paper on the Integration of EU Mortgage Credit Markets in December 2007 (EC, 2007b), focusing on a number of areas in which new legislative measures or recommendations for self-regulation could be considered. The main policy objectives set out in the White Paper are: *i)* to facilitate the cross-border supply

Box 2.1. **Obstacles to integration in EU mortgage markets**

European mortgage markets continue to be characterised by considerable differences across countries, restricting the level of cross-border activity and hence market competition in the EU as a whole. Technological changes and financial innovation have helped to stimulate the supply of new mortgage products, but no single country in the euro area offers a complete range of all the products available in the area as a whole (ECB, 2008a). The latter may among other things stem from national preferences, consumer protection rules or obstacles to integration.

Mortgage debt levels differ markedly across the EU. As of the end of 2006, mortgage debt to GDP ratios amongst member states then in the euro area ranged from almost 100% of GDP in the Netherlands, and 70% of GDP in Ireland to under 30% of GDP in Greece and Austria. Owner-occupation rates also varied widely, from an owner-occupation rate only a little over 40% in Germany, up to rates of 80% or more in Italy and Spain. The Netherlands and Austria, which have very different mortgage debt ratios, have similar owner-occupation ratios (EMF, 2007). Mortgage interest rates also continue to differ across countries (ECB, 2008a).

Mortgages are an important source of income in retail banking in the EU, accounting for around 30% of total gross bank income (EC, 2007b). Tying and cross-selling are common in mortgage credit markets in many member states, with mortgage provision often tied to the sale of insurance products or the payment of salaries into an account held at the mortgage provider. On average, as of 2006, a consumer purchasing a mortgage bought two additional products from the mortgage lender. This may reflect an ability to benefit from reduced transaction costs, but it also serves to reduce market competition.

The characteristics of mortgages vary widely across countries as well. In some they are typically fixed rate throughout the term of the mortgage, whereas in others they are typically variable and linked to market interest rates. Other differences arise from different tax structures, notably the tax treatment of interest payments on housing loans, and institutional features, such as the maximum loan-to-value ratio and the extent to which lenders can make use of capital market funding to improve the funds available for mortgage credit.

For institutions looking to supply mortgages across borders, important cross-country differences include the existence of different legal structures, including the cost and duration of foreclosure procedures, and the extent to which lenders can access national credit and land registries (Catte *et al.*, 2004; Sørensen and Lichtenberger, 2007; ECB, 2008a). Estimates by Sørensen and Lichtenberger (2007) suggest that cross-country differences in enforcement procedures, tax subsidies and loan-to-value ratios all help to account for cross-country differences in mortgage rates on standardised products, although they do not account for all of the differences.

Some diversity across countries in mortgage rates may be expected to persist, even if barriers to cross-border mortgage supply and demand are reduced. Factors such as demographics, the age of the existing housing stock, the provision of social housing and cultural differences such as language, will affect the range of products demanded in different locations. The main impetus to integration will thus have to come from cross-border mortgage supply, with policy makers concentrating on the removal of impediments to the take-up of mortgages supplied by lenders headquartered in other countries, rather than from cross-border mortgage demand.

It is likely to take some time to make substantive progress in the integration of mortgage market given the range of factors that act to differentiate national markets.

and funding of mortgage credit, *ii)* to increase the diversity of products that meet consumers' needs, *iii)* to improve consumer confidence, and *iv)* to facilitate customer mobility. Progress in this area may be slow, reflecting the many institutional factors that are different across national housing markets in the EU, but it is important that the Commission fully follows through, and possibly eventually expands, on the range of measures proposed in the White Paper. The Commission is presently working on the different work streams announced in the White Paper. Integration in retail banking is most likely to occur via the entry of foreign providers to national markets, as lending to households and small businesses is often reliant on subjective information about borrowers, which requires geographical proximity. However, it is generally thought that retail financial services will remain predominantly local for the foreseeable future. Even in domestic markets customers use local providers rather than those situated at a distance from them. The main reasons for this preference for local financial services are language, culture and customers' familiarity with the features of certain products and domestic conditions as well as with their provider or adviser. While the Commission should focus attention on removing regulatory obstacles to the supply of cross-border investments (subject to adequate safeguards for consumers), it should take account of these non-regulatory barriers.

Continued moves towards additional financial integration should be growth-enhancing for the euro area and the EU as a whole. The gains need not be automatic, but the balance of recent cross-country evidence suggests that financial development is beneficial for growth (Hartmann *et al.*, 2007; Jappelli and Pagano, 2008). The OECD Economic Growth project also found that the scale of financial market development and well-functioning financial systems can have an important impact on long-run economic growth. In particular, they can help to ease the external financial constraints faced by firms who want to make long-term investments (OECD, 2003). The findings of Guiso *et al.* (2004) imply that if the extent of financial development in the EU was to reach that in the United States, for the particular financial structure at that time, it could add 0.2 percentage point per annum to the annual rate of GDP growth in the EU. However, it remains an open question whether aggregate financial development is what matters for growth, or whether the composition of it is also important. For instance, work at the OECD suggests that equity-based financial systems offer much more stimulus to business sector innovation than do credit-based financial systems (Jaumotte and Pain, 2005).

There is also scope for further efficiency gains in European financial services (González-Páramo, 2008). Early results using the EU KLEMS database suggest that the growth of total factor productivity in financial and business services in the United States and the United Kingdom was positive over the decade from 1995-2005, whereas in the two largest euro area member states, Germany and France, it was negative (O'Mahony and Robinson, 2007). Stronger competitive pressures and regulatory reforms should both have a positive impact on value-added and productivity growth. Evidence for OECD countries suggests that removing anti-competitive regulations in the banking sector, and improving contract enforcement, access to credit and the efficiency of bankruptcy procedures in securities markets would also have a significant positive impact on productivity growth (de Serres *et al.*, 2007).

Financial innovation

Financial deepening and enhanced market contestability have been accompanied by marked financial innovations in global and European financial markets, at least until recently. New financial products and actors have emerged, as have new ways of pricing and managing financial transactions and financial risks (Tufano, 2003; Visco, 2007). The current ongoing financial turmoil appears to have considerably reduced the usage of many of the new financial products.

Theoretically, the principal effect of financial innovations is to make financial markets more complete, thereby lowering transaction costs, benefiting output growth prospects and increasing the opportunities for risk sharing. During the past decade, financial innovation in Europe and elsewhere has facilitated the decomposition of risk into different subcomponents and the recombination of these subcomponents into new structured financial products with different risk characteristics (Blundell-Wignall, 2007). In principle this should be beneficial for the euro area economy, but recent developments show that financial sectors should be carefully supervised at a time of rapid innovation. The broader range of financial products enables a closer match to be made between the supply of risky products and the demands of investors, offering the eventual prospect of lower risk premia and greater financial efficiency. In turn this should lower the cost of capital to firms and improve the ability of households to smooth their incomes and their consumption over time and also to insure against unexpected outcomes. This need not happen immediately; financial innovation in Europe and elsewhere has also led to greater risk-taking by financial institutions (Rajan, 2006; Borio and Zhu, 2007), potentially offsetting the benefits from the greater opportunities for risk diversification, at least temporarily. The relative opacity of many new structured products may also delay the extent to which they can be put to effective use.

The extent of income and consumption smoothing in response to country-specific output shocks in the euro area, and the impact on this of financial market deepening, is explored by Kalemli-Ozcan *et al.* (2004) and Demyanyk *et al.* (2008). Their results suggest that income and consumption smoothing have both risen somewhat since the formation of the euro area, although smoothing is far from complete, and considerably less than found in related exercises using data for US states.[5]

There is some evidence that the extent of income smoothing in the euro area is positively related with increased holdings of foreign assets, with cross-border investment outside the euro area by euro area residents having a greater effect than cross-border investment within the euro area (Demyanyk *et al.*, 2008). More tentatively there is some weak evidence that internal financial integration, as measured by banking consolidation, may also have beneficial effects, although the estimated gains are small. One implication of these findings is that additional policy actions by the Union to remove remaining (non-prudential) impediments to cross-border investment and financial development would help to promote risk sharing in the euro area.

The asset securitisation market began much later in the euro area than in the United States, at the end of the 1990s. As elsewhere, the increased demand from institutional investors to invest in credit risk and technological changes raising the feasibility of issuing asset-backed securities have been important factors underpinning the growth of off-balance sheet securitisation. But the creation of the euro, with the reduction in exchange rate risk, has provided additional impetus. Deregulation has also contributed, with several member states passing specific laws to remove obstacles to the issuance of asset-backed securities.[6]

A growing use of securitisations has been made in European financial markets over the past decade, although the volume of new issuances has remained well below that in the United States (Figure 2.8). On average, issuance in the euro area from 2005 to the first semester of 2007 was equivalent to around 2% of area GDP, compared to just under 10% of GDP in the United Kingdom and close to 25% of GDP in the United States. Within the euro area, issuances differed considerably across member states. In relative terms, the largest issuers have been financial institutions from the Netherlands, Spain, Luxembourg and Ireland, all countries that have experienced strong property price growth over the past decade. Estimates produced by the European Securitisation Forum (ESF) indicate that the total value of outstanding securities at the end of the first quarter in 2008 was EUR 540 billion (5.9% of GDP), with just over three-fifths of these being residential mortgage-backed securities (ESF, 2008).[7] Earlier survey evidence for 2005-06 indicated that over half of all euro area asset-backed securities were held by investors from outside the euro area, with around one-third being bought by UK investors (Altunbas *et al.*, 2007). More recently, the financial market turmoil has been associated with a drop in securitisation issuance in both the EU and the United States.

Figure 2.8. **Securitisation issuance**

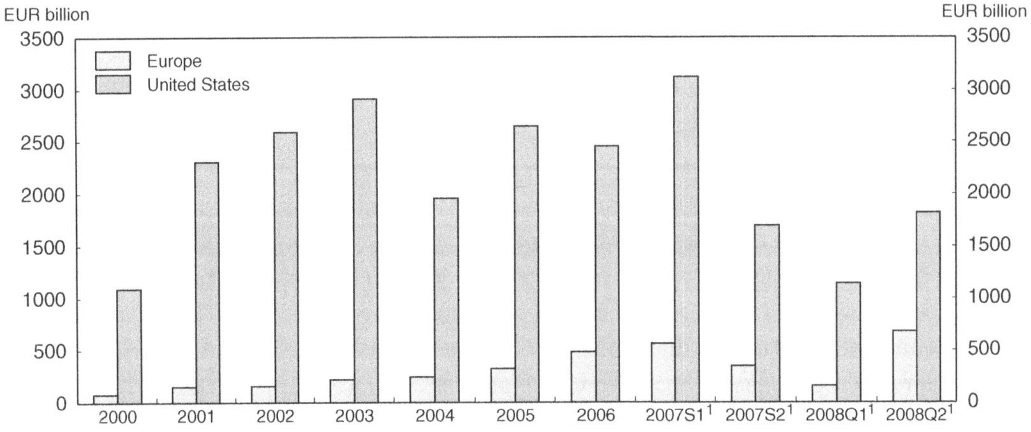

1. Semi-annual and quarterly figures are expressed at an annualised rate.

Source: European Securitisation Forum, *ESF Securitisation Data Report* – Q2:2008.

StatLink http://dx.doi.org/10.1787/518545310804

The securitisation statistics understate the amount of such activities in the euro area (ECB, 2008a). In some countries there are large markets in covered bonds, which are similar to asset-backed securities but which are kept on the balance sheet of the issuer, typically a bank. Within the euro area, securitisation via covered bonds is comparatively large (relative to total bonds and loans outstanding) in Germany, Luxembourg, Ireland and Spain. In Germany the amount of outstanding covered bonds is almost 50% of GDP. However, the euro area covered bond market remains fragmented, reflecting continued differences across member states in their legal frameworks for such products.

The increasing use of securitisations to manage credit risks has been accompanied by the increasing use of derivatives to hedge interest rates and currency risk and exposure to commodity prices. Globally, the outstanding notional value of interest rate swaps and other derivatives was USD 516 trillion in 2007, more than twice the amount outstanding in 2004 (BIS, 2007). The market for euro denominated interest rate derivatives quadrupled between 1999 and 2006 (ECB, 2008a). Financial innovation has also been facilitated by the increasing impact of actors such as hedge funds, private equity funds and special purpose vehicles. These have facilitated the placement of structured credit products originated by the banking sector. They also influence the provision of bank loans by changing the extent to which loans can be hedged or sold. These new financial actors have become a more important presence in financial markets. At the end of 2006, just under one-quarter of global hedge fund assets were in European-based funds (Visco, 2007).

Financial innovations have also occurred in retail banking, with increasing use being made of cashless financial transactions, helped by the progress that has been made in integrating payment systems in the euro area. Such payments should help to minimise the cost of transactions for consumers and make markets function more efficiently. Cashless payments per capita have risen in the euro area over the past decade, but are still only around three-quarters of the level in the United Kingdom and half the level in the United States (ECB, 2008a), suggesting that further growth might be possible.[8] The implementation of the Payment Services Directive by member states by November 2009 should provide further stimulus.

Overall, financial innovations have begun to weaken the long-held distinction between bank-based and market-based financial systems. Banks remain relatively more important in euro area financial markets than they do in the United States, but the banking sector has begun, at least until recently, to make greater use of market-based funding to finance their loans. For euro area MFIs as a whole, the difference between their loans to the non-financial private sector and their deposits from that sector (one measure of the "funding gap") was equivalent to 13.7% of their total loans to that sector, as of August 2008 (ECB, 2008e). This gap was smaller than at the onset of the financial crisis in August 2007, but considerably above the level a decade earlier, when the gap was negligible.

The combination of financial innovation and financial development has also altered the nature of risks in euro area financial markets. Market deepening and the emergence of large cross-border banking groups should facilitate risk diversification. But risk-taking has also increased, as has the overall complexity of the financial system and the emergence of large cross-border groups adds to the potential for systemic risks within the area as a whole. This has implications for the monetary policy transmission mechanism in the euro area, as discussed below, and also for the design of financial market regulation and supervisory activities, as discussed in Chapter 3.

Financial innovation and competition affect the channels of monetary policy transmission

The overall consequences of financial market growth and financial innovation have been to widen the range of financing and investment opportunities available to households and companies. These changes affect the speed and extent to which monetary policy decisions are transmitted to the euro area economy. It is likely that some channels of policy transmission will have been strengthened over the past decade, and some new channels have appeared, while others may have become weaker (Cournède *et al.*, 2008). Potential non-linearities in the transmission of policy have also been enhanced. The balance of such changes is difficult to evaluate, given the comparatively short time period for which data are available; but it would seem sensible to revisit and update the analytical work of the Eurosystem Monetary Transmission Network, conducted soon after the formation of the euro area (Angeloni *et al.*, 2003). The ECB has already begun work on some aspects of this.

Monetary transmission is normally viewed as operating through two broad channels – the interest rate channel, which includes the direct effects of interest rates on real activity, through credit demand, asset prices and exchange rates, and the credit channel, based on the hypothesis that owing to the potential presence of credit market imperfections and non-perfect substitutability of bank *versus* non-bank assets and liabilities, banks may play a distinct role in amplifying the effects of changes to monetary policy (ECB, 2008d). Other channels, such as the influence of financial conditions on risk-taking behaviour, may now be gaining greater importance. The size of these channels does not only depend on financial factors. For instance, the higher degree of price rigidity found in the euro area compared to the United States, which was found by the Eurosystem Inflation Persistence Network (Álvarez *et al.*, 2006) implies, *ceteris paribus*, that a change in the monetary policy stance has a larger impact on the real interest rate and hence on output.

All of these channels are inter-related. For instance, asset prices also play an important role in the credit channel, as they affect the value of the collateral that firms and households can present when obtaining credit. If there are financial frictions, such as information or agency costs, declining collateral values will increase the premium borrowers must pay for external finance, magnifying the direct effects from changes in interest rates. Such effects will be present in the euro area, but may be smaller than in countries such as the United States, Canada and the United Kingdom, as there has been comparatively less use made of housing assets as collateral for mortgage-related loans (equity withdrawal). Collectively, there has continued to be net investment into housing in the euro area, although this is not the case in all member states (ECB, 2008a).

A key conclusion of the earlier work undertaken for the Eurosystem Monetary Transmission Network was that the impact of monetary policy shocks on euro area output was driven primarily by changes in investment (Angeloni *et al.*, 2003). In contrast, for the United States, monetary policy shocks appeared to have a comparatively stronger effect on household consumption than on business investment. Possible reasons for this include the greater dependence of euro area firms on bank financing and larger wealth effects on household consumption in the United States. Overall, however, there was little difference in the aggregate impact of monetary policy on output in the euro area and the United States. A similar conclusion was obtained from a meta-analysis of a large number of individual studies (De Grauwe and Costa Storti, 2005). Over the first decade of the euro, financial deepening and innovation may well have changed the importance of some of the key channels of monetary policy transmission and possibly also led to the emergence of new channels as well.

The interest rate channel

Bank interest rates have often been found to be sticky, responding to changes in reference market rates with some delay and with incomplete pass-through. The enhanced competitive pressures from the expansion in the euro area financial market and the gradual reduction in barriers to market entry are likely to have strengthened the speed at which changes in market rates are passed through to bank interest rates for retail clients (van Leuvensteijn *et al.*, 2008). There is also evidence that aspects of financial innovation may have raised interest rate pass-through in the euro area, with Gropp *et al.* (2007) finding that access to risk management technologies via securitisation and derivative markets serves to enhance the pass-through of market rates to bank rates on mortgages and long-term corporate loans. All else equal, higher debt levels in the private sector also serve to make changes in interest rates more powerful than before.

Enhanced financial integration has also increased the importance of financial market expectations of future monetary policy actions (Visco, 2007). Signals of future policy actions can affect asset prices and the term structure of interest rates. All else equal, this will improve the effectiveness of monetary policy, with market rates and retail rates responding both to current intervention and to changes in expectations of the future policy stance, underlining the importance of clear communication by the monetary authorities. But it may also mean that monetary policy changes perceived to be only temporary now have a smaller effect on market rates than before. The enhanced role of expectations also makes it more difficult to measure the immediate effect of monetary policy changes.

The wealth channel of policy transmission, arising from monetary-policy induced movements in asset prices and exchange rates, is likely to have been amplified by the changes that have occurred in euro area financial markets over the past decade. For households, the rising importance of net wealth relative to incomes and the compositional shift of asset holdings from deposits to assets whose valuation is sensitive to market prices, both serve to raise the direct impact of asset price movements on net wealth and hence, all else being equal, on expenditure. For companies, greater recourse to external capital markets for funding might also raise the sensitivity of investment decisions to changes in asset prices.

Studies for individual euro area member states have frequently found that there are significant long-run effects from household net wealth on consumption (Annex 2.A1). These effects differ across countries, both in terms of magnitude and in the particular importance of changes in different components of wealth. On balance, there is somewhat more firmly based evidence for the impact of changes in net financial assets, than for an impact from changes in housing wealth, possibly because of the comparative stability of real house prices in some euro area countries over time. It is also important to allow for structural change in financial markets, with wealth effects found to become larger after financial deepening (Barrell and Davis, 2007). The empirical evidence in Annex 2.A1 is based on data for the first decade of EMU. The results confirm the existence of a significant impact from net financial wealth on household consumption in the euro area in this period,[9] with a permanent 10% decline in net financial wealth ultimately reducing consumption by 0.9%, all else being equal.[10] The implied marginal propensity to consume out of wealth is between 3½-4 cents per euro of wealth, which is comparable with the estimates of the Federal Reserve for the United States.

Underlying the aggregate impact of changes in household wealth on expenditure there are likely to be considerable cross-country differences. Chirinko *et al.* (2008) find marked cross-country heterogeneity in the euro area in the response of household consumption and residential investment to changes in house prices and equity prices, both in terms of the size of the responses and in terms of the relative importance of housing and equity price shocks.[11] Such asymmetries reflect both different institutional settings across countries, especially in housing markets (Hoeller and Rae, 2007), but also differences in financial structures and the composition of household portfolios (Bartiloro *et al.*, 2007).

These latter differences may have been accentuated by the different pace of financial market deepening across euro area member states in the past decade.

Although the wealth channel has become more important for monetary policy transmission, the impact may have been offset by weaker income effects. As financial markets become more complete, fewer households should be credit constrained (consuming from their current incomes) and companies may need to rely less on internal funding through cash-flow, which in the past has been an important mechanism of policy transmission in the euro area (Angeloni *et al.*, 2003), although cash-flow continues to be an important influence on fixed investment in many euro area member states (Martinez-Carrascal and Ferrando, 2008). The speed at which expenditure adjusts to economic shocks may also have changed as financial development has progressed. For instance, debt and equity integration, measured as cross-border holdings of assets and liabilities relative to GDP, have both been found to raise the speed at which industry fixed investment reacts to changes in the net returns on capital (EC, 2008).

The internationalisation of portfolios also helps to magnify the valuation effects from exchange rate movements, although the direction of such effects will depend on the currency composition of assets and liabilities. If assets are held in foreign currencies and liabilities are held in domestic currencies, an exchange rate depreciation will reinforce the impact of a monetary policy easing by raising the domestic currency value of net foreign assets. This appears to be the case for the euro area, based on data for the international portfolio investment position. At the end of 2006, euro-denominated portfolio investment liabilities of the euro area were almost twice the size of euro-denominated portfolio investment assets (ECB, 2008b, Table 3). The value of euro deposits in euro area banks by depositors from outside the area also exceeded the value of euro-denominated loans by euro area banks to borrowers outside the area (ECB, 2008b, Box 3).

The overall impact of the greater internationalisation of European financial markets on the interest rate channel and the rising proportion of extra-euro area assets in the portfolios of investors is ambiguous. In general, stronger cross-border linkages mean that domestic monetary policy may need to react less to any country-specific (or region-specific) "shocks", since a larger proportion of such "shocks" will have to be absorbed by foreign economies via changes in trade levels or more risk sharing, or from revaluation effects on foreign asset holdings in the domestic economy (Hervé *et al.*, 2008). A corollary of this is that, over time, any given change in euro area monetary policy may have a smaller direct effect than before on the euro area economy. Global financial integration should increase the extent to which market interest rates in the euro area are determined by worldwide conditions in financial markets. The increasing presence of large global banking groups in the euro area may reinforce such effects. Evidence for the United States suggests that global banks are more likely to absorb national changes in monetary policy through use of internal sources of funding from affiliates elsewhere (Cetorelli and Goldberg, 2008).

The credit channel

Within the credit channel, financial frictions give rise to two principal effects. In the bank-lending channel, monetary policy affects credit supply by changing deposit levels or by changing the value of bank capital. In the balance sheet channel, the agency costs of lending change endogenously with monetary policy due to changes in the perceived net worth of potential borrowers.[12] The credit channel has been relatively important in the euro area in the past, reflecting the relative importance of bank financing for households and companies (Angeloni *et al.*, 2003; Stark, 2007).

Financial innovations, such as securitisation, have reduced financial frictions and made markets more complete. By giving banks easier access to non-deposit sources of funding, securitisation should be expected to weaken the (credit) transmission mechanism. Enhanced globalisation should have related effects, giving banks greater access to international capital markets and allowing them to manage their balance sheet comparatively independently of their loan portfolios. In the euro area, lending by banks with securitisation activities appears to be relatively more insulated from changes in monetary policy (Altunbas *et al.*, 2007). The emergence of new non-bank financial actors such as hedge funds and special purpose vehicles has also helped financial intermediation to become more market-based, which should also reduce the importance of the credit channel.

Evidence from a sample of almost 3 000 euro area banks suggests that securitisation activity reduces, but does not eliminate, the impact of monetary policy changes on bank lending (Altunbas *et al.*, 2007). Weighting the banks in the sample by market share indicates that a 1 percentage point rise in money market rates reduces loan supply by 0.7% in the long term, an effect about half the size of that found in related exercises prior to the introduction of the euro (Ehrmann *et al.*, 2003). Although it is not possible to meaningfully test the statistical significance of these differences, the findings provide an indication of the potential structural changes in euro area monetary policy transmission over the past decade.

Despite this, the credit channel undoubtedly remains relevant in the euro area. The expansion in bank assets, and the corresponding increase in private sector liabilities, means that overall credit risk exposure need not have declined, even if the risk of any given activity has done so. Collateral effects from asset price fluctuations have become more important and uncertainty about default rates remains; both are likely to be influenced by monetary policy. Reserve and capital requirements continue to impact on bank decisions, so that banks' balance sheet constraints will still eventually impact on bank lending, and bank lending standards fluctuate over time. The financial disruptions since mid-2007 have led to a reduction in the use made of securitisations, higher money market spreads, tighter bank lending standards and moves to bring off-balance sheet items back onto the balance sheet (ECB, 2008a).

The recent decline in the extent of securitisation issuance in the euro area is likely to have dampened the effects of financial innovation on the supply of bank loans and hence, at least temporarily, raised the importance of the bank lending channel for monetary policy transmission. Estimates in ECB (2008d), using the results of Altunbas *et al.* (2007), suggest that if securitisation activity dropped back permanently to its average level since the introduction of the euro, the growth rate of bank credit to the private sector would drop by 1.5 percentage points.

Changes in financial regulation, such as the introduction of International Financial Reporting Standards (IFRS) in the European Union, may also act to raise the size of bank capital and corporate balance sheet effects (Weber *et al.*, 2008). The IFRS requires that assets and liabilities be recorded at market values (or "fair values" if market indicators are unavailable), rather than at historical cost. This can be expected to raise the overall sensitivity of bank capital and the net worth of potential corporate borrowers to movements in market interest rates and asset prices.

A number of factors can make the bank lending channel asymmetric. Capital regulations may be more stringent during economic expansions, especially if there are limits on the extent of leverage banks can have. Informational asymmetries may matter more during economic downturns, with banks having greater uncertainty about the creditworthiness of potential borrowers. If so, the impact of tighter monetary policy would be expected to be greater than that of an accommodative policy stance. Gambacorta and Rossi (2007) find that the negative effect of a temporary interest rate increase on euro area output and consumption after two years is around twice the size of the positive effect from a temporary interest rate reduction.[13]

The risk-taking channel

The risk-taking channel of monetary policy transmission is one which has only just begun to be examined in detail. The underlying idea is that the effects of monetary policy on asset values and liquidity may also affect risk perceptions and risk tolerance in the financial sector. To this extent, the effects of monetary policy changes may be amplified by changes in risk-taking behaviour by banks and other financial institutions (Borio and Zhu, 2007; ECB, 2008d). Changes in monetary policy may also affect risk premia on market interest rates and asset prices. There is some evidence that banks tend to engage in riskier lending at times in which monetary policy is accommodative (Jimenez *et al.*, 2007; ECB, 2008d) but this may also be because riskier borrowers also can offer improved collateral at such times. The euro area Bank Lending Survey also indicates that bank lending standards in the euro area are affected by the economic cycle, with standards becoming tighter during a cyclical downturn, which is consistent with monetary policy having an effect on risk perceptions and risk-taking. Recent OECD work for the United States shows that more stringent bank lending standards are associated with tighter financial conditions (OECD, 2008).

The extent to which the risk-taking channel is distinct from the conventional credit channel effects that stem from fluctuations in bank balance sheets and changes in agency costs is unclear, and requires empirical testing. However, financial innovation and financial market deepening are likely to have increased the influence and impact of changes in risk perception and management on economic developments. This increases the need for additional research on this channel of monetary transmission.

If the risk-taking channel matters, it will generate non-linear effects in the monetary transmission mechanism. For instance, if monetary policy is perceived as providing some downside insurance against asset price risks, then the changes in risk-taking behaviour would be stronger during periods of accommodative policy than in periods of policy tightening. Alternatively, if risk-taking behaviour by financial institutions is more sensitive to the perceived chances of solvency or liquidity problems, risk-taking effects may be accentuated at times when markets for risk are functioning poorly.

The net effects on the transmission mechanism are uncertain and may be non-linear

On balance, the available evidence suggests that financial deepening and greater market competition have raised the speed at which changes in policy interest rates are passed through to retail clients, and improved the transmission mechanism more generally. The comparative importance of different channels has changed, at least until

OECD ECONOMIC SURVEYS: EURO AREA – ISBN 978-92-64-04824-9 – © OECD 20

recently, with the influence of asset prices becoming enhanced and the credit channel less influential. Financial innovations have also facilitated risk-taking, potentially amplifying the direct impact of monetary policy changes and increasing non-linearities in the transmission of policy. It remains to be seen whether these changes will still be present once the current financial turmoil fades.

Monetary policy clearly continues to have a powerful influence on economic stabilisation in the euro area, but it is too soon to say with certainty whether the overall impact of policy decisions has become more powerful than before. Even if changes in financial markets have raised the efficacy of monetary policy, other developments may have reduced it. Globalisation has brought many structural changes in addition to those in financial markets, and the influence of domestic cyclical conditions on price-setting appears to have waned (Box 2.2). Weber *et al.* (2008) suggest that the aggregate impact of monetary transmission on euro area inflation since 1999 is not very different from that in earlier years. Findings for six major euro area economies in Boivin *et al.* (2008) suggest that the overall impact of area-wide monetary policy shocks may even have diminished over the past decade, although it has become more homogenous across countries than previously.

Structural changes in the monetary transmission mechanism in the euro area are likely to be evolutionary, making them hard to quantify. Changes such as securitisation, the disintermediation of credit formation, the changing mix of household portfolios and the financing of residential investment have all occurred gradually. Their full impact on the transmission mechanism will become apparent only over relatively long periods of time. So the scope for formal tests of structural change is somewhat limited, although any evidence of such changes is more powerful as a result. Nonetheless, the changed financial landscape of the euro area makes it imperative to maintain a continual and up-to-date assessment of the monetary policy transmission mechanism.

Box 2.2. **Structural changes in price setting in the euro area**

This box reviews some of the channels through which global factors have an increased influence on domestic wage and price setting and discusses the implications for the transmission of monetary policy.

Over the past 25 years price and wage inflation have moderated considerably in the euro area member states, as in other OECD economies. At the same time, the production of many goods and services has become increasingly internationalised and the level of trade between the euro area and non-OECD economies has risen markedly. The extent to which the increasing integration of non-OECD economies into the global economy has changed the effects of cost pressures and product market competition on price setting in the euro area and other OECD economies is explored in Pain *et al.* (2006) and Koske and Pain (2008). The results of these analyses show that import prices have become a more important influence on domestic consumer prices since the mid-1990s, helped by continued rises in import penetration. This increased sensitivity to foreign economic conditions has been accompanied by declines in the sensitivity of inflation to domestic economic conditions, as reflected in the economy-wide output and unemployment gaps. The degree of inflation persistence in the euro area has also declined in recent years (Altissimo *et al.*, 2006).

Box 2.2. **Structural changes in price setting in the euro area** *(cont.)*

While globalisation has put downward pressure on prices via lower non-commodity import prices, it has put upward pressure on prices via higher commodity prices. Until recently, the former effect dominated in most OECD economies. Calculations by Pain *et al.* (2006) suggest that consumer price inflation in the euro area could have been up to 0.3 percentage points higher per annum over 2000-05 had the estimated effect of globalisation not occurred, all else being equal. The various influences on inflation suggest that policy makers should examine developments in headline inflation as well as core inflation (Bean, 2006). The latter is usually regarded as a better signal of ongoing inflationary pressures, but the former reflects both influences from globalisation.

The effects of low-cost production on trade prices are likely to be concentrated in particular sectors of the economy. Using data for the euro area from 1995 to 2005, estimates produced by the European Central Bank indicate that the combined impact of the rising import penetration of low-cost producers in the manufacturing sector, and the differentials in inflation between them and other producers, has dampened euro area manufacturing import price growth by approximately 2 percentage points per annum (ECB, 2006). Although this would appear to suggest that trade with lower-cost producers is placing downward pressure on domestic prices in OECD economies, the eventual effect on inflation is less clear as such calculations show only *ex ante* effects. The extent to which they eventually lead to lower consumer price inflation will depend on the effect they have on the behaviour of other competitors and domestically generated inflation. The latter will depend on whether the initial impacts are accommodated by the stance of monetary policy in the importing economy.

Globalisation also affects supply-side developments in national economies, and hence potential output or the NAIRU, through enhanced competitive pressures, greater net inward migration and the potential productivity gains from outsourcing and offshoring. As with any structural change, the difficulties in estimating such effects precisely and in a timely fashion may force policy makers to place greater emphasis on the actual behaviour of prices and costs and reduce the attention paid to signals from estimates of the current state of the domestic economic cycle.

The observed flattening of the Phillips curve over time suggests that whilst changes in the output gap may have only a limited short-term direct impact on inflation, it has become much more costly or difficult for monetary policy to bring inflation back to target after the point at which it has begun to rise or decline markedly. In some circumstances, such as the perceived risk of deflation, signals from the gap may thus lead to a more aggressive policy action to minimise the risk of having to make long and costly adjustments at a later time. These factors need to be weighed against the broader uncertainty about the levels of potential output and gaps resulting from the flattening of the Phillips curve; at times this could result in such measures being given a reduced role in policy formulation, especially if they appear at odds with other cyclical indicators, such as surveys, or observed inflationary pressures (Mishkin, 2007).

Box 2.3. **Main recommendations on financial market integration**

- The Commission should follow through on the measures to improve competition and efficiency proposed in the White Paper on Integration of EU Mortgage Credit Markets. Areas for action include the need to improve the access of foreign institutions to national credit and land registries, greater harmonisation of the cost and duration of foreclosure proceedings and measures to reduce tying and cross-selling of products in mortgage markets.
- Further moves should be made to remove other obstacles to market integration in other retail financial services.
- The authorities should continue to reduce fragmentation of payment infrastructures at EU level to improve competition in the provision of financial services. The Single European Payments Area and implementation of the Payment Services Directive in 2009 will help this process.
- The analysis undertaken for the Eurosystem Monetary Transmission Network should be revisited to see whether enhanced competition and financial innovation have led to structural changes in the speed and impact of monetary policy changes in the euro area and, in particular, the importance of wealth-related effects. It would also be useful to investigate whether asymmetries across the euro area countries in the transmission mechanism have risen or diminished and how the globalisation of financial markets has influenced the various channels of transmission.

Notes

1. At the end of 2006, the largest five banking groups held 43% of euro area banking assets, up from 39% in 2002 (ECB, 2007b).
2. International liabilities comprise cross-border liabilities in all currencies and foreign currency liabilities to domestic residents. Euro-denominated cross-border liabilities contracted within the euro area are excluded.
3. A real-time gross settlement system is one in which payments are not subject to a waiting period and transactions are dealt with individually rather than grouped together.
4. Examples include Chi-X, Turquoise and Nasdaq OMX Europe.
5. Income and consumption smoothing would be complete if country-specific changes in gross national income and consumption (government plus private) were respectively uncorrelated with country-specific output changes. The results obtained in the empirical analysis are sensitive to the model specification and estimation procedures used.
6. Examples include Belgium, France, Germany, Greece, Italy, Portugal and Spain (Altunbas *et al.*, 2007).
7. A time series of the outstanding stock of securities in Europe is available only since mid-2007. The value in the first quarter of 2008 is estimated to be 9% lower than that at the end of the third quarter of 2007.
8. Within the euro area, the greatest use of cashless payments is in Finland, the Netherlands, Austria and France, all of whom have levels similar to that in the United Kingdom. The least frequent use is in Greece, Italy and Spain.
9. It was not possible to test directly the impact of housing wealth because of the absence of published data for the euro area as a whole.
10. Estimates from the European Central Bank in August 2008 indicate that at the end of the first quarter of 2008, euro area household net financial wealth was just over 6% lower than at the end of the second quarter in 2007, prior to the onset of financial market turmoil.

11. A limitation of their work is that it is carried out using a data set ending in 1998, leaving open the issue of whether any changes have occurred since the advent of monetary union.
12. Changes in capital adequacy regulations can have related effects, either by affecting bank capital requirements or by changing the perceived value of the collateral of potential and actual borrowers.
13. Some caution is needed in interpreting their results as the majority of their sample uses synthetic euro area data for the pre-EMU period. It is possible that financial integration has moderated the channels leading to asymmetric behaviour.

Bibliography

Altissimo, F. *et al.* (2005), "Wealth and Asset Price Effects on Economic Activity", *ECB Occasional Paper*, No. 29, ECB, Frankfurt.

Altissimo, F., M. Ehrmann and F. Smets (2006), "Inflation Persistence and Price-Setting Behaviour in the Euro Area", *ECB Occasional Paper*, No. 46, ECB, Frankfurt.

Altunbas, Y., L. Gambacorta and D. Marqués (2007), "Securitisation and the Bank Lending Channel", *Banca d'Italia Working Paper*, No. 653, Rome.

Álvarez, L. *et al.* (2006), "Sticky Prices in the Euro Area: A Summary of New Micro-evidence", *Journal of the European Economic Association*, May, 4(23).

Angeloni, I., A. Kashyap and B. Mojon (2003), *Monetary Policy Transmission in the Euro Area*, Cambridge University Press.

Barrell, R. and E.P. Davis (2007), "Financial Liberalisation, Consumption and Wealth Effects in Seven OECD Countries", *Scottish Journal of Political Economy*, Vol. 54.

Bartiloro, L., M. Coletta and R. De Bonis (2007), "Italian Household Wealth in a Cross-country Perspective", in *Household Wealth in Italy*, Banca d'Italia, Rome.

BIS (Bank for International Settlements) (2007), *Foreign Exchange and Derivatives Market Activity in 2007*, BIS, Basel.

Bean, C. (2006), "Comments on 'The Impact of Globalisation on Monetary Policy'", presented at the Federal Reserve Bank of Kansas City 30th Annual Economic Symposium, Jackson Hole, Wyoming.

Blundell-Wignall, A. (2007), "Structured Products: Implications for Financial Markets", *OECD Financial Market Trends*, Vol. 92, OECD, Paris.

Boivin, J., M.P. Giannoni and B. Mojon (2008), "How Has the Euro Changed the Monetary Transmission?", *NBER Working Paper*, No. 14190.

Borio, C. and H. Zhu (2007), "Capital Regulation, Risk-taking and Monetary Policy: a Missing Link in the Transmission Mechanism?", paper presented at the conference on The Implications of Changes in Banking and Financing on the Monetary Policy Transmission, ECB, Frankfurt, November.

Catte, P. *et al.* (2004), "Housing Markets, Wealth and the Business Cycle", *OECD Economics Department Working Paper*, No. 394, OECD, Paris.

Cetorelli, N. and L. Goldberg (2008), "Banking Globalization, Monetary Transmission and the Lending Channel", *NBER Working Paper*, No. 14101.

Chirinko, R.S., L. de Haan and E. Sterken (2008), "Asset Price Shocks, Real Expenditures and Financial Structure: a Multi-country Analysis", *CESifo Working Paper*, No. 2342.

Christiansen, C. (2007), "Volatility-Spillover Effects in European Bond Markets", *European Financial Management*, Vol. 13.

Cournède, B., R. Ahrend and R. Price (2008), "Have Long-Term Financial Trends Changed The Transmission of Monetary Policy?", *OECD Economics Department Working Paper*, No. 634, OECD, Paris.

De Grauwe, P. and C. Costa Storti (2005), "Is Monetary Policy in the Eurozone Less Effective Than in the US?", *CESifo Working Paper*, No. 1606.

Demyanyk, Y., C. Ostergaard and B.E. Sorensen (2008), "Risk Sharing and Portfolio Allocation in EMU", *European Commission Economic Paper,* No. 334, Brussels.

Deutsche Bank (2008), "Mobility of Bank Customers in the EU: Much Ado About Little", *Deutsche Bank EU Monitor,* No. 60.

European Commission (EC) (2007a), *European Financial Integration Report 2007*, European Commission Staff Working Document, No. SEC(2007)1696.

EC (2007b), *White Paper on the Integration of EU Mortgage Credit Markets*, European Commission, Brussels.

EC (2008), *EMU@10: Success and Challenges after 10 Years of Economic and Monetary Union*, European Commission, Brussels.

European Central Bank (ECB) (2006), "Effects of the Rising Trade Integration of Low-cost Countries on Euro Area Import Prices", *ECB Monthly Bulletin*, August.

ECB (2007a), *Financial Stability Review*, ECB, Frankfurt.

ECB (2007b), *EU Banking Structures*, ECB, Frankfurt.

ECB (2007c), "Monetary Policy and Financial Integration", in *Financial Integration in Europe*, ECB, Frankfurt.

ECB (2008a), *Financial Integration in Europe*, ECB, Frankfurt.

ECB (2008b), *The International Role of the Euro*, ECB, Frankfurt.

ECB (2008c), *Financial Stability Review*, June 2008, ECB, Frankfurt.

ECB (2008d), "The Role of Banks in the Monetary Policy Transmission Mechanism", *ECB Monthly Bulletin*, August.

ECB (2008e), *Aggregated Balance Sheet of Euro Area Monetary Financial Institutions, excluding the Eurosystem;* August, *www.ecb.int/stats/money/aggregates/bsheets/html/outstanding_amounts_2008-08.en.html*

Ehrmann, M. *et al.* (2003), "The Effects of Monetary Policy in the Euro Area", *Oxford Review of Economic Policy*, Vol. 19/1.

European Mortgage Federation (EMF) (2007), *HYPOSTAT 2006: A Review of Europe's Mortgage and Housing Markets*, European Mortgage Federation.

European Securitisation Forum (ESF) (2008), *ESF Securitisation Data Report Q1:2008*, European Securitisation Forum.

Eurostat (2008), "Intra-EU Share of International Trade in Services Amounts to 57% in 2007", *Eurostat Statistics in Focus*, No. 57/2008.

Gambacorta, L. and C. Rossi (2007), "Modelling Bank Lending in the Euro Area: a Non-linear Approach", *Banca d'Italia Working Paper*, No. 650, Rome.

Giovannini, A. (2008), "Why the European Securities Market is not Fully Integrated", *NBER Working Paper*, No. 14476.

González-Páramo, J.M. (2008), "Financial Systems, New Technologies and Productivity Growth", speech at Ronda, July.

Gropp, R., C.K. Sorensen and J.-D. Lichtenberger (2007), "The Dynamics of Bank Spreads and Financial Structure", *ECB Working Paper*, No. 714, ECB, Frankfurt.

Guiso, L. *et al.* (2004), "Financial Market Integration and Economic Growth in the EU", *Economic Policy*, Vol. 19.

Hartmann, P. *et al.* (2007), "The Role of Financial Markets and Innovation in Productivity and Growth in Europe", *ECB Occasional Paper*, No. 72, ECB, Frankfurt.

Hervé, K. *et al.* (2008), "The Macroeconomic Policy Challenges of Continued Globalisation", *OECD Economic Studies*, Vol. 44, forthcoming, OECD, Paris.

Hoeller, P. and D. Rae (2007), "Housing Markets and Adjustments in Monetary Union", *OECD Economics Department Working Paper*, No. 550, OECD, Paris.

Jappelli, T. and M. Pagano (2008), "Financial Market Integration Under EMU", *European Commission Working Paper*, No. 312, European Commission, Brussels.

Jaumotte, F. and N. Pain (2005), "Innovation in the Business Sector", *OECD Economics Department Working Paper*, No. 459, OECD, Paris.

Jimenez, G. *et al.* (2007), "Hazardous Times for Monetary Policy: What do Twenty-Three Million Bank Loans Say about the Effects of Monetary Policy on Credit Risk?", *CEPR Discussion Paper*, No. 6514.

Kalemli-Ozcan, S., B. Sorensen and O. Yasha (2004), "Asymmetric Shocks and Risk Sharing in a Monetary Union: Updated Evidence and Policy Implications for Europe", *CEPR Discussion Paper*, No. 4463.

Koske, I. and N. Pain (2008), "The Usefulness of Output Gaps for Policy Analysis", *OECD Economics Department Working Paper*, No. 621, OECD, Paris.

van Leuvensteijn, M. *et al.* (2008), "Impact of Bank Competition on Interest-rate Pass-through in the Euro Area", *ECB Working Paper*, No. 885.

Martinez-Carrascal, C. and A. Ferrando (2008), "The Impact of Financial Positions on Investment: an Analysis for Non-financial Corporations in the Euro Area", *ECB Working Paper*, No. 943.

McGuire, P. and N. Tarashev (2008), "Global Monitoring with the BIS International Banking Statistics", *BIS Working Paper*, No. 244.

Mishkin, F.S. (2007), "Estimating Potential Output", speech at the Conference on Price Measurement for Monetary Policy, Federal Reserve Bank of Dallas, May.

OECD (2003), *The Sources of Economic Growth*, OECD, Paris.

OECD (2006), *Competition and Regulation in Retail Banking*, Competition Committee Policy Roundtable, OECD, Paris.

OECD (2007), *OECD Economic Survey: European Union*, OECD, Paris.

OECD (2008), *OECD Economic Outlook*, Vol. 2008/1, No. 83, OECD, Paris.

O'Mahony, M. and C. Robinson (2007), "UK Growth and Productivity in an International Perspective: Evidence from EU KLEMS", *National Institute Economic Review*, No. 200.

Pain, N., I. Koske and M. Sollie (2006), "Globalisation and Inflation in the OECD Economies", *OECD Economics Department Working Paper*, No. 524, OECD, Paris.

Rajan, R. (2006), "Has Finance Made the World Riskier?", *European Financial Management*, Vol. 12.

de Serres, A. *et al.* (2007), "Regulation of Financial Systems and Economic Growth", *OECD Economics Department Working Paper*, No. 506 (reissued version), OECD, Paris.

Sørensen, C. and J.-D. Lichtenberger (2007), "Mortgage Interest Rate Dispersion in the Euro Area", *ECB Working Paper*, No. 733, ECB, Frankfurt.

Stark, J. (2007), "The Monetary Policy Transmission Mechanism: In Light of Recent Changes in Banking and Financial Innovation", speech at conference on The Implication of Changes in Banking and Financing on the Monetary Policy Transmission Mechanism, Frankfurt, November.

Trichet, J.-C. (2007), "The Process of European Economic and Financial Integration", speech at the European Central Bank Symposium "Konvent für Deutschland", Berlin, December.

Tufano, P. (2003), "Financial Innovation", in G. Constantinides, M. Harris and R. Stulz (eds.), *Handbook of the Economics of Finance*, Elsevier, North Holland.

Vajanne, L. (2007), "Integration in Euro Area Retail Banking Markets – Convergence of Credit Interest Rates", *Bank of Finland Research Discussion Paper*, No. 2007/2.

Visco, I. (2007), "Financial Deepening and the Monetary Policy Transmission Mechanism", paper presented at the Joint High-Level Eurosystem and Bank of Russia seminar, Moscow, October.

Weber, A., R. Gerke and A. Worms (2008), "Has the Monetary Transmission Process in the Euro Area Changed? Evidence Based on VAR Estimates", presented at 7th Annual BIS Conference, Luzern, June.

ANNEX 2.A1

Wealth effects on household consumption in the euro area

This annex presents new empirical evidence about the impact of wealth effects on household consumption in the euro area, using data for the first decade of EMU. A limitation of this approach is that it reduces the available degrees of freedom in estimation, but it serves to obviate the need to allow for possible structural changes that might coincide with the formation of EMU.

Based on a comprehensive survey of the empirical evidence for wealth effects on consumption in euro area member states and other OECD countries, Altissimo *et al.* (2005) conclude that wealth effects do have a significant impact on household consumption in euro area member states, although the magnitude of the effects may differ across countries. The estimated marginal propensity to consume out of wealth is typically found to be a little smaller than in the United States, although this finding is not universal to all studies, and little is known about whether such differences are statistically significant.

For a sample of OECD countries including five euro area member states, Catte *et al.* (2004) find significant long-run effects from net financial wealth in all of the euro area economies, but long-run effects from housing wealth in only some. Movements in housing wealth appear to be important in the Netherlands, Spain and, to a lesser extent, Italy but not in Germany or France. In part, such differences are likely to reflect cross-country differences in the institutional features of national housing and mortgage markets in the euro area. If European mortgage markets become more integrated, and more competitive, such differences will be reduced, which can be expected to make the link between house prices, housing wealth and consumption more important.

Studies have also demonstrated that it is important to allow for structural changes in financial markets in empirical work. Barrell and Davis (2007) illustrate the extent to which financial liberalisation has been associated with significant structural changes in the relative importance of the different drivers of household consumption, typically raising the long-run importance of changes in wealth for consumption. A related possibility is that the formation of EMU may have led to important changes in the impact of different factors on consumption in the euro area.

The consumption functions reported here are consistent with those used frequently in macroeconomic models, with allowance being made for possible income, substitution and wealth effects on household consumption. A dynamic error-correction model is estimated, with the combined long-run elasticities with respect to real disposable household income and real net household sector financial wealth being imposed at unity. The initial model also allowed for lagged dynamic effects from past consumption (habit persistence), plus current and lagged income growth, consumer price inflation (which some studies suggest has a direct negative impact on consumption) and a measure of the *ex post* real interest rate. The latter was defined as the benchmark 10-year euro area government bond rate less consumer price inflation.

All data are taken from the *OECD Economic Outlook database*, with the exception of the wealth data, which come from the ECB. A limitation of the wealth data available for the euro area as a whole is that comprehensive and timely data on tangible asset holdings are not yet available. The approach adopted was therefore to derive a benchmark model, and then test separately for the presence of additional effects from the growth of real euro area house prices, as well as real euro area equity prices.

After removing a number of variables that were individually and jointly insignificant in the initial model estimated, the parsimonious specification shown in column [1] of Table 2.A1.1 remained. There is clear evidence of a significant impact from net financial wealth on euro area consumption, with an elasticity of 0.09%. Using the sample mean values, this translates into a marginal propensity to consume 3¾ cents of every euro of wealth, which is within the range of results from earlier studies (Altissimo *et al.*, 2005). There is also evidence of a negative impact from the *ex post* real interest rate, so that an increase in real interest rates would have a negative effect on consumption over and above the indirect impacts via income and wealth. No evidence was obtained for a separate significant impact from inflation.

Subsequent analysis augmented this benchmark model with additional dynamic terms in real equity and housing prices. The house price series is a GDP-weighted aggregate of the national country data reported in OECD (2008). An illustrative model is shown in column [2] of Table 2.A1.1. It is clearly difficult to identify well-determined dynamic effects from wealth in the euro area, as suggested by the findings in earlier studies for individual countries (Catte *et al.*, 2004). It is noticeable that the inclusion of the dynamic wealth terms results in the coefficient on the real interest rate becoming insignificant, suggesting that it might be picking up some kind of asset market effect in [1] rather than a pure substitution effect. The equity price, house price and real interest rate variables are jointly significant at the 10% level (p-value 0.063) suggesting that they all pick up related effects.

The estimated equations can be used to obtain an accounting decomposition of the influences of different factors on consumption growth. This is illustrated in Figure 2.A1.1, which uses the first equation in Table 2.A1.1 to decompose the year-on-year growth of consumption into contribution from income growth, changes in net wealth and changes in real interest rates. The difference between the sum of these contributions and the actual growth of consumption is shown in the category "Other" in the figure. Income effects are the dominant direct influence on consumption growth, but wealth and interest rate effects are both important, having both a positive and negative influence at different times.

Table 2.A1.1. Determinants of euro area household consumption

	[1]	[2]
$\Delta\ln(y)_t$	0.371 (2.9)	0.406 (2.2)
$\ln(c/w)_{t-1}$	–0.542 (4.4)	–0.561 (2.7)
$\ln(c/y)_{t-1}$	–0.053 (4.6)	–0.057 (3.0)
r_{t-1}	–0.001 (2.1)	–0.001 (1.3)
$\Delta\ln(c)_{t-1}$		0.133 (0.9)
$\Delta_4 \ln(rpeq)_t$		0.007 (1.3)
$\Delta_4 \ln(rpeq)_{t-1}$		–0.007 (1.4)
$\Delta_4 \ln(rph)_t$		–0.028 (0.1)
$\Delta_4 \ln(rph)_{t-1}$		0.016 (0.1)
constant	0.648 (4.6)	0.691 (2.8)
Long-run parameters:		
Income	0.91 (63.8)	0.91 (21.6)
Net wealth	0.09 (6.2)	0.09 (2.2)
R-bar squared	0.45	0.44
Standard error	0.25%	0.25%
Serial correlation (p-value)	0.48	0.08
Normality (p-value)	1.00	0.69

Notes: Dependent variable $\Delta\ln(c)$, $\Delta\ln$ = log difference. The sample period is 1999Q2 to 2007Q4.

1. Student-t statistics are shown in parentheses.
2. The variables are real household consumption (c), real household disposable income (y), real household net financial wealth (w), the real interest rate (r), real equity prices (rpeq) and real house prices (rph).

Figure 2.A1.1. Contributions to annual consumption growth

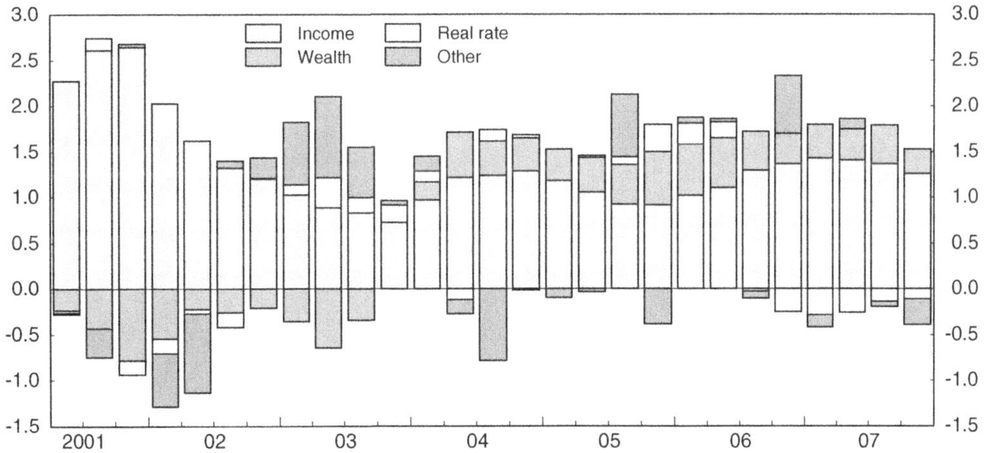

Source: OECD calculations based on the model shown in column [1] of Table 2.A1.1.

StatLink http://dx.doi.org/10.1787/518548308086

ISBN 978-92-64-04824-9
OECD Economic Surveys: Euro Area

Chapter 3

Financial market stability: Enhancing regulation and supervision

Financial innovation and integration have spurred financial development and enhanced consumer choice. Financial integration has also been associated with the emergence of large, complex, cross-border financial institutions (LCFIs). This has changed risk profiles and made cross-border contagion more likely. An important challenge for the EU is to manage systemic risks and cross-border contagion to ensure financial stability in an integrated financial market. The financial market turmoil has also highlighted some gaps in the regulatory and supervisory framework. Although the European authorities should be commended for the progress they have made in updating and improving frameworks and responding to the financial turmoil, more can be done. In particular, further steps are needed to remove the mismatch between integrating European financial markets on the one hand, and largely national supervision on the other. Attention should also be given to the question of which measures are adequate to dampen the pro-cyclicality of the financial system. New regulations should not impose unnecessary costs on consumers, businesses and financial institutions, nor create obstacles to further market integration.

Introduction

Financial integration spurs financial development, improves economic outcomes and enhances consumer welfare. By providing greater diversification, financial integration and development can reduce risks. However, integration can also accentuate systemic risks by increasing the complexity of the financial system as institutions become more interconnected, and by encouraging the growth of large cross-border financial institutions (LCFIs), of which there were just under 70 in Europe in 2007.[1] Such institutions can heighten risks by increasing the impact of bank failures, by acting as a conduit for shocks between markets or by being seen as "too big to fail", thereby worsening moral hazard. The more integrated economic environment in which banks function may also increase the correlation of financial sector developments across Europe (Decressin, 2007). Although the trend towards financial integration is putting pressure on financial stability arrangements in many countries, the challenges facing the Union are unique because integration has proceeded more rapidly in the EU than in most other countries. This will probably continue, as past initiatives and proposals for additional legislation are likely to further stimulate integration.

Cross-border financial groups increasingly organise themselves beyond national boundaries and legal structures, as they seek to increase efficiency and minimise costs. They tend to centralise liquidity, risk and asset-liability management, and to ignore or downplay the distinctions between branches and subsidiaries in their business model. However, the overall stability of the financial system remains primarily a national responsibility, with cross-border financial institutions mostly supervised by the authorities in the country where they are licensed. This division of responsibility can create tensions between countries where a financial institution is active, particularly where there is a large foreign bank presence in a local market. Though based on the Basel Accords and several directives, national supervisory frameworks vary across the EU and no consistent supervisory framework has yet emerged at the EU or euro area level. This might create an uneven playing field, as regulations and enforcement practices differ across jurisdictions. Having to deal with different regulatory and supervisory practices within a financial group can also increase costs.[2] More importantly, although colleges of supervisors have access to supervisory information on EU-wide cross-border banks, a fragmented supervisory framework could fail to prevent or respond adequately to a major financial crisis.

The euro area together with other major economies has experienced the turning of a prolonged credit cycle, which was driven by a combination of low global interest rates and financial innovation, and led to a rapid expansion of credit and booming asset prices. A feature of the credit cycle was strong demand for relatively new, risky asset classes such as subprime residential mortgage-backed securities. As default rates on subprime mortgages increased, uncertainty mounted about the quality of the underlying assets and the distribution of losses. This has led to a drying up of liquidity in markets for structured products, and made banks reluctant to lend. Although some features of the current crisis will probably be addressed by the market itself, the recent financial turmoil suggests that there is scope for improving prudential frameworks.

This chapter reviews the adequacy of the existing prudential framework in the EU, as well as recent proposals to reform the framework, in the light of the rapid integration of EU financial markets and the recent financial turmoil. Although recent reforms improve on the current framework, more can be done to simplify the system and align EU prudential regulation and supervision with the increasingly cross-border business models of European financial institutions. There is also scope to reduce the pro-cyclicality of the financial system.

Why prudential regulation is necessary

Asymmetric information between borrowers and lenders, as well as other market failures, make the banking and broader financial sector susceptible to bouts of instability (Box 3.1).[3, 4] Because the negative externalities generated by such instability are not easily overcome by the private sector, and because governments have tended to be the "provider of solvency" of last resort, banks have been regulated for a long time. However, the extent to which public sector agencies should intervene in the market is difficult to establish.

Box 3.1. **Sources of banking instability**

Banks have a critical role within the economy helping to transfer capital and risk efficiently between borrowers and savers. However, banking systems are also prone to bouts of instability, which can have negative flow-on effects to the real economy. Explanations for the instability of the banking system are often grounded in theories of asymmetric information; in markets for debt, lenders usually know less than borrowers about the riskiness of investment projects. This makes it difficult for lenders to discriminate between high quality and low quality borrowers.

There are a number of ways that asymmetric information impairs banking systems (Mishkin, 1990), including:

- Allowing low-quality borrowers (high-quality borrowers) to pay lower (higher) interest rates than is optimal, leading to an inefficient allocation of capital.
- Making the banking system pro-cyclical because tighter monetary conditions and lower collateral values make it harder for banks to identify borrowers with profitable investment opportunities.
- Accentuating moral hazard by giving borrowers an incentive to engage in activities that make default more likely.
- Encouraging contagion of bank runs by making it harder for depositors and investors to distinguish between solvent and insolvent institutions.

Other structural features of banking systems also contribute to their instability. For example, financial market participants may poorly measure changes in risk over time and have incentives to ignore the build-up of longer term risks when making investment decisions (Borio *et al.*, 2001). Adrian and Shin (2007) see the pro-cyclicality of banks' leverage as a source of instability. In their model, when balance sheets are marked to market, increases in asset prices show up immediately as reductions in banks' leverage. This provides banks with surplus capital that they can use to expand their balance sheets. On the asset side they do this by taking on large amounts of short-term debt, while on the liability side banks look for new sources of lending. When asset prices and collateral begin to fall, liquidity dries up.

Box 3.1. **Sources of banking instability** *(cont.)*

An alternative view is that incomplete financial markets are the ultimate source of banking crises (Allen and Carletti, 2008). When financial markets are incomplete (intermediaries cannot hedge all aggregate risks) liquidity provision is inefficient; it can only be provided by selling assets when required. However, because providers of liquidity have to be compensated for the opportunity cost of holding it in states where it is not needed, asset prices must be low, when banks need liquidity. Thus, inefficient liquidity provision becomes responsible for asset price volatility and can turn liquidity crises into solvency crises.

Recent innovations in banking markets may have accentuated banking instability. Traditionally, banks' long-term relationships with borrowers have helped them to discriminate between low and high risk borrowers, while holding loans on their balance sheet provides an incentive for banks to adequately screen borrowers. However, the trend over recent years for some commercial banks to bundle the loans they originate into securities, and sell them to investors, may have dulled the incentives to internalise the risks associated with these loans.

Finally, although the large potential economic cost of market failures in the banking sector provides a justification for government regulation, regulation can itself encourage destabilising behaviour. For example, deposit insurance (or other implicit government guarantees), which is designed to reduce the likelihood of bank runs, can generate moral hazard, because banks have an incentive to engage in excessively risky lending practices because the costs will be shared with the insurance fund or taxpayers, and depositors have little incentive to monitor their bank. Regulatory arbitrage can also be a source of instability. This occurs when regulated banks have an incentive to find loopholes in existing regulations or differences in regulation between countries, shift their activity to more lightly regulated jurisdictions, or where activity shifts from banks to less regulated institutions. Regulation may fail to keep pace with developments in banking markets. For example, over the past decade the number of large banks with an important presence in many countries has increased significantly. However, prudential regulation has remained based on national boundaries, making crisis resolution potentially more difficult.

Regulation of the banking and financial system should proceed with a clear understanding of the market failures it is trying to offset, and how specific regulations will address such failures, without unduly increasing risk elsewhere in the system.

There are three central objectives of regulation and supervision:

- Maintaining the stability of, and confidence in, the financial system by ensuring the solvency and soundness of financial institutions (prevention of systemic risk).
- Protecting investors, borrowers and other users of the financial system against undue risk of loss and other financial harm that may arise from failure, fraud, malpractice, manipulation and other misconduct on the part of providers of financial services (consumer/investor protection).
- Ensuring an efficient, reliable and effective functioning of financial markets, including a proper working of competitive market forces (conduct of business).

More generally though, it is difficult to determine where the line between statutory and self-regulation should be drawn, as a balance must be struck between promoting soundness on the one hand and wealth creation on the other. Unnecessary regulation may damage the functioning of financial markets, stifle innovation and hamper economic growth (de Serres *et al.*, 2006). Badly designed regulation can also enhance instability through regulatory arbitrage or by encouraging excessive risk taking. Moreover, just as lenders have less information about the riskiness of borrowers' investment projects, regulators and supervisors do not have complete information about the riskiness of banks' balance sheets, or the market conditions in which they operate. It is also difficult to accurately undertake cost-benefit analysis of banking regulations because bouts of instability can be infrequent and the costs of regulation diffuse. Consequently, regulation should proceed with a clear sense of its own limits.

Recent financial innovations and greater integration have also made regulation more difficult. Traditional distinctions between different activities – banking, securities dealing, insurance and asset management – have become blurred and national distinctions are evaporating in many markets. Although traditional banking is still the main activity of most banks and most operate within a single country, integration has increased the exposure of banks to systemic risk and the greater inter-linkages in the financial system have made cross-border contagion more likely. The increase in the number of large cross-border financial institutions may also mean that there are more institutions that are "too big to fail". Innovation has rendered the financial system and its oversight much more complex. Many of the new instruments are not regularly traded, which makes it more difficult to assess the soundness of institutions' balance sheets – a problem accentuated by the increase in institutions' off-balance sheet activities. All of these issues emphasise the need for a fresh look at the current functioning of the financial system as well as the regulatory and supervisory framework.

Recent turmoil in financial markets

The euro area together with other major economies has experienced the turning of a prolonged credit cycle, which was driven by a combination of low global interest rates and financial innovation, and led to a rapid expansion of credit and booming asset prices (Chapter 1). The turning of the cycle has coincided with a sharp drop in confidence in financial institutions and a prolonged period of turmoil in international financial markets. Against the backdrop of historically low interest rates on traditionally low-risk investments, institutional and retail investors had moved into new and more risky assets in search of higher yield. This was evident in a number of developments, including the increase in "carry trades", the growth in alternative investment vehicles such as hedge funds, and strong demand for relatively new asset classes such as subprime residential mortgage-backed securities and other types of structured financial products, such as collateralised debt obligations (CDOs). This demand together with favourable regulatory capital requirements on mortgages held in the trading account rather than as loans on the banks' balance sheet supported the rapid growth of the "originate-and-distribute" model of credit intermediation, in which underlying credit risk is first unbundled and then repackaged, tiered, securitised, and distributed to investors. As default rates on US subprime mortgages increased beyond expectations in the early summer of 2007, and it became clear that there had been insufficient due diligence on securitised assets, uncertainty mounted about the quality of the underlying assets and the distribution of losses. In the search for yield, the leverage taken on by many institutions increased and the collateral to back the outstanding loans declined in quality.

The current market dislocations partly reflect a lack of knowledge as to who is ultimately bearing the losses. The opacity of many structured products makes it difficult for investors and third parties to fully understand and value them. Not only were ratings of these products based on overly optimistic assumptions, but changes to these ratings occurred too slowly. Widespread uncertainty about the distribution of losses and the financial situation of various participants led to a drying up of liquidity in markets for structured products. With growing concerns about counterparty risk, banks became reluctant to lend even at very short horizons and are hoarding liquidity. As time passed, weaknesses in underlying asset quality have become more evident.

Some of the more idiosyncratic characteristics of the current crisis will probably be addressed by the market itself, as investors learn to avoid the same mistakes. What is more interesting is the extent to which the current turmoil is similar to previous episodes, since the similarities are likely to reflect the more enduring features of the dynamics of financial instability (Reinhart and Rogoff, 2008). Most episodes of financial distress of a systemic nature, with potentially significant implications for the real economy, stem from excessive risk-taking and rapid expansion of balance sheets in good times, with risks masked by a vibrant economy (Borio, 2008). Rising exposure to risk generates financial vulnerabilities revealed only once the economic environment becomes less benign, in turn contributing to its further deterioration. The risks that build up in good times materialise in the downturn. This build-up and unwinding of financial imbalances has been coined the "excessive pro-cyclicality" of the financial system (Borio *et al.*, 2001 and Goodhart, 2004).

Effects of the financial crisis on European banks

The institutions most visibly affected by the financial crisis have been banks. In the United States and elsewhere many have announced large write-downs both directly and indirectly linked to the troubled subprime mortgage market, been forced to raise new capital through rights issues and other exceptional measures, and undergone an involuntary expansion of their balance sheets, as borrowers draw on pre-agreed credit lines or off-balance sheet entities are being brought onto the balance sheet. A number of institutions have failed, been sold cheaply to other financial institutions, and been nationalised or received large capital injections from governments. The strains have also spread to insurers and hedge funds. Further deteriorations in asset quality are possible if property prices continue to soften, credit terms are tightened further and the overall economy also weakens further. Early in 2008, the OECD (2008) estimated that overall losses will reach USD 420 billion, based on a 40% recovery on defaulting loans and a scenario for the economy and house prices benchmarked on previous episodes. The recent intensification of the turmoil means that these losses will almost certainly be larger than this estimate, though the enormous uncertainty about how the current episode will play out makes forecasting losses very difficult.

Europe appeared to weather the first phase of the financial crisis reasonably well, aided by ECB actions to extend and broaden liquidity provision. European investors did not appear to have a disproportionate exposure to toxic assets, though some institutions made substantial losses. Further, among the world's largest 30 banks, the decline in capital-to-assets ratios for euro area banks over 2007 was noticeably less than for US banks (The Banker, 2008). This was supported by evidence from the ECB's July 2008 Bank Lending Survey, which suggested that for most euro area banks capital has not been affected by the financial market turmoil (Chapter 1). However, the intensification of the financial crisis in mid-September 2008 changed the outlook for Europe dramatically. Spreads on interbank lending rates and credit default swap rates surged, financial stocks collapsed, and a number of large cross-border European banks had to be rescued by governments (Figure 3.1). This in turn brought about further liquidity injections by the ECB and prompt co-ordinated action from European governments to safeguard the short-term stability of their financial systems (see Box 3.2). According to the ECB's October Bank Lending Survey, the financial turmoil hampered access to money markets and debt securities to a much greater extent than in the second quarter of 2008. Lending to enterprises was more affected than lending to households. Although financial markets have stabilised more recently, the European banking sector remains exposed to further risks. Many euro area banks have low capital-to-asset ratios and low credit ratings. Moreover, because the credit and economic cycle turned later in the EU than in the United States, conditions in the European banking sector could worsen as conditions in housing markets and the broader economy deteriorate.

The proximate cause of the financial market turmoil lay in the US subprime market, but there are a number of Europe-specific risks that could materialise in the future as well as the broader concern about the turning of the international credit cycle. Firstly, European financial institutions have been at the forefront of the large increase in the issuance of structured equity products (*e.g.* Constant Proportion Portfolio Insurance) to retail investors since 2003. With these products, the client's capital is guaranteed even though it is exposed to risky assets such as equities. Even though the product is distributed by small banks, the guarantee is provided by a prime broker that issues and manages it, often hedging the risk

Figure 3.1. **Share price indices**[1]

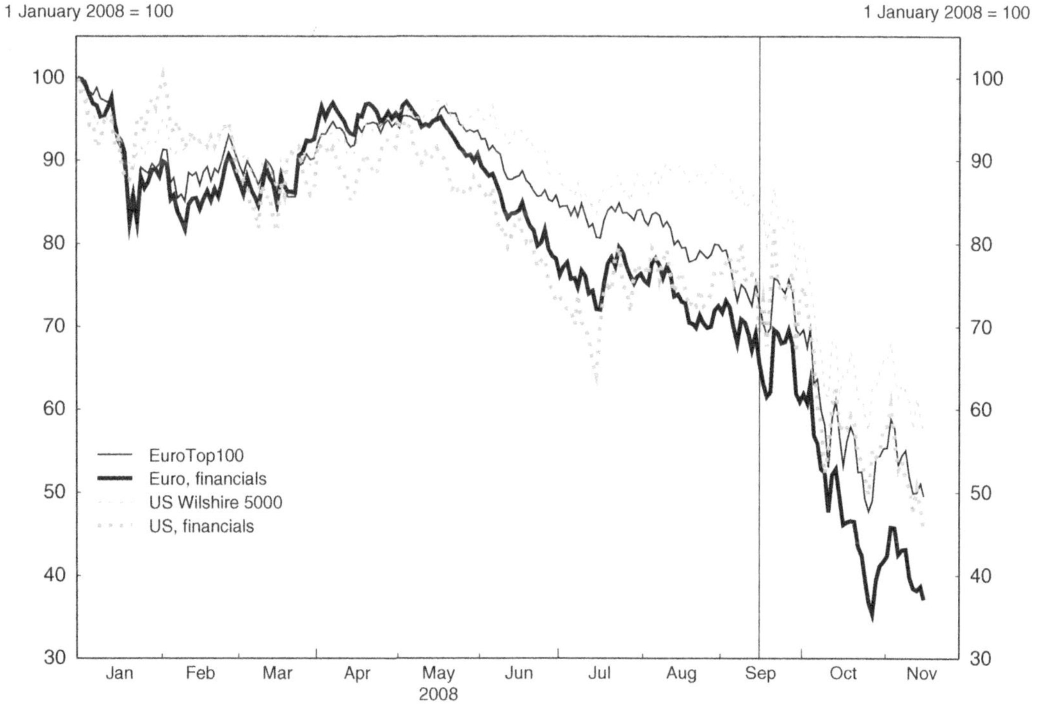

1. All series are denominated in USD.

Source: Datastream, November 2008.

StatLink http://dx.doi.org/10.1787/518570442117

Box 3.2. Co-ordinated action by European governments to safeguard the stability of the financial system

In October 2008, European governments agreed to the following set of guidelines for specific actions to stabilise the financial sector:

- Ensure appropriate liquidity conditions for financial institutions.
  - Facilitate the funding of banks by making available a government guarantee of new medium-term (up to 5 years) bank senior debt issuance.
  - Depending on market conditions in each country, actions may be targeted at some specific and relevant types of debt issuance.
  - The price of instruments should reflect their value in normal market conditions.
  - All financial institutions incorporated and operating in euro area countries and subsidiaries of foreign institutions with substantial operations will be eligible.
  - The scheme will be limited in amount, temporary and will be applied under close scrutiny of financial authorities, until 31 December 2009.
- Provide financial institutions with additional capital resources and allow for efficient recapitalisation of banks.
  - Each member state will make Tier 1 capital available by acquiring preferred shares or other instruments including non dilutive ones.
  - Price conditions shall take into account the market situation of each institution.
  - Governments will provide capital when needed but prefer private capital to be raised.
  - Financial institutions should face additional restrictions to prevent abuse of arrangements at the expense of non beneficiaries.
  - Prudential rules should be implemented by national supervisors with a view to stabilising the financial system and allowing for an efficient recapitalisation of distressed banks.
  - Emergency recapitalisation of a given institution shall be followed by an appropriate restructuring plan.
- Ensure sufficient flexibility in the implementation of accounting rules given current exceptional market circumstances.
- Enhance co-operation procedures among European countries.

These measures form part of what the European Commission has called "A New Financial Market Architecture at EU Level". Other measures include previously announced proposals relating to deposit guarantees, capital requirements, and countering the pro-cyclicality of regulation and accounting standards. These are discussed later in the chapter.

Individual governments have since released details of how these measures will be carried out in their country. While the response to the deterioration in financial conditions is welcome, it remains to be seen whether they will be sufficient to unfreeze interbank lending markets or prevent further tightening of lending standards. Although European governments have now set aside funds for the recapitilisation of banks, to date, few have actually made use of these funds. This seems appropriate in the short term because banks should first be given the opportunity to find private funding. However, if private funds are not forthcoming, governments may have to be proactive in forcibly recapitalising banking systems.

Box 3.2. **Co-ordinated action by European governments to safeguard the stability of the financial system** *(cont.)*

In addition, some countries' decisions to provide blanket guarantees of deposits, or guarantee that no institution, whether systemic or not, will be allowed to fail, could sow the seeds of future banking problems. More broadly, as set out by the European authorities, interventions should be timely and temporary, mindful of taxpayers' interests, ensure that existing shareholders bear the consequences of interventions, and prevent management from receiving undue benefits. Detailed consideration will also have to be given to how countries exit from the commitments they have made when the turmoil eventually dissipates. While differences in liquidity and solvency concerns mean that it is appropriate for countries' responses to the crisis to differ, countries should keep externalities for other European countries to a minimum, and competition should not be distorted.

through complex options replication programmes and derivatives contracts backed by hedge funds. If a major market break occurs and counterparties fail, the guarantee will fall on prime broker's capital (OECD, 2008). If the current crisis spills over into these products, Europe's heavy exposure would represent a risk to the financial system. However, no estimates of potential losses exist. Secondly, during the recent credit cycle euro area banks may have increased the riskiness of their lending by increasing the proportion of their loans to non-investment grade and non-rated borrowers (ECB, 2008d). Should the subsequent default rates of these "leveraged loans" be higher than expected, the solvency of some institutions could be affected. Thirdly, a sharp housing market correction is underway in Spain and Ireland, which could put their financial markets under strain. Finally, some EU banks have large cross-border exposures to the Central and Eastern European economies (Box 3.3).

Areas for policy action arising from the financial turmoil

Proposals on how to deal with the shortcomings in the regulatory framework revealed by the recent turmoil have been put forward by a number of international bodies. The Financial Stability Forum (FSF, 2008) has identified several underlying weaknesses,[5] and stressed the importance of dealing with the forces that contribute to the pro-cyclicality of financial systems. It proposes concrete actions to enhance the resilience of markets and financial institutions. The IMF also identified a number of short-run actions that should be taken to reduce the duration and severity of the crisis and the need for more fundamental changes to the regulatory frameworks in the longer run (IMF, 2008). The financial industry itself has proposed ways to address market weaknesses to rebuild market confidence (IIF, 2008). European countries have contributed to the international policy debate and reflected on their own systems of financial regulation. The international consensus on the necessary steps includes:

- Improving transparency by increasing the quality of information available in the market and enhancing disclosure by market participants about risk exposure, valuation methods and off-balance sheet entities. Accounting practices could also be improved by enhancing audit guidance standards. The lack of market confidence during the turmoil, and the difficulties associated with fair valuation in circumstances in which markets become dislocated, have become apparent during the financial market stress.

Box 3.3. **Emerging risks in eastern European countries**

The eastern European countries have been converging rapidly on countries in the euro area in recent years. Growth was underpinned by strong capital inflows and structural reforms, *inter alia* the implementation of the *acquis communautaires* and financial market liberalisation. At the same time real short-term interest rates were relatively low in most countries helping to fuel rapid credit growth. Output is now growing at a slower pace in most of the Eastern European countries, reflecting slower export market growth and a tightening in monetary policy and in credit standards. A re-appraisal of risk is underway with increased bond spreads and a rising cost of protection against default.

A salient feature of the financial systems of these countries is the strong presence of foreign ownership. Another important feature is that the share of foreign currency in total loans is important in many, though not all, countries. Servicing debt could become very costly, should a country's currency depreciate significantly.

Several regulators have tightened prudential regulations and other requirements to slow credit growth. Other measures include higher capital adequacy ratios, tighter supervision and enhancing cross-border co-operation agreements (World Bank, 2008). In most countries foreign bank credit has been growing faster than domestic bank credit. The large presence of foreign banks exposes the countries to contagion risks from the home country or sudden stops if sentiment turns sharply. This underlines the importance of close co-operation between the home and host supervisors. World Bank (2007) suggests that home country supervisors could enhance their understanding of the risks posed by their subsidiaries, while host country supervisors could improve their understanding of the health of foreign bank entities in their countries. Memorandums of understanding, when they exist, could be complemented by more reciprocal visits and better information sharing. Taking discretionary action, like lowering loan-to-value ratios, is made difficult, if not impossible, by the fact that branches of foreign banks would not be affected, thus making the playing field between foreign and domestic credit suppliers less even.

- Changing the role and use of credit ratings. Credit rating agencies (CRAs) play an important role in evaluating and publishing information on structured credit products, and investors have relied heavily on their ratings. Although CRAs insist that ratings measure only default risk, and not the likelihood or intensity of downgrades or mark-to-market losses, many investors were seemingly unaware of these warnings and disclaimers. Moreover, poor credit assessment by rating agencies leading, in particular, to high ratings for complex structured subprime debt turned out to be misleading. When products were downgraded, investors lost confidence in ratings of all securitised products.
- Strengthening risk management standards and practices. The market turmoil has revealed weaknesses in risk management at banks and securities firms and in the system of incentives that regulators and supervisors provide through capital and liquidity requirements and oversight, especially with respect to the light regulatory capital treatment of structured credit and off-balance sheet activities. Moreover, liquidity risk management should be improved to better cope with sustained system-wide stress in funding markets.
- Strengthening the authorities' responsiveness to risks. Authorities need to be able to take proper actions when recognising excessive risk-taking in individual banks or

markets. This requires state-of-the-art knowledge about financial intermediation, good communication and international co-operation to establish best practices.

- Strengthening arrangements to deal with stress in the financial system. Timely liquidity provision by the central banks in times of tension is important and their role as a lender of last resort should be well-defined.
- Clarifying and strengthening national and cross-border arrangements for ensuring prompt corrective action occurs before banks fail. The FSF also recommends setting up colleges of supervisors at the international level to better address cross-border issues.
- Ensuring adequate deposit insurance schemes are in place. The main issues are the size of the potential pay-out, the speed of the pay-out and whether the scheme should be funded up-front.
- Reducing pro-cyclicality. The possibilities for the regulatory framework to "lean against the wind" through smoothing capital requirements and provisioning should be investigated.

The Economic and Financial Affairs Council (ECOFIN) has issued a roadmap, discussed in the next section, which addresses many of these issues.

The prudential framework for the single European capital market

The objective of prudential regulation is to limit the number of failures of financial institutions, in order to protect depositors and the stability of the financial system, while not impeding improvements in efficiency or hindering competition. It has both a micro dimension – ensuring that individual institutions do not pose a risk to the financial system and a macro dimension – ensuring that institutions collectively do not pose excessive risk. These are already difficult tasks, but the euro area and the wider European Union face additional challenges from having an integrated capital market but with supervision remaining primarily a national responsibility, albeit within a common framework. This raises issues both for the effectiveness of the single market and the risks to the European financial system.

The current prudential framework for the EU banking market emerged from the creation of the single European market. Regulation has focused on removing barriers to the integration of EU financial markets, and harmonising regulatory standards to support a level playing field between financial institutions in different countries. Within this framework, financial stability arrangements have remained primarily national because governments have wanted to keep decision making about supervision and fiscal bail-outs on the same level. However, the long-standing efforts towards harmonisation and convergence have given both an increasingly European character. Since the 1970s, the hub of financial regulation has been shifting towards the EU level, as a series of directives and a number of other legal instruments created a framework for national prudential regulation across the European Union.

The 27 EU member states each have their own institutional and legal supervisory frameworks. National prudential authorities are set up differently and have different powers and accountability arrangements. There is some trend towards centralising supervision across sectors (banking, securities markets and insurance), with a fully integrated single supervisor now in place in 15 out of 27 member countries (Figure 3.2). Of these countries, 10 have an independent supervisory structure, while in 5 other countries banking supervision is the responsibility of the central bank. In the other member states, supervisory responsibilities are divided between specialised agencies that deal with

Figure 3.2. **Supervisory models in EU Countries**

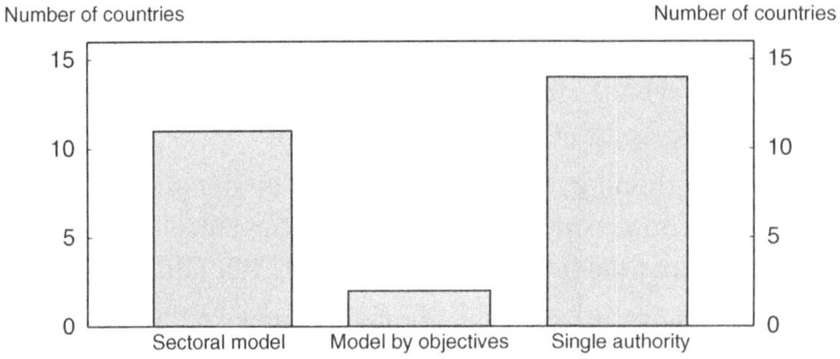

Source: IMF (2008), "Euro Area Policies: Selected Issues", *IMF Country Report*, No. 08/263, August.

StatLink http://dx.doi.org/10.1787/518686083488

particular sectors (banking, securities markets or insurance) and/or particular functions (regulation, supervision, licensing or conduct of business).

The Second Banking Directive,[6] which entered into force in 1993, set out the key drivers of banking market integration and cross-border supervision. It introduced the single EU banking passport[7] together with the principles of minimum harmonisation, mutual recognition and home-country control. The "home-host" principle was established whereby the home-country supervisor has responsibility for the supervision of institutions they licence, *including* their foreign branches and the direct cross-border provision of banking services from the home country to other EU member states. Subsidiaries of non-domestic banks are local corporate citizens and therefore subject to local licensing and prudential oversight. The Capital Requirements Directive[8] (CRD) from 2006 confirmed this principle.[9]

Deposit guarantee schemes are also primarily the responsibility of the home country but the host country is allowed to take additional measures. For example, under "topping-up" arrangements, branch depositors enjoy the advantages of the host country's guarantee scheme in cases where the level of coverage provided by the host country is higher. In addition, foreign depositors are treated in the same way as domestic depositors. For example, the UK government guaranteed Northern Rock depositors fully both at home and in other EU countries.

However, the home/host principle does not apply to all elements of regulation (Table 3.1). In particular the host country retains responsibility for issues that closely relate to local market conditions, such as local liquidity management. If a financial institution facing insolvency problems needs to be reorganised or wound down and liquidated, this is the responsibility of the home country for branches and the host country for subsidiaries. Bankruptcy procedures follow national law and only some countries have special

Table 3.1. **Division of responsibility between home and host country**

	Oversight of the financial system	Solvency supervision	Deposit guarantee scheme	Emergency liquidity assistance	Reorganisation and winding-up authority
Home country					
Bank	Home country	Home country	Home country	Home country	Home country
Host country					
Branch	Host country	Home country	Home country	Host country	Home country
Subsidiary	Host country	Host country	Host country	Host country	Host country

bankruptcy regimes for banks. For cross-border banks, this division of labour creates several layers of regulation.

A considerable degree of consistency of regulation is achieved through the financial sector directives issued under the EU Financial Services Action Plan (FSAP) launched in 1999.[10] These established the basic regulatory framework that national legislation and supervisors currently implement and apply. The EU legal framework sets out minimum standards that must be met, but allows individual countries to pursue a more stringent approach if they wish. Important aspects of the FSAP included the CRD for banking and investment firms and the Markets in Financial Instruments Directive (MiFID) for financial markets. The CRD, which implements the provisions of the Basel II accord, requires member states to limit some of the national discretions allowed by Basel I, thereby promoting regulatory convergence. The directive also consolidates many of the provisions of the earlier prudential directives. Solvency II, which overhauls solvency requirements for insurance companies, is expected to achieve similar convergence in the insurance sector.

Many legislative and regulatory actions are undertaken through the framework of the Lamfalussy committees (Box 3.4). The Lamfalussy process, which focuses on the development and implementation of legislation, has given a boost to the integration process particularly with respect to facilitating the FSAP initiatives. The Lamfalussy process puts in place a more efficient and flexible EU-level regulatory structure that can be used to adapt the body of regulation on an ongoing basis. This is particularly important for financial regulation, where the pace of innovation is rapid and can give rise to new risks that regulation should be able to respond to quickly. It applies a four-level structure to financial regulation: legislative (level 1), technical implementation (level 2), the exchange of information, co-operation, and convergence of supervisory practices (level 3) and strengthened enforcement (level 4). Both Solvency II and the MiFID are Lamfalussy directives; that is, principles-based framework directives that leave detailed regulation to the level 2 and level 3 committees. In banking, the scope for regulation through the Lamfalussy process is more limited, because the CRD is not a Lamfalussy directive (although some provisions can be adjusted via comitology procedures, which make it easier to develop a detailed set of regulations).[11]

Box 3.4. **The Lamfalussy framework**

The Lamfalussy process was launched in 2001. It put in place efficient procedures to deal with rapidly changing financial markets and the legislative burden produced by the FSAP. The goal was to facilitate decision-making on financial sector legislation and regulation and to achieve faster progress towards harmonisation by moving much of the discussion from the political level to "downstream" technical committees. Originally designed to address the challenges in securities regulation, it was later extended to the banking and insurance sector in 2004. As it was recognised that new institutional arrangements were needed, a four-level EU financial rulemaking architecture for each of the three sectoral pillars (banking, insurance and securities) was established.* Under the new approach financial regulation consists of two elements. The first contains basic principles, which do not need frequent amendment or high-level political agreement by the EU Council and Parliament. The second consists of more detailed technical features that might need more frequent amendments to follow market developments (Figure 3.3).

Box 3.4. **The Lamfalussy framework** *(cont.)*

- At level 1 the core principles of legislation take the form of directives and regulations adopted by the political bodies, the European Council and the European Parliament, on the basis of proposals prepared by the European Commission.
- At level 2 the technical implementation of framework directives and regulations is done by the European Commission, on the basis of recommendations made by high-level regulatory committees, in consultation with level 3 committees and users and experts from industry. The level 2 committees are the European Securities Committee (ESC), the European Banking Committee (EBC) and the European Insurance and Operational Pensions Committee (EIOPC).
- At level 3 the implementation of EU legislation at the national level is made by expert committees composed of national regulators and central banks. Level 3 committees are responsible for supporting a consistent day-to-day implementation of EU legislation by issuing guidelines and reviewing national regulatory practices. The level 3 committees are the Committee of European Securities Regulators (CESR), the Committee of European Banking Supervisors (CEBS) and the Committee of European Insurance and Occupational Pensions Supervisors (CEIOPS).
- At level 4 the European Commission enforces the timely and correct transposition of EU legislation into national law.

The level 2 committees essentially act as regulators, as they put in place secondary legislation with and through the European Commission that constitutes the basis for regulation at the national level. As the level 2 committees take into account industry advice delivered through the level 3 committees, secondary legislation can be modified relatively rapidly to adapt to changing circumstances, without having to go through the full legislative process. However, these advantages are somewhat limited for the banking sector as the CRD was not devised as a Lamfalussy framework directive. Instead, the extensive regulatory framework is established by the EU's legislative bodies.

Harmonised regulation is only effective if supervisors interpret and implement them in a co-ordinated way. Achieving convergence of supervisory practices – established practices as well as those related to new laws and regulations – is the main objective of the level 3 committees. These committees bring together national supervisors and seek harmonisation through, *inter alia*, 1) exchange of ideas and experience, 2) issuance of non-binding guidelines and recommendations on regulations, and 3) standard setting areas not covered by level 1 and 2 legislation.

CEBS is the main actor in the effort to achieve harmonised implementation of the CRD. Its work in this respect encompasses, *inter alia*, common guidance on the supervisory review process (Pillar 2 of Basel II), as well as guidance for accreditation of rating agencies, guidelines on prudential reporting by banks, validation of internal ratings-based credit risk, and operational risk approaches. Common implementation of Pillar 3 of Basel II is being facilitated through a common framework for supervisory disclosure. Beyond the CRD, CEBS established guidelines on prudential adjustments ("prudential filters") in the context of the introduction of the International Financial Reporting Standards (IFRS), to avoid that the changes in accounting standards will have undesirable effects on prudential indicators.

Since the end of 2005, cross-sectoral co-operation is being developed between the three level 3 committees, under the label "3L3 work programme". This work focuses on improving and facilitating the supervision of conglomerates and on other issues of common interest.

* See Davis and Green (2008) for a more detailed description of changes in the institutional arrangements.

Source: IMF (2007), "Integrating Europe's Financial Markets" and European Commission (2007).

Box 3.4. **The Lamfalussy framework** *(cont.)*

Figure 3.3. **The Lamfalussy four-level process**

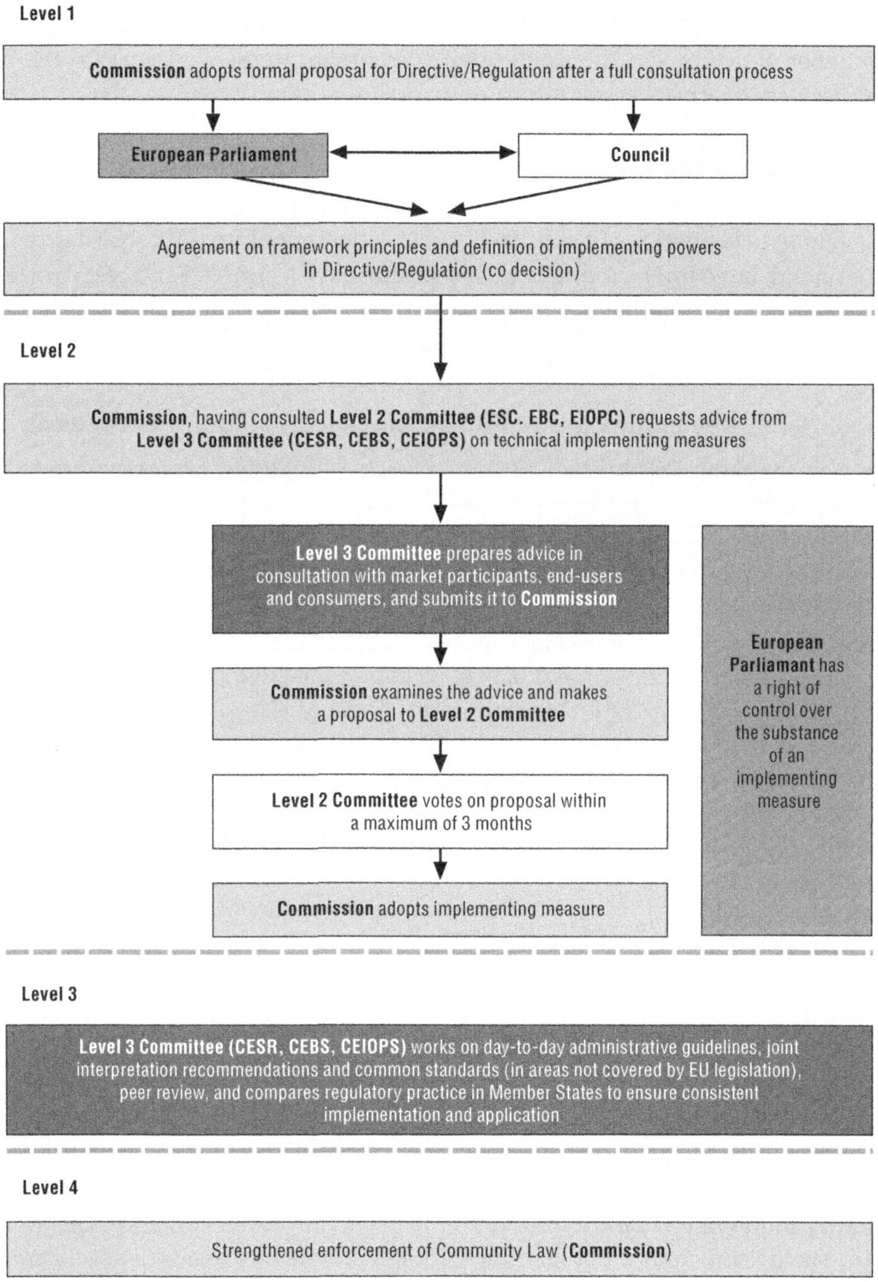

Source: Commission of the European Communities (2007), "Review of the Lamfalussy Process – Strengthening Supervisory Convergence", *Communication from the Commission*, COM (2007) 727 final, Brussels.

The application of these regulations in a coherent manner across countries, and the supervision of cross-border financial institutions are major challenges. Given the roles of national institutions, a high degree of co-operation between the many institutions is essential. To foster this, many committees at the EU level bring together the supervisors, finance ministries and central banks that have important prudential roles (Box 3.5). Most of the focus of the prudential authorities is on the country and institution/group level. The large number of actors and their potentially divergent interests complicate the decision-making process, both in crisis situations and in general matters related to financial stability. There is also the potential for regulatory capture due to the close relationship between regulators and the financial industry, as well as the industry's resources and economic importance. Differences in the regulatory regime across jurisdictions will persist if each adapts its regulations to suit its dominant incumbent institutions (Hardy, 2006). On the other hand, large internationally active groups have a stronger interest in streamlined financial stability arrangements across countries than local domestic banks.

Box 3.5. **Key bodies in the EU banking sector stability framework**

European Banking Committee (EBC): It consists of high-level representatives of the ministries of finance of member states and is chaired by the European Commission. The ECB, the chair of CEBS, and (optionally) national central banks may participate as observers. The EBC is a level 2 Lamfalussy committee that advises the European Commission on policy issues related to banking activities and on commission proposals in the banking area.

Committee of European Banking Supervision (CEBS): It comprises representatives of supervisory authorities and central banks, including the ECB, although only supervisory authorities have voting rights. Although the focus of CEBS, as a level 3 Lamfalussy committee, is mainly on regulatory and supervisory convergence, it also plays a role in promoting supervisory co-operation and as a conduit and organiser for the exchange of information between supervisors on individual financial institutions, including in situations of distress. Recently, CEBS as well as the other level 3 committees have been invited to gather relevant information for regularly assessing key financial developments, risks and vulnerabilities that could affect the stability of the EU financial system; in this work, CEBS should closely collaborate with the BSC.

European Central Bank (ECB): The ECB's main role in financial stability is monitoring, in co-operation with national central banks and supervisory agencies. It publishes an annual report on "EU Banking Sector Stability" and a twice-yearly Financial Stability Review for the euro area (both documents are prepared with the BSC). It also advises on financial rulemaking on EU and national laws and provides its technical input within the Lamfalussy structure and participates in the Basel Committee on Banking Supervision (BCBS), EBC and CEBS (observer status).

Banking Supervision Committee (BSC): It brings together national central banks, banking supervisory authorities, and the ECB. It monitors and assesses developments in the euro area from a financial stability perspective, analyses the impact of regulatory and supervisory requirements on financial system stability, and it promotes co-operation and exchange of information between central banks and supervisory authorities on issues of common interest, including the prevention and effective handling of financial crises. Preparatory work is performed in four working groups: macro-prudential analysis, structural developments in the EU banking sector, crisis management and credit registers.

OECD ECONOMIC SURVEYS: EURO AREA – ISBN 978-92-64-04824-9 – © OECD 20

Box 3.5. **Key bodies in the EU banking sector stability framework** *(cont.)*

Economic and Financial Committee (EFC): It includes representatives of ministries of finance, the European Commission, the ECB and central banks. It provides high-level assessments of developments in financial markets and services and advises ECOFIN and the European Commission.

Financial Stability Table (FST): The EFC meets twice a year (in April and September) to discuss financial stability issues in a special configuration as the FST, in a group including the Chairs of the BSC and the level 3 Lamfalussy committees – CEBS, CESR and CEIOPS. The discussion of banking issues is based primarily on ECB reports, including its Financial Stability Review, the FSC and the Commission's input and on regular input from CEBS, CEIOPS, CESR and the BSC. The FST brings together the broadest group of actors in matters of financial stability (prudential, monetary and fiscal authorities) and is a forum that can provide policy co-ordination.

Financial Services Committee (FSC): It is composed of representatives of the ministries of finance and the European Commission, joined by a representative of the ECB and the chairpersons of the 3 Lamfalussy committees as non-voting observers. The FSC discusses and provides guidance on cross-sector strategic and policy issues, especially technical and political aspects, and assists the EFC in preparing ECOFIN meetings.

Figure 3.4. **Key bodies in the EU banking sector stability framework**

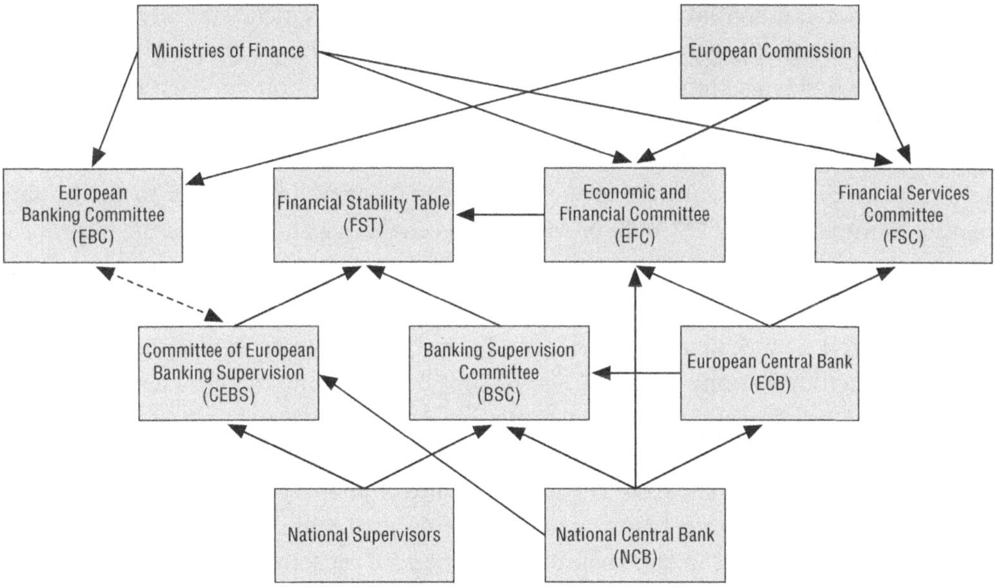

Source: IMF (2007), "Integrating Europe's Financial Markets".

The EU has attempted to address the mismatches between the country-based prudential setup and the emergence of LCFIs by shifting some responsibility for the regulation and supervision of cross-border financial groups to the home country. For financial conglomerates and banking groups, the Financial Conglomerate Directive (FCD) and the CRD[12] assign special tasks and responsibilities to the co-ordinating/consolidating supervisor of the conglomerate or banking group.[13] The directives require the relevant authorities to have written arrangements in place for co-ordination and co-operation between supervisors involved with a conglomerate. Both directives foresee also the exchange of information and consultation in the application of major sanctions. The resulting network of bilateral agreements aims to foster co-operation by laying down practical arrangements on information exchange. Additionally, for all EU-wide cross-border institutions, "colleges of supervisors" have been established in which home- and host-country supervisors meet, discuss supervisory issues and take decisions with regard to specific LCFIs (for instance for Nordea, Fortis and Sampo). As already mentioned, the CEBS, which has been entrusted with the task of promoting the co-operation among supervisors and the convergence of supervisory practices, plays an active role to strengthen the functioning of the colleges of supervisors. The existence of the colleges of supervisors should receive a proper legal basis in the upcoming revision of the CRD.

Nonetheless, the existing framework has shortcomings in providing a level playing field across the Union as considerable cross-country differences persist in the legal and regulatory frameworks for banks. National discretion is preserved by national specificities in transposing directives (there are almost one hundred specificities for the CRD (Kager, 2006)), and the practice of "goldplating" by national authorities, which adds further national requirements over and above those prescribed by EU directives.[14] In addition to stability concerns, the lack of convergence in national frameworks means that cross-border financial institutions face a considerable regulatory burden, adding to their costs.

Information is essential for the effective monitoring of financial stability and as a basis for taking decisions. Timely access to accurate information helps regulators and markets overcome the problems stemming from asymmetric information between regulators and financial institutions. However, gaining access to adequate information can be difficult even in the domestic market and improving the exchange of information between authorities in different countries is seen as one of the main challenges to the financial stability framework in the EU. To help address this challenge and enhance the information flow between supervisors also on a cross-border level, colleges have been set up.

The attempts at managing the institutional mismatch have not been complete and have introduced new challenges. The control that home-country authorities have gained over the foreign operations of the LCFIs has not been accompanied by a corresponding degree of responsibility and accountability for financial stability in the host country where those LCFIs operate. In countries with a significant foreign banking presence, the host authorities might no longer have meaningful control of the institutions active in their market, though they retain responsibility for financial stability within their borders. Although a host country can still require some financial reporting by banks present in the country, a full overview of the situation would require deeper co-operation with the home country than can be achieved within the college of supervisors.

The wider macro-prudential framework

Maintaining financial stability involves a wider set of institutions and arrangements. Besides the prudential authorities – regulators and supervisors – monetary and fiscal authorities have an important role to play. Fiscal authorities need to be involved in financial stability because they are the "solvency providers of last resort" and taxpayers may need to fund the recapitalisation of banks following financial crises. The central bank's involvement is crucial, even if it has no prudential responsibilities, because of its role as "lender of last resort". Moreover, the activities of the fiscal and monetary authorities affect the conditions for financial stability. This division of responsibility requires national authorities to co-operate and exchange information.

There is an ongoing debate about whether central banks should be directly involved in the supervision of financial institutions (*e.g.* Goodhart, 2000 and Maciandaro, 2008). Even without this, the national central banks and the European Central Bank (ECB) have a prominent role in the safeguarding of financial stability by ensuring price stability, and also by their provision of liquidity and oversight of payment systems. For the euro area, the European System of Central Banks (ESCB) has a statutory responsibility to "contribute to the smooth conduct of policies pursued by the competent authorities relating to the prudential supervision of credit institutions and the stability of the financial system".[15] This gives the ECB a monitoring and advisory role, but no supervisory mandate.[16] The ECB performs its tasks with the assistance of the BSC. The central banks and the ECB also have a central role in managing an eventual crisis; national banks can provide liquidity support to individual firms, while the ECB can provide liquidity support to the market as a whole.

The activities of the ECB in the monitoring and assessment of financial stability are based on three pillars (ECB, 2008a). *First*, the publication of the Financial Stability Review which draws attention to the main risks and vulnerabilities, and assesses whether the euro area financial system is capable of withstanding shocks and disruptions that are severe enough to significantly impair its intermediation function. *Second*, the macro-prudential analyses performed by the BSC of the EU banking sector, the findings of which are published in an annual report. The BSC also reviews structural developments in the EU banking sector that are relevant to central banks and supervisory authorities, publishing a separate annual report. *Third*, the ECB and the national central banks are closely involved in, and contribute to, the work of other institutions and bodies that monitor financial stability in Europe and worldwide. Given the ESCB's tasks in financial stability and especially in macro-prudential monitoring, information flows from and to the central banks, and within the ESCB system, are essential and should be improved (Bini Smaghi, 2008).[17] For instance, prior to the crisis, little was known about the role and activities of structured investment vehicles and their relationships with banks.

Recent European prudential initiatives

The European financial regulatory architecture remains work in progress. There are four major policy initiatives currently underway at the EU level. First, the ECOFIN adopted a roadmap in December 2007 to enhance the functioning of the Lamfalussy framework, especially the functioning of the Committees of Supervisors (referred to here as the "Lamfalussy Roadmap"). Second, ECOFIN has drawn up a list of policy responses to the recent financial market situation in a decision in October 2007 (referred to as the "Financial Turmoil Roadmap". Third, another roadmap was adopted in October 2007 to strengthen the financial stability framework, and in particular crisis management arrangements (referred to as the "Financial Stability Roadmap"). Finally, the de Larosière Group has been set up to examine how the European financial supervisory system can be improved to provide better macro-prudential oversight.

The Lamfalussy roadmap

The roadmap enhancing the Lamfalussy framework aims to improve the operation of the current EU supervisory framework (EC, 2007). In formulating its assessment, the Council took into account earlier evaluations of the Lamfalussy framework by various EU institutions and fora.[18] The Lamfalussy framework is widely supported by stakeholders. Nevertheless, the Council considered that, without changing the inter-institutional balance between the European Parliament, the Council and the Commission, further improvements should be introduced at all levels of the framework. Accordingly, recommendations were endorsed by the ECOFIN Council concerning: *a)* the arrangements for regulation (levels 1 and 2 of the Lamfalussy framework); and *b)* the institutional setting of the level 3 committees.

As regards level 1 (the legislative level of the Lamfalussy framework), several measures to limit the use of national options and discretion in EU directives and the implementation of legislation have been put forward. Moreover, the Council also stressed the importance of setting realistic transposition and implementation deadlines for level 2 measures. Finally, open and transparent consultations with all interested stakeholders were to be encouraged.

To strengthen the level 3 committees, whose main tasks are to exchange information and to facilitate co-operation and convergence of supervisory practices, several proposals have been made (and subsequently endorsed by ECOFIN), including improvements to accountability and decision-making:

- To strengthen the political accountability of these committees, their objectives should be better specified and accompanied by a reporting procedure to the EU institutions. Moreover, an EU dimension should be taken into account by national supervisors. This should intensify work towards supervisory convergence and co-operation. The enhanced EU dimension will allow financial supervisory authorities to consider financial stability concerns in other member states.
- To improve the committees' decision-making processes, the level 3 committees have been mandated to introduce in their charters the possibility of applying qualified majority voting, with the obligation for those who do not comply to explain their decision publicly.
- The ECOFIN Council has also asked the Commission to undertake further analysis "to clarify the role of the level 3 committees and consider all different options to strengthen the working of these committees, without unbalancing the current institutional structure or reducing the accountability of supervisors". It requested supervisors to report back regularly on their achievements, and to explain any non-compliance. The Commission is working on a revision of the Commission Decisions establishing the three Committees of supervisors. By the end of 2008, these Committees will be assigned specific, practical tasks, such as: *i)* mediation, *ii)* drafting recommendations and guidelines, and *iii)* an explicit role to strengthen the analysis and responsiveness to risks to the stability of the EU financial system.

Financial Turmoil Roadmap

The Financial Turmoil Roadmap is broadly consistent with proposals advanced by the Financial Stability Forum. It identified four priorities: *i)* enhancing transparency for investors, markets and regulators, *ii)* improving valuation of financial products –

particularly for complex, illiquid financial instruments, *iii)* strengthening the prudential framework and banks' risk management, and *iv)* making markets function better, in particular by reviewing the role of credit rating agencies.

The absence of accurate and timely information on exposures to credit risk has been a key factor in explaining the rapid loss of investor confidence during the turmoil. Both the industry itself and prudential authorities have not kept pace with the development of new financial instruments and techniques. Some immediate measures to reduce the duration and severity of the turmoil are under way. For example, to enhance transparency the financial industry was expected, by the time of publication of mid-year results in 2008, to have made full and prompt disclosure of on- and off-balance sheet risk exposures and losses (write-downs, and fair value estimates for complex and illiquid assets), consistent with best disclosure practices. By the end of October 2008, the industry is expected to adopt guidelines to promote consistent and comparable disclosures for 1st quarter 2009 results. Moreover, progress is being made on industry initiatives to strengthen investor information. The Commission has requested that the Committee of European Banking Supervisors (CEBS) and the industry bodies formulate a plan to provide more detailed information on securitisation exposures. In February 2008, European industry associations[19] published a joint position paper outlining how they planned to respond to the transparency-related issues of the roadmap. The paper covered sound and consistent implementation of the securitisation related CRD disclosure requirements, transparency and the provision of public information, and a commitment by the European industry to increase transparency to investors in the securitisation markets. In July 2008, the industry published valuable data and statistics on the securitisation market. These initiatives are welcome. Work by the Basel Committee of Banking Supervisors (BCBS) on guidance on how to strengthen disclosure requirements further under Pillar 3 of the Basel II accord should be followed closely with the goal of implementation in the CRD.

The management of risk through appropriate valuation and accounting treatment of assets is ultimately the responsibility of the institution that holds them. Nevertheless, accounting standards set by the supervisors and other relevant authorities play an important role from a prudential perspective. At the EU level, initiatives to find agreement on a common approach to the accounting valuation of illiquid assets and implication for risk management practices by banks have been taken. Work is underway at the international level on ways to ensure the reliable valuation and auditing of assets, particularly of those assets where markets are potentially illiquid in times of stress, while maintaining compatibility with international financial standards. Positive steps have been recently taken at international level on the complex issue of fair valuation. The International Accounting Standards Board set up an expert advisory panel on fair valuation in close co-operation with the Financial Stability Forum. This panel has now delivered input to the Board. In addition, a roundtable of stakeholders will also be organised by the International Accounting Standards Board to provide input on off-balance sheet items. However, because the Board will have to follow its due process including consultations, before it can issue final outcomes, concrete deliverables should not be expected before 2009.

With respect to strengthening the prudential framework and banks' risk management, the roadmap comprises the revision of the CRD. On 1 October 2008, the Commission adopted the proposals for amendments to the CRD, covering areas such as limiting banks' concentration risk, improving their capital quality, increasing co-operation through supervisory colleges for cross-border groups, enhancing co-operation and information exchange between supervisors, finance ministries and central banks for crisis management to further strengthening the existing prudential framework, as well as proposals to ensure that the risks associated with the "originate-and-distribute model" (ODM) are properly mitigated.

The Financial Turmoil Roadmap calls for an examination of the role of credit rating agencies (CRAs) and the use of credit ratings, in particular regarding structured financial instruments, conflicts of interest, transparency of rating methods, time-lags in rating reassessments and regulatory approval processes. In June 2008, the European Commission concluded that the industry's initiative put forward in the revised International Organisation of Securities Commissions' (IOSCO) Code of Conduct[20] is a step in the right direction but lacks the necessary teeth to effectively address the challenges posed. Because a strengthened oversight regime for rating agencies might be necessary to remedy these shortcomings, the Commission adopted a proposal to regulate CRAs on 12 November 2008. The main elements of the Commission's proposal are that the credit rating agencies (CRAs) should be subject to an EU registration system and that an oversight regime for CRAs should be put in place, whereby regulators will supervise the policies and procedures followed by the rating agencies. In addition, corporate and internal governance issues will come under scrutiny, especially the remuneration structure of analysts. The proposal also attempts to strengthen competition by encouraging entry of new players.

There is a debate about whether greater scrutiny of CRAs is the most efficient way to deal with the flaws in the current system. For example, under Basel II, credit rating agencies are referenced in capital adequacy rules and many investment funds are permitted to buy only highly-rated bonds. This has triggered a discussion about how ratings are used.[21] The Basel-based Joint Forum has launched a stocktaking of the uses of credit ratings, which is due at the end of 2008. However, changing the rule-based credit ratings is seen as harder than changing the ratings process itself, since the former requires an overhaul of Basel II. Moreover, it is also recognised that there is no good alternative to using ratings in many cases, which is why they need to be credible.

The Financial Stability Roadmap

Crisis prevention and management are key challenges for regulators and supervisors. There is considerable scope to strengthen the current arrangements in this area. The Financial Stability Roadmap sets out a work programme and proposals to address these issues. In September 2006, an *ad hoc* working group of the EFC was formed to explore ways to further develop financial stability arrangements in the EU, on the basis of the insights provided by the EU-wide financial crisis simulation exercise of April 2006. The group identified a number of actions that would improve consistency between the arrangements for crisis management and resolution, on the one hand, and the arrangements for crisis prevention, on the other. The proposals by the group were approved and subsequently endorsed as part of the strategic roadmap for strengthening the arrangements for financial stability at both the EU and national level. The strategic roadmap comprises the following measures (Council Press Release 9 October 2007 and ECB (2008b)):

- Common principles for financial crisis management. The EU countries have agreed on a set of nine common principles to be followed in the management of any cross-border financial crisis involving at least one banking group that: *i)* has substantial cross-border activities; *ii)* is facing severe problems which are expected to trigger systemic effects in at least one member state; and *iii)* is assessed to be at risk of becoming insolvent. Three important elements are set out. First, cross-border crisis management is a matter of common interest to member states. Second, private sector solutions should be given primacy in the resolution of a crisis. Third, the use of public money to resolve a crisis can never be taken for granted and will only be considered to remedy serious disturbances in the economy. If public resources are used, the direct budgetary costs will be shared among affected member states on the basis of equitable and balanced criteria, including the economic impact of the crisis and the framework of home/host countries' supervisory powers.

- An extended Memorandum of Understanding (MoU) on cross-border financial stability. The new MoU, issued in June 2008, replaces and extends the 2005 MoU. First, it incorporates the common principles on crisis management described above. The second component is a common analytical framework for the assessment of systemic implications of a cross-border crisis which has been developed by the BSC in co-operation with the CEBS. The third component consists of common practical guidelines for crisis management, which reflect a common understanding of the steps and procedures that need to be taken and followed in a cross-border crisis situation. In addition, the extended EU-wide MoU also encourages the authorities in different countries that share financial stability concerns to set up voluntary co-operation agreements for crisis management.

To preserve financial stability and to facilitate co-operation and information exchange among authorities, enhancements to the legal framework might be required. Several fields are being examined and in some areas changes to the regulatory framework have already been proposed:

- The Capital Requirements Directive (CRD). The objective of the proposed revision of the legal framework is to: *i)* clarify the existing obligations of supervisory authorities, central banks and ministries of finance to exchange information and co-operate in crisis situations; *ii)* increase the information rights and involvement of host countries; *iii)* clarify the role of the home or consolidating supervisor and facilitate the timely involvement of relevant parties in a crisis situation; and *iv)* include an EU-dimension in the national mandates of supervisory authorities, *i.e.* a requirement to co-operate and to take into account financial stability concerns in all member states. The amendments will also require the establishment of colleges of supervisors. Colleges comprising authorities supervising group entities in different member states will address potential conflicts and supervisory overlap. This will be aided by reinforced powers of the consolidating supervisor. In crisis situations, stakeholders will benefit from enhanced supervisory co-operation and a clearer allocation of responsibilities. Mediation mechanisms will ensure conflict resolution while regular exchanges will allow for early detection of financial stress.
- Cross-border transfer of assets. Since the subsidiaries of a banking group are separate legal entities subject to the legislation of the country where they are established (host country), national law may hinder the transfer of assets between them for the purpose of protecting creditors and depositors. The Commission is looking into the possibility of reducing barriers to cross-border asset transferability, while introducing appropriate safeguards within banking, insolvency and company law, taking into account that the reallocation of assets in a crisis affects the ability of stakeholders in different legal

entities to pursue claims. The overall objectives are to reinforce the primacy of private sector solutions, avoid counterproductive ring-fencing of assets, and facilitate the smooth management of a crisis. Changes would be implemented in the Winding-up Directive.

- Winding-up of banking groups. The present directive on the reorganisation and winding-up of credit institutions could be amended to also include subsidiaries. The objective is to increase the efficiency of any reorganisation and winding-up of cross-border banking groups. As the current directive does not cover subsidiaries, the reorganisation or the winding-up of a cross-border banking group will necessarily involve various national regimes. A revision of the current directive could facilitate the winding-up of subsidiaries by providing joint insolvency proceedings.
- Early intervention. The Commission has outlined plans for a White Paper on Early Intervention to deal with ailing banks. The main focus of the White Paper will be on assessing whether the current range of crisis prevention/resolution/stabilisation tools available to authorities can and should be complemented by additional tools and whether there is a case for further convergence of such tools at EU level. The Commission will also consider the appropriateness of tools for dealing with both cross-border and domestic institutions. Publication of the White Paper is planned for mid-2009.
- Deposit guarantee schemes (DGS). The European Commission has put forward a revision of EU rules on deposit guarantee schemes on 15 October 2008. The new rules are designed to improve depositor protection and to maintain the confidence of depositors in the financial safety net. Under the new rules, the minimum level of coverage for deposits will be increased within one year from EUR 20 000 to EUR 100 000, and initially to EUR 50 000 in the intervening period. Individual member states can choose to add to these minimum levels. In addition, the payout period in the event of bank failure will be reduced. The proposal now passes to the European Parliament and the Council of Ministers for consideration.
- The Commission has clarified the application of the state aid rules of the EC Treaty in crisis situations in the banking sector. The basic principles are that any selectively granted aid to individual banks in difficulties must comply with the rules of the Rescue and Restructuring Guidelines, which is the general framework of guidelines applied to all sectors, in order to prevent market distortions. While the Commission has no specific provisions of state aid rules for the banking sector, it acknowledges the special character of the banking sector in terms of spill-over effects and implications for financial stability. This special character requires a rapid reaction from the Commission, when faced with a notification of state aid. However, systemic risk has never been accepted by the Commission as a justification for state aid in respect of an individual bank in difficulties. On the contrary, a general measure targeted at the entire sector/industry could be deemed compatible with the specific case of "serious disturbance to the economy". Serious economic disturbance would be unlikely to be remedied by intervention in favour of just one bank. Moreover, the serious economic disturbance must already exist before aid can be justified to be accepted as "serious disturbance to the economy".

Areas for improvement in Europe's prudential framework

Crisis prevention

Adequate supervision of financial institutions is a key requirement for ensuring financial market stability. One purpose of supervision is to ensure that risks taken by financial institutions are commensurate to their capacity to bear them. Another purpose is to gather information about financial institutions, so that, in the event of a crisis, the authorities can make informed decisions on the best way to handle and resolve the crisis. A well-functioning supervisory system is also a prerequisite for effective crisis management and resolution. As early remedial action against delinquent, unsafe or unsound institutions is essential to keep down the potential costs of a crisis, continuous surveillance is crucial.

Efficient supervision in a landscape with major cross-border banks requires supervisors in different countries to co-ordinate their activity and share information. Understanding the risks in a banking group necessitates a clear picture of all its various activities on a consolidated basis. As cross-border banks set up financial institutions in different countries, co-ordination of supervision becomes vital. Currently, the national foundations of prudential arrangements imply (notwithstanding the increasingly harmonised accounting and reporting framework) that information about the European Union's financial system is collected locally, using different methodologies. No centralised store of prudential information exists, in part because of national confidentiality rules. According to some authors, supervisors are in a position to control information during crisis situations to the potential harm of other parties. Indeed, research suggests that supervisors may face significant incentives to withhold information in a crisis (Čihák and Decressin, 2007). This can be costly if it delays an intervention and could create tensions between countries as trust is important in cross-border supervision.

Some arrangements for information-sharing do exist, however. The CRD[22] requires information-sharing and co-operation between all the authorities responsible for the supervision of the entities comprising the banking group. The proposed changes to the CRD (described above) will enhance information exchange between home and host supervisors of a group, as colleges of supervisors will share and gather information in order to have a comprehensive view of the health of a cross-border financial institution. However, the directive currently falls short, as no requirement for full information sharing is included. In the CRD for example, there is a distinction between essential and relevant information. The former should be provided by supervisors on their own initiative, the latter upon request.

The ESCB has the responsibility for overseeing financial stability at the macroeconomic level. The ESCB has access to information from various sources, including of supervisory nature. Indeed the Banking Supervision Committee of the ESCB, which brings together National Central Banks (NCBs) and supervisory authorities, provides access to supervisory information for the ECB's financial stability assessment. Moreover, NCBs and the ECB are members of the CEBS. The CRD requires national authorities to communicate information to central banks in an emergency. Arrangements for exchange of information are evolving and a number of central banks perform supervisory functions, and therefore have access to supervisory information.

Preventing a crisis requires appropriate sanctions in cases of non-compliance. The CRD and other directives provide only the baseline standards with which banks must comply and oblige the member states to impose the sanctions if they fail to comply.

Aligning the responsibility and accountability of national supervisors of cross-border institutions is a major challenge. In a first-best world, host countries would be confident that the controlling home country will take early action where necessary. Providing home-country supervisors with explicit financial responsibility (and accountability) for the economic impact of problems stemming from their banks' activities in the host country could also help. In practice, achieving these goals would be difficult both economically and politically.

The recent initiative – expressed in both the proposed changes to the Capital Requirements Directive (CRD) and the review of the Lamfalussy framework – to introduce an EU dimension into the mandates of national supervisory authorities, is a step in the right direction. The member states will need to ensure that an EU dimension, including the intensification of work towards enhancing supervisory convergence and co-operation at the EU level, is taken into account in the mandates of national supervisors. Moreover, the proposed changes to the CRD would require supervisors to take into account financial stability concerns in all member states. However, this will only address some of the tensions between home and host authorities, since little will be done to align the incentives of the separate supervisory authorities.

The proposed changes to the CRD require the consolidating supervisor to establish Colleges of Supervisors. Colleges of supervisors bring together all supervisors that have an interest in a specific cross-border institution, and there are a rising number of them in the European Union. Their establishment should be an instrument for stronger co-operation whereby competent authorities reach agreement on key supervisory tasks. The colleges should facilitate the handling of ongoing supervision and emergency situations. The competent authorities responsible for the supervision of subsidiaries of an EU parent credit institution or an EU parent financial holding company, the competent authorities of a host country where systemically relevant branches are established, and authorities of third countries where appropriate, may participate in colleges of supervisors. The Committee of European Banking Supervisors should provide, where necessary, for non-binding guidelines and recommendations in order to enhance the convergence of supervisory practices. It is important that colleges remain effective and efficient for the supervision of banking groups. Therefore, the Commission considers that the increased information flows should be accompanied by the eventual decision for two key aspects being entrusted to the consolidating supervisor (Pillar 2 capital requirements and reporting requirements). Setting up colleges will enhance co-operation, but the problem of aligning responsibility and accountability for financial stability will persist. Moreover, there is still no mechanism for sharing the cost of bank failures.

Even though processes for co-operation between supervisors from different countries have improved, the current European supervisory framework may still be inadequate in detecting emergent systemic risk. Moreover, enhanced co-operation through the colleges will not necessarily address the problem of differences in supervisory structures across the EU countries. It is crucial for financial stability assessments to be effectively integrated into supervisory priorities, and that these lead to tangible actions to address weaknesses and mitigate the associated risks. Conversely, macro-prudential analysis should rest on solid micro-level information. Early identification of trends and risks by the micro-level monitoring should be reflected in the agenda for macro-prudential oversight.

Crisis management

Quick, but effective decisions are required during a financial crisis. A clear line of command is also important. The relevant authorities need adequate powers and an ability to act. As a crisis might involve providing liquidity to solvent but illiquid banks, the central bank has an important role in the management of a crisis. Generally, emergency liquidity assistance (ELA) would consist of the support given by national central banks in exceptional circumstances and on a case-by-case basis to temporarily illiquid but solvent institutions and markets, and against adequate collateral to prevent any potential systemic effects or disruption of the smooth functioning of payment and settlement systems.

Currently, crisis management is largely a national responsibility, although increasingly supported by cross-border arrangements for co-ordination and information exchange.[23] The CRD and the FCD provide a basic framework, but both existing provisions and new proposals relating to the non-supervisory aspects of crisis management (such as central bank involvement and liquidity support) lack teeth. The FCD[24] prescribes the gathering and exchange of information to the home or co-ordinating supervisor, but leaves full power to the host-country authorities to use their own crisis-management tools when needed. The CRD[25] gives the consolidating supervisor responsibility for planning and co-ordinating supervisory actions in emergency situations, and requires the lead supervisor to alert all supervisors and central banks concerned as soon as is practicable when an emergency situation arises that could jeopardise the stability of the financial system in any member state. Supporting guidelines by the CEBS provide concrete guidance for the effective and consistent implementation of the revised legal framework for cross-border banking groups, and enhance the practical operational networking of national supervisors. They have been designed to follow a risk-based and proportional approach. For instance, the degree of information exchange and co-operation between supervisors should be related to the systemic relevance of the entities, both in relation to the host's market and the group as a whole.

The co-operation among EU authorities in the area of crisis management has been enhanced through voluntary agreements in the form of MoUs between various authorities. Such agreements, which set out procedures for co-operation and information-sharing in potential crisis situations, have been adopted at the regional and national levels with respect to individual institutions.

In addition, a series of multilateral MoUs set out the general framework for crisis management, bringing together all the relevant supervisory parties. The first was signed in 2003 between the ECB, banking supervisors and the EU national central banks. It sets out high-level principles for procedures and co-operation in crisis management situations, but focuses mainly on information sharing. It gives the home-country authority responsibility for informing other supervisors and for making most crisis-management decisions. To address systemic crisis-management issues that may include a fiscal burden, a second MoU was signed in 2005. This MoU involves ministries of finance along with national central banks, the ECB and EU banking supervisors. Its focus remains on information sharing, although it also encourages the development of crisis-management tools. Following the recommendations of an *ad hoc* working group of the EFC, a third MoU was signed by EU supervisory authorities, finance ministries and central banks on 1 June 2008. It replaces the 2005 MoU and contains common principles on crisis management including on the conditions for the use of public funds and on the subsequent possible burden-sharing, a common analytical framework and practical guidelines for crisis management. Financial crisis simulation exercises of the 2003 and 2005 MoUs have taken place to test the overall financial stability arrangements. They identified potential weaknesses in the co-ordination of responses to a crisis and suggested improvements to better manage liquidity and avoid breakdowns in payment systems.

In the past, relatively little attention has been paid to liquidity management, which remains largely an issue for national host supervisors. However, the recent financial market turmoil has thrown the spotlight on the importance of maintaining adequate liquidity. In principle, there may be a need to provide emergency liquidity to rescue a systemically important bank to prevent contagion to the rest of the financial market. The ECB has played an important role during the turmoil in providing liquidity to the market as a whole, but emergency liquidity assistance (ELA) to individual banks is the responsibility of national central banks. Within the Eurosystem, a national central bank deciding to provide liquidity support to individual institutions needs to inform the ECB and the other central banks *ex post* for small operations and needs the *ex ante* consent of the Governing Council of the ECB for large operations that could have an impact on monetary policy. The treasuries (*i.e.* taxpayers) carry the risks involved in ELA operations.

For cross-border banks, host countries are technically responsible for liquidity oversight for both subsidiaries and branches, though home countries are able to provide liquidity to groups. For EU countries outside the euro area, this is also important because liquidity support interacts with monetary policy, as it may require the provision of large amounts of money in local currency. Within the Eurosystem, national responsibility is driven by the possibility that ELA operations could generate losses for the central bank that may need to be compensated by the fiscal authority. There is no concrete mechanism yet for sharing this burden at the EU level. There is a tension from giving the main responsibility to the host country for ELA to branches operating in its territory, while the supervisory information about these banks is held by the home country. Assessing the risks of an ELA operation would thus be difficult. Moreover, as funds flow within a group, liquidity support to a local bank may be costly, especially in the case of a branch, as the ring-fencing of assets in the local entity is not allowed within the Union.

Crisis resolution

A financial safety net is important for preventing financial crises, limiting their cost once they occured and helping to resolve them quickly and efficiently. Safety nets usually involve a combination of deposit insurance, ELAs (discussed earlier) and other regulatory procedures. Deposit insurance is designed to help overcome the asymmetric information between depositors and financial institutions about the solvency of financial institutions and hence the safety of deposits. During bouts of financial uncertainty, unprotected depositors may have difficulty distinguishing between solvent and insolvent financial institutions and rapidly withdraw funds from both types of institutions. This can make financial crises self-fulfilling and more damaging. Although deposit guarantee schemes (DGS) protect depositors and can reduce the incentives for depositors to run on banks, they also induce moral hazard by reducing the incentives for depositors to monitor risk-taking by financial institutions. However, empirical evidence on the relationship between deposit insurance and risk-taking by banks is mixed. Demirguc-Kunt and Huizinga (2004) find that in countries with explicit deposit insurance, required interest rates are lower, but there is also greater risk-taking by banks. They therefore argue that there is a trade-off between the benefits of depositor protection and the dangers of moral hazard. In contrast Gropp and Vesala (2004) find that within Europe, when explicit deposit insurance schemes have replaced implicit insurance, market risk-taking by banks that are not "too big to fail" has actually fallen.

Designing a DGS also involves trade-offs. Although in principle the optimal coverage is that which reaches an appropriate balance between reducing the probability of bank runs and limiting moral hazard, in practice it is difficult to determine what this level should be. Other design features also affect this trade-off. Demirguc-Kunt and Huizinga (2004) find that co-insurance, joint management of the DGS by the public and private sectors and coverage of foreign currency deposits dampen risk-taking, while higher coverage and protection of inter-bank deposits enhance risk-taking. Governments should also be wary of providing more insurance *ex post* than was designated by the insurance schemes *ex ante,* as it may damage the longer run credibility of schemes and accentuate moral hazard. Finally, crises are more likely to be resolved quickly when arrangements are in place that gives depositors near-immediate access to their insured deposits (which is the case in the United States but not in European countries, which pay out within three months with an optional three-months delay).

An important issue for the EU is that while its capital markets have become more integrated, there is significant variation in the design of deposit insurance schemes across countries. Although European countries recently agreed to raise the ceilings on their insurance schemes to a common level, some countries have also committed to guaranteeing all retail banking deposits. There are also variations in the types of deposits covered, the amount of coverage, co-insurance, risk-based premia and funding arrangements. This matters because it gives depositors and banks incentives to engage in regulatory arbitrage. Depositors may seek the most generous coverage or avoid being covered by a foreign deposit insurance system. Moreover, increasingly mobile banks have an incentive to seek coverage by unfunded, and thus inexpensive, schemes in normal times as well as an incentive to relocate during crises. Variation also creates uncertainty and may amplify cross-country spillovers from bank failures.

To reduce moral hazard problems, it is important to signal that financial institutions should not necessarily expect a bailout and that tough conditions will be placed on shareholders if such action is undertaken. If a financial institution is facing insolvency problems, an effective method of resolution can help to avoid more severe tensions elsewhere in the financial system. A resolution requires that the failing institution be returned to health, restructured or wound down and liquidated. In the latter case, arrangements are needed to allocate losses, and compensate insured creditors, particularly depositors. Resolving a crisis in a cross-border bank also poses challenges in co-ordinating activities and decisions by authorities in different countries and in dealing with conflicts of interest. In recent history, the collapse of the Bank of Credit and Commerce International (BCCI) in 1991 revealed how difficult the problem can be if an institution is active in several countries where crisis resolution is a national responsibility. Large cross-border institutions that assume that they are "too big to fail" may also have greater incentives to load-up on risk. With some European countries appearing reluctant or unwilling to close even small, non-systemic, insolvent banks, moral hazard may be correspondingly high.

Efficient bank resolution would involve speed, specialist expertise, and a focused view on the interest of depositors and the general welfare. Having insolvency procedures specifically adapted to banks might facilitate this. In some European countries, banking supervisors have the right to petition for bankruptcy. However, in many others, bank failures are covered by general bankruptcy proceedings (Eisenbeis and Kaufman, 2007). This is problematic because general bankruptcy procedures can be very slow and vary widely between member states. The collapse of Parmalat, a non-financial corporation but the most prominent European large cross-border bankruptcy, shows that general bankruptcy procedures become extremely complex when there are cross-border elements. While some European countries have bank-specific provisions, no country goes as far as the United States, which has a separate insolvency regime for banks and where the Federal Deposit Insurance Corporation (FDIC) has legal closure authority (Eisenbeis and Kaufman, 2007). In the US system, banks are closed when equity capital to total balance sheet assets drops below 2%, and shareholders lose everything. Even if a bank is legally closed, it is kept open physically, either by bringing in another bank quickly or by operating a newly chartered bridge bank. This practice has helped to avoid bank runs and has minimised the pay-out from the deposit insurance fund. At the same time, moral hazard issues are also limited because banks are allowed to fail. In the United States, prompt corrective action aims to turn troubled banks around before insolvency. Progressively harsher and more mandatory sanctions are applied by the bank regulators on weak financial institutions as their net worth declines. Sanctions include a change in senior management, reductions in dividends or restrictions on growth and acquisitions. These measures attempt to slow a bank's deterioration and buy time, so that regulators may be ready to close them when necessary. The recent crisis has shown, however, that while such a model may be useful to deal with a slow-developing crisis affecting a small institution, it may remain inefficient to counter a very rapid crisis affecting a large institution. The European Commission is currently preparing a White Paper on Early Intervention.

Special bankruptcy procedures might not be sufficient in the case of a LCFI where the rights of claimholders may be in conflict with the need to take into account broader economic and systemic considerations. Addressing failures of cross-border banks at the EU level is handled currently by national insolvency frameworks, on the basis of the principles established by the 2001 Reorganisation and Winding-Up Directive.[26] It provides that in the case of the insolvency of a cross-border financial group, the parent company and its EU branches should be considered a single company subject to home-country insolvency proceedings, whereas subsidiaries should be subject to host-country insolvency proceedings. The directive also prescribes equality of treatment for claimants from different countries, imposes information requirements, and establishes some limited minimum standards for the winding-up legislation of member states. Some of the drawbacks in the winding-up directive are currently being addressed in the Financial Stability Roadmap. These include the different treatment of subsidiaries and branches, which is inefficient as it does not follow company organisation. Untangling the different parts of an integrated group could cause significant loss of value, limit the options of each of the separate receivers, and would be time-consuming. In a few countries, insolvency law differs by financial sector, which would hamper a consistent and effective resolution of a financial conglomerate (Hadjiemmanuil, 2005).

Due to the potential costs of a failure of one or more LCFIs and the lack of capacity in deposit insurance systems, which are not designed to deal with systemic failures, it is important to consider cost-efficient ways of liquidating a failing LCFI.[27] A cost minimising resolution of a failing bank would probably involve ensuring continuity in many of the operations of the institution. This might not be possible without a solvency package that includes taxpayer money or public guarantees. This raises the thorny issue of how the financial burden of the solvency package should be shared between taxpayers of different countries. On the one hand, *ex ante* decisions on burden sharing may accentuate moral hazard. In this case it is best to decide *ex ante* on the general procedures to follow, for example, an allocation formula for sharing of potential losses. The latter should of course not entail that governments will always step in. On the other hand, *ex post* decisions, which characterise the current arrangements in Europe, may lead to an under-provision of recapitalisation, because countries have an incentive to understate their share of the problem to incur a smaller share of the costs (Freixas, 2003). This leaves the largest country, almost always the home country, with the decision of whether to shoulder the costs on its own or to close the bank. Even though the new EU-wide MoU sets out principles on burden sharing for cross-border institutions, it is not legally binding and it remains to be seen whether the home country authorities will use taxpayer's money to the benefit of host countries or if they have the capacity to do so.[28]

Dampening the pro-cyclicality of the financial system

As the financial system has developed and become more complex, concern has increased about systemic risks and these have been heightened by recent events in financial markets. These result not just from what happens to a single financial institution but also from how problems can spread from one institution to another or are correlated across markets. Despite significant advances in the management of credit and other risks, banks' assessment of risks tends to vary with the business cycle; risk are underestimated in good times and overestimated in bad times. This increases the potential for credit and asset market booms and busts. These risks may be higher in the euro area because individual countries cannot use monetary policy to influence cycles in their own economies and fiscal policy may be constrained. It is therefore especially important for these countries to have financial systems that are robust to shocks.

Regulations can contribute to credit cycles if inappropriately designed, particularly where the focus is on achieving micro-prudential objectives aimed at individual institutions rather than the macro-prudential stability of the system as a whole. There is a risk that with the implementation of the Basel II Capital Accord, the financial amplification of the business cycle could become even larger (Lowe, 2002; Borio and Shim, 2007). Under the Basel I Accord, minimum capital requirements on a given portfolio were fixed and they became binding with a fall in a bank's capital following credit losses. Under the new risk-based capital system, requirements become binding through an increase in minimum requirements as loans migrate to higher risk classes. At the point in the cycle when banks are most likely to record losses, the minimum capital requirements could themselves increase, which would accentuate any slowdown in credit growth brought about by capital losses and perceived declines in the creditworthiness of potential borrowers.

From a macro-prudential perspective, the time dimension and the endogeneity of risk are important. Cushions should be built up in upswings to be relied upon in rough times. This would enhance an institution's ability to weather deteriorating economic conditions when access to external financing becomes more costly and constrained. Moreover, by "leaning against the wind", it would reduce the amplitude of the financial cycle, limiting the risk of financial distress in the first place. The Basel II Accord has seen a number of technical adjustments to the original proposals to address pro-cyclicality concerns and strengthen the supervisory pillar. It is now possible for supervisors to impose higher capital standards if stress tests imply increasing risks. The jury is out on whether Basel II will perform better than Basel I from a macro-prudential perspective. But there will be one important improvement: Basel II imposes provisioning for credit lines extended to structured investment vehicles and similar institutions, undercutting incentives to perform financial transactions in the unregulated shadow banking system.[29]

Pronounced pro-cyclicality is illustrated by the strong inverse relationship between GDP growth and bank provisioning (Figure 3.5). Dobson and Hufbauer (2001) observe that: "Banks are often reluctant to make adequate provisions for their loan losses, and bank regulators are often hesitant to push banks to recognize losses before it becomes plain that borrowers are in trouble. No bank loan officer wants to admit she made a mistake, and few supervisors want to cry 'fire' when there is only smoke. As a consequence, published loan-loss provisions usually lag the eruption of a financial crisis. Hence, when the crisis strikes, banks typically have inadequate cushions of equity plus reserves to absorb the loss." Empirical work focusing on loan loss provisions and capital buffers tend to confirm this behaviour (Ayuso *et al.*, 2004 for Spain; Lindquvist, 2004 for Norway; Stolz and Wedow, 2005 for Germany and Bikker and Metzemakers, 2003 and Jokipii and Milne, 2006 for a large sample of European countries).

Figure 3.5. **Loan loss provisioning tends to have pro-cyclical effects**

Average for eight euro area countries, per cent[1]

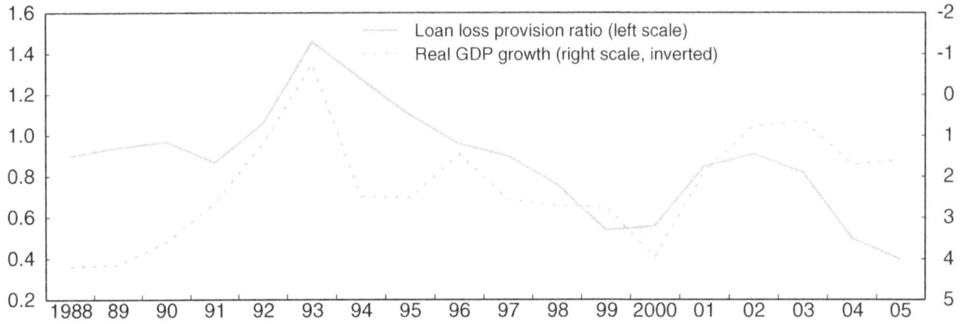

1. Weighted average based on 2000 GDP and purchasing power parities of the following countries: Belgium, Finland, France, Germany (Western Germany prior to 1993), Italy, Netherlands, Portugal (commercial banks) and Spain.

Source: OECD (2005), *Bank Profitability: Financial Statements of Banks* and OECD (2008), *OECD Economic Outlook*, No. 83.

StatLink http://dx.doi.org/10.1787/518702876603

Several approaches have been suggested or implemented to reduce the pro-cyclicality of the financial system (Borio and Shim, 2007 and Borio, 2008):

- Regulators can impose a leverage ratio (the ratio of tier 1 (core) capital to total assets) on large banks, in addition to risk-weighted capital ratios. The leverage ratio caps the extent to which banks' assets can exceed its capital base. Although the leverage ratio approach runs counter to the decade-long trend to assess riskiness on the basis of sophisticated models, an additional transparent, complementary constraint may help to redress the asymmetric information between banks and regulators.

- The Spanish authorities have introduced a second tier of prudential provisioning that complements specific provisioning arrangements (Fernández de Lis *et al.*, 2001 and Fernández Ordóñez, 2008). This sets a floor to the fall in provisions during a credit boom. Bank provisions to non-performing loans have indeed been the highest among the 90 countries that report such ratios to the IMF (IMF, 2008), about four times higher than in the other euro area countries and double those reported by the United States. No other country has implemented such a scheme, largely because tax authorities regard them as profit-smoothing schemes and they are disliked by accounting standard setters. In Spain, it was possible to implement the scheme because the regulator (the Bank of Spain) also sets accounting standards for financial institutions.
- Capital requirements could themselves be varied over the economic cycle to lean against the pro-cyclicality of the financial system. By forcing financial institutions to build capital buffers during upturns, counter-cyclical macro-prudential policy could reduce the incentives for excessive risk-taking, while also allowing them to draw down on those buffers during downturns when external finance is costly and difficult to obtain (Borio, 2003).
- Many banks paid bonuses to traders and executives for deals that subsequently incurred large losses. Compensation arrangements have often encouraged risk-taking with insufficient regard to long-term risks, thus amplifying the financial cycle. The FSF (2008) has encouraged supervisors to work with market participants to mitigate risks arising from inappropriate incentive structures.
- A more radical option would be to give banks the option of either accepting a higher capital buffer or of taking out insurance against large aggregate write-downs of asset values by other banks (Kayshap *et al.*, 2008). Such insurance could be less costly than having to permanently hold excess capital on institutions' balance sheets, thereby reducing the benefits of regulatory arbitrage. In addition, by basing insurance on *aggregate* write-downs, moral hazard problems are reduced. It is unclear, however, which non-bank institutions would have balance sheets large enough to provide such insurance, and how the insurance could be accurately priced.

The Commission and the ECB will present a report to the Council and the European parliament at the end of 2009 on the possible pro-cyclical effects of the banking legislation and its impact on the EU economy, together with proposals for change.

An additional consideration is whether policies to reduce the pro-cyclicality of the financial system should be rules-based or discretionary. Rules-based approaches have the benefit of being transparent. However, they could also be blunt and not improve the incentives for institutions to improve their measurement of the time-dimension of risk (Borio, 2003). Discretionary approaches have the advantage of being potentially more finely tuned to the nature and risks of a particular credit cycle. However, they could appear *ad hoc*, create unnecessary uncertainty for financial institutions and raise the risk of regulators/supervisors acting too late, if at all. As Box 3.6 shows, regulators/supervisors undertook some, albeit limited action in the run-up to the recent financial market turmoil.

A key difficulty for the euro area and the European Union is that no institution has responsibility for area-wide macro-prudential risk. The ECB produces half-yearly *Financial Stability Reviews* but these only raise awareness of issues. Although the Banking Supervision Committee (BSC) brings together banking supervisors and central banks in a single forum, such an arrangement may not be suited to quickly identifying emerging EU-wide systemic risks and does not have the authority to maintain financial stability in the area as a whole.

Box 3.6. **Leaning against the wind in the build-up to the financial market turmoil**

Some European regulators took actions during this credit cycle to "lean against the wind" or dampen the cycle. These were generally fairly modest and late-on in the cycle. These actions included:

- In Belgium, new liquidity rules, emphasising a qualitative approach and better reporting were introduced in December 2006.
- Estonia increased the risk weighting of all loans secured by mortgages on residential property and limited mortgage interest rate deductibility (World Bank, 2007).
- In Ireland, in 2006 the supervisor raised the risk weighting on high loan-to-value mortgages for owner-occupiers and for exposure secured by properties that are not occupied by the borrower. It also raised the risk weight applied to speculative commercial estate lending. Moreover, a new forward-looking liquidity mismatch approach was introduced replacing the focus on the stock of liquid assets. A new consumer protection code specific to the banking sector was implemented and Minimum Competency Requirements for persons who provide advice on or sell retail financial products were introduced. The new consumer protection code was extended to the (unregulated) subprime market. Finally, stress testing was ramped up, including for liquidity risks.
- Latvia raised reserve requirements (World Bank, 2007).
- In the Netherlands, concerns about persistently high levels of household debt led to the introduction of a new Code of Conduct for Mortgage Lenders in 2007 with the explicit goal of dealing with rising loan-to-value and loan-to-income ratios.
- Portugal tightened rules governing general provisions, large exposures, connected lending and capital adequacy. The risk weighting for housing loans with loan-to-value ratios above 75% was raised and provisioning for consumer loans was tightened.
- Apart from implementing dynamic provisioning, the Bank of Spain has taken a cautious approach to off-balance sheet investment vehicles. The development of investment vehicles was not prohibited, but if banks were to set up such vehicles, these should be consolidated within the group, and therefore be subject to capital requirements and provisions. Under these conditions, no such vehicles were set up. The same rules apply in the Netherlands and Denmark.

What regulatory architecture for the European banking industry?

A variety of market failures make the banking sector susceptible to bouts of instability. Because the negative externalities generated by such instability are not easily overcome by the private sector, and because governments are the ultimate guarantor of the banking system's solvency, there is a role for governments in designing regulation to improve the stability of the system. However, regulating the financial industry is different from regulating many other markets in that there is no clear "bottom line" or standard by which regulation can be judged (Goodhart, 2006). In particular, there is often a trade-off between promoting soundness on the one hand and wealth creation on the other. Unnecessary regulation may damage the functioning of financial markets, stifle innovation and hamper economic growth. Badly designed regulation can also enhance instability through regulatory arbitrage or by encouraging excessive risk taking. Moreover, because of information asymmetry, it will always be challenging for regulators and supervisors to stay informed about the institutions they supervise and to keep pace with innovations and their potential impact on the stability of financial markets. For these reasons, regulation and changes to regulations should proceed cautiously with a clear sense of its own limits, the market failures it is trying to offset, and how it will address such failures.

Notwithstanding these caveats, there are important areas in which EU financial supervision could improve. Although the European Union has made great strides towards creating an integrated financial market with the euro area at its heart, financial market supervision remains primarily the responsibility of national authorities. This fragments responsibility, results in co-ordination problems and also raises regulatory costs for financial enterprises operating in more than one jurisdiction. Although there is a great deal of information sharing, there are still gaps as information does not flow sufficiently between different regulators and there are insufficient incentives to provide timely and relevant information, particularly at difficult times. Adding a European dimension to the mandate of the national regulators may help to align incentives at the margin.

Although recent initiatives to enhance colleges of supervisors, the role of co-ordinating supervisor within these groups, MoUs and the role of the Lamfalussy level 3 committees provide a clearer set of principles on how to act, the EU system of prudential regulation could be improved further by:

- Further integrating and centralising the supervision of LCFIs.
- Aligning incentives, authority and information sharing with the need to deal with solvency and liquidity. An effective system of crisis management with responsibility apportioned so as to avoid such problems *ex ante* and deal adequately with them *ex post* should be put in place.
- Keeping the overall regulatory burden for firms low.
- Ensuring that supervisors, ministries of finance and the monetary authorities collaborate closely to manage systemic risks and financial market crises.
- Investigating possibilities for reducing the pro-cyclicality of financial markets – such as counter-cyclical adjustments to capital ratios and complementing risk-weighted capital ratios with leverage ratios.

Determining the appropriate institutional structure to supervise LCFIs is complicated. The Commission's recent proposals to supplement the existing national structure with supervisory colleges have the key advantage of ensuring that supervisors are closer to the institutions they supervise and keeping supervision at the same level as fiscal responsibility. The decentralised approach also facilitates a more level playing field between a country's local banks and cross-border banks.

However, a centralised supervisory structure would have key benefits. Centralisation is more consistent with maintaining a single market in the face of increased cross-border activity. It would ensure that LCFIs were supervised consistently, make it easier to pool information and analysis, and reduce reporting burdens. It would also make it easier to align the incentives of supervisors with the underlying risks. Although centralised supervision for LCFIs would make the playing field between local and cross-border banks less even, that may actually be the appropriate outcome given the different risks that the two types of institutions pose.

Before a more centralised supervisory structure can be put in place, a number of issues would have to be resolved. These include:

- Aligning fiscal responsibility with supervisory responsibility.
- Maintaining accountability.

- Determining how a centralised structure would be financed.
- Ensuring consistency with national laws.
- Linking with national supervisors.
- Determining the appropriate organisational structure.

Although all of these issues will take time to resolve, perhaps the most difficult to resolve will be the optimal organisational structure. Here, there are a number of options. One is the establishment of a European banking charter to function alongside national regimes (Čihák and Decressin, 2007). The charter would set out a complete European regulatory and legal framework for financial institutions and be designed to be attractive to those heavily engaged in cross-border business. Banks would be free to choose between operating under national banking charters or the European charter. Although giving institutions the freedom to choose which charter to operate under would promote competition among regulators, this freedom could also undermine the goal of consistent supervision.

An alternative approach would be to develop a European system of supervisory agencies (Schoenmaker and Oosterloo, 2008). In such a system, the national prudential agencies would be brought together in a single supervisory system with a cross-border structure, along the lines of the European System of Central Banks. A European Prudential Supervisory Agency at the centre would be responsible for key supervisory decisions (for example, the assessment of potential cross-border mergers and acquisitions, or crisis management decisions) as well as the design of policy. It could also help to resolve disputes between home and host country supervisors. Day-to-day prudential supervision would be delegated to the national supervisors close to the financial firms. Cross-border financial firms would be supervised by the lead supervisor from the home country (*e.g.* the BaFIN for Deutsche Bank). The home supervisor would also be the single point of contact for the cross-border financial firm (for example, on reporting schemes, capital and liquidity, and on-site inspections). The home supervisor could ask host supervisors to perform on-site inspections of the host country operations. The home supervisor would feed its information into a common database of the system. This common database would enable the European Prudential Supervisory Agency to have an overall view of the stability of cross-border financial firms across Europe. The system would deal with financial firms that operate cross-border. Small and medium-sized financial firms (banks and insurance companies) that are primarily nationally-oriented would continue to be supervised by the national prudential supervisors. By bringing the national supervisors into a European system under the oversight of a central agency accountable to Brussels, the advantages of both centralisation and decentralisation could be balanced. However, fundamental questions, including burden sharing, would also need to be resolved. Moreover, if such a system were unable to balance the interests of home and host countries, or adequately resolve disputes between them, moving toward a single supervisor could also be considered.

Progress in strengthening financial regulation is important as the current regulatory framework increases the likelihood of severe financial market problems. These can cause substantial macroeconomic dislocation, which could be worse still for members of the monetary union, as they have fewer policy instruments at hand. The fiscal burden could also be very large should a systemically important institution fail. Such crises are rare, but it is important that this does not give a false sense of security or misleading picture about the strength of the regulatory architecture.

The Commission has launched work on how the European financial supervisory system can be improved to provide scope for effective macro-prudential oversight through the de Larosière Group. The mandate of the group is to consider the organisation of European financial institutions to ensure prudential soundness, the orderly functioning of markets and stronger European co-operation on financial stability oversight, early warning mechanisms and crisis management, including the management of cross-border and cross-sectoral risks. It will also look at co-operation between the EU and other major jurisdictions to help safeguard financial stability at the global level.

Box 3.7. **Main recommendations on financial stability and regulation**

Financial market regulation should be strengthened, particularly in the light of the international financial market turmoil:

- Implement the actions as set out in ECOFIN's "Financial Turmoil Roadmap" and, with due consideration, reforms emanating from the Financial Stability Forum's review of prudential and supervisory powers.
- Swiftly and efficiently implement near-term measures to stabilise the European financial system and think carefully about an exit strategy once the stress in financial markets has dissipated.
- Allow sufficient time for banks to recapitalise themselves using private funding sources, but consider forcible recapitalisation of banking systems if private funding is not forthcoming.
- Implement insolvency procedures specifically adapted to banks, and ensure that such regimes allow for early intervention before insolvency occurs.
- Improve the functioning of deposit guarantee schemes by ensuring that pay-outs occur promptly and ensure that the schemes are properly funded.
- Spell out the principles and procedures for burden sharing in a situation of public intervention in a cross-border financial institution in greater detail.
- Investigate possibilities to reduce the pro-cyclicality of financial markets – such as counter-cyclical adjustments to capital ratios and leverage ratios to complement risk-weighted capital ratios.

Despite on-going progress in improving the regulatory and supervisory architecture, further measures are required to improve supervision. The long-run goal should be a more centralised structure for the supervision of large complex financial institutions (LCFIs). Because this is not likely to be feasible in the short run, intermediate steps should be taken towards this goal:

- Add a European dimension to the mandates of national supervisory authorities.
- Harmonise national regulatory standards for large complex financial institutions (LCFIs) and systemically important financial institutions and further strengthen the colleges of supervisors and the role of lead supervisors.
- Strengthen the role of the level 3 committees by enhancing their role in monitoring the functioning of the colleges of supervisors and increasing the resources they have to fulfill their tasks.

Notes

1. According to the European Commission (2007) there were 68 "financial conglomerates" with a head of group within the EU/EEA as of November 2007.
2. Schüler and Heinemann (2005) find that the absence of scale economies in supervision adds 15% to the cost of banking in Europe. Additional costs are created as banks need to cope with different requirements and reporting systems.
3. A World Bank study shows that there were 112 systemic crises in 93 countries between the late 1970s and the end of the twentieth century (World Bank, 2001).
4. Reinhart and Rogoff (2008) estimate the average drop in output per capita to be over 2%. The worst crisis have reduced growth by five percentage points from their peak, and it takes more than three years for growth to regain the pre-crisis level. In the most extreme cases the costs of banking crises can easily run into double digits of GDP (Hoggarth and Saporta, 2001).
5. The underlying weaknesses identified by the FSF include: poor underwriting standards; shortcomings in firms' risk management practices; poor investor due diligence; poor performance by the credit rating agencies with respect to structured products; incentive distortions; weaknesses in disclosure; feedback effects between valuation and risk-taking; and weaknesses in regulatory frameworks and other policies.
6. Directive 89/646/EEC.
7. Any bank licensed in an EU country is free to open branches in any other EU country, subject only to the regulation and supervision of the country that had issued the licence. Some exceptions exist, such as host country responsibility for liquidity and oversight.
8. Directive 2006/48/EC and Directive 2006/49/EC.
9. The CRD also applies to non-deposit taking investment banks. The share of investment banks in Europe is considerably smaller than in the US, where they are not regulated.
10. The follow-up to the FSAP, the European Commission's White Paper on "Financial Service Policy 2005-10" seeks to move this process, with a focus on implementation rather than on new regulatory and legal initiatives.
11. Comitology is a procedure in which the Council and European Parliament delegate to the Commission the power to adopt implementing measures of European laws, subject to consultation with the parliament and representatives of the member states.
12. In the directives there is a difference in terminology and applicability between the FCD and CRD. The former uses the term "co-ordinating supervisor" and the latter "consolidating supervisor" for what is essentially the same basic function. The FCD applies to a limited number of cross-sector conglomerates and the CRD to banking groups. Many, but not all, of these conglomerates are also banking groups.
13. Solvency II goes further than the CRD in giving power to home-country supervisors, turning the home-country supervisor of an insurance group into a "group supervisor" who supervises all the group's EU branches and subsidiaries in co-ordination with host-country supervisors.
14. Goldplating refers to the process whereby EU regulations are extended or applied earlier than intended when passed into law in individual countries within the EU.
15. Article 105(5) of the Treaty on European Union.
16. However, the Treaty foresees the possibility of transferring specific supervisory tasks to the ECB following a simplified procedure without the need to amend the Treaty (Article 105(6)).
17. Bini Smaghi also emphasises the importance of supervisory information in the conduct of monetary policy and in assessing credit risk in providing liquidity.
18. See ECB (2008b) for a short review of some of the contributions.
19. The European Banking Federation (EBF), the Commercial Mortgage Securities Association (CMSA), the International Capital Markets Association (ICMA), the European Association of Co-operative Banks (EACB), the European Savings Banks Group (ESBG), the Securities Industry and Financial Markets Association (SIFMA), the London Investment Banking Association (LIBA) and the European Securitisation Forum (ESF).
20. *www.iosco.org/library/pubdocs/pdf/IOSCOPD270.pdf.*

21. The US Securities and Exchange Commission (SEC) has already proposed to downgrade many of its rules that depend on ratings and encourage investors not to rely on credit ratings, especially for complex structured products.
22. Articles 129 to 132 of the CRD set out the requirements concerning the division of labour and the co-ordination and co-operation between home and host supervisors for banking groups, both in normal times and in emergency situations.
23. For an in-depth discussion of current arrangements, see ECB (2007).
24. Articles 11 and 12.
25. Articles 130 and 132.
26. Directive 2001/24/EC.
27. This is the case even beyond the EU context (Hüpkes, 2005).
28. History shows that bailouts of foreign depositors are rare. For example, in the rescue of the Italian bank Banco Ambrosiano in 1982, the rescue operation covered the Italian operation, while the Luxembourg subsidiary was not originally included (Goodhart and Schoenmaker, 1995).
29. On the other hand, reputation risks will remain. As Julie Dickson (2008), the Superintendent of the Office of the Superintendent of the Financial Institutions Canada put it: "Regulators are just figuring out how significant reputation risk is for a bank. Global regulators agreed when banks said that they could transfer risk to third-party investors via asset-backed commercial paper conduits or structured investment vehicles. Because we were armed with legal opinions and accounting opinions, we believed that off-balance sheet meant off-balance sheet. But since last summer, we have seen banks support off-balance sheet vehicles, and we have seen them step in to protect investors in money market funds."

Bibliography

Adrian, T. and H.S. Shin (2007), "Liquidity and Financial Cycles", Paper for the 6th Annual BIS Conference "Financial System and Macroeconomic Resilience", Basel, 18-19 June.

Allen, F. and E. Carletti (2008), "The Role of Liquidity in Financial Crises", Federal Reserve Bank of Kansas 2008 Symposium "Managing Stability in A Changing Financial System."

Ayuso, J., D. Pérez and D. Saurina (2004), "Are Capital Buffers Pro-cyclical?", *Journal of Financial Intermediation*, No. 13.

Beltran, D.O., L. Pounder and C. Thomas (2008), "Foreign Exposure to Asset-Backed Securities of US Origin", *Board of Governors of the Federal Reserve System International Finance Discussion Papers*, No. 939.

Bikker, J. A. and P.A.J. Metzemakers (2003), "Bank Provisioning Behaviour and Procyclicality", *DNB Staff Reports*, No. III/2003.

Bini Smaghi, L. (2008), "Supervision and Central Banking: Improving the Exchange of Information", Remarks at the Workshop "Financial Turmoil and Missing Tisks: New Challenges for Bankers and Regulators", Milan, 12 June.

Borio, C., C. Furfine and P. Lowe (2001), "Procyclicality of the Financial System and Financial Stability: Issues and Policy Options" in "Marrying the Macro- and Micro-Prudential Dimensions of Financial Stability", *BIS Papers*, No. 1, March.

Borio, C. (2003), "Towards a Macroprudential Framework for Financial Supervision and Regulation?", *BIS Working Papers*, No. 128, February.

Borio, C. (2008), "The Financial Turmoil of 2007–?: a Preliminary Assessment and Some Policy Considerations", *BIS Working Papers*, No. 251, March.

Borio, C. and I. Shim (2007), "What Can (Macro-)Prudential Policy Do to Support Monetary Policy?", *BIS Working Papers*, No. 242.

Čihák, M. and J. Decressin (2007), "The Case for a European Banking Charter", *IMF Working Paper*, WP/07/173.

Davis, H. and D. Green (2008), "Global Financial Regulation. The Essential Guide", Polity Press, 2008.

De Brant, O. and P. Hartmann (2000), "Systemic Risk: A Survey", *ECB Working Paper*, No. 35, ECB, Frankfurt.

Decressin, J. (2007), "Bank Business Correlations", in *Integrating Europe's Financial Markets*, edited by J. Decressin, H. Faruqee and W. Fonteyne, IMF.

Demirguc-Kunt, A. and H. Huizinga (2004), "Market Discipline and Deposit Insurance", *Journal of Monetary Economics*, 51.

Department of Treasury (2008), "Blueprint for a Modernized Financial Regulatory Structure".

Diamond, D. W. and P. Dybvig (1983), "Bank Runs, Deposit Insurance and Liquidity", *Journal of Political Economy*, No. 109.

Dickson, J. (2008), "Challenges Facing Financial Institutions and Regulators", Remarks by the Superintend to the Langdon Hall Financial Services Forum, Ontario, 6 May.

Dobson, W. and G.C. Hufbauer (2001), *World Capital Markets. Challenges for the G-10*, Institute for International Economics, Washington.

European Commission (2007), "Review of the Lamfalussy Process. Strengthening Supervisory Convergence", Communication from the Commission, COM(2007) 727 final, Brussels.

European Central Bank (ECB) (2007), "The EU Arrangements for Financial Crisis Management", *Monthly Bulletin*, Frankfurt, February.

ECB (2008a), "Financial Stability and Oversight", *Monthly Bulletin*, 10th Anniversary of the ECB.

ECB (2008b), "Developments in the EU Arrangements for Financial Stability", *Monthly Bulletin*, April.

ECB (2008c), Keynote speech by Jean-Claude Trichet at the Second Symposium of the ECB-CFS Research Network on "Capital Markets and Financial Integration in Europe", 13 February.

ECB (2008d), "The Role of Banks in the Monetary Policy Transmission Mechamism", *Monthly Bulletin*, August.

Eisenbeis, R. A. and G. G. Kaufman (2007), "Cross-border Banking: Challenges for Deposit Insurance and Financial Stability in the European Union", *Federal Reserve Bank of Atlanta Working Paper Series*, No. 2006-15a.

European Financial Stability Round Table (EFR) (2007), "Monitoring Progress in EU Prudential Supervision", *A Report by the EFR*, September, *www.efr.be/members/upload/publications/97338EFR-september2007%20(final).pdf.*

Fernández de Lis, S., J. Martinez Pagés and S. Saurina (2001), "Credit Growth, Problem Loans and Credit Risk Provisioning in Spain", in: Marrying the Macro- and Microprudential Dimensions of Financial Stability, *BIS Papers*, No. 1, Basel.

Fernández Ordóñez, M. (2008), "Turbulence in the World Markets: a Spanish View (Five Lessons and Some Homework)", Address delivered to the "Círculo Financiero", Barcelona, 14 May.

Financial Stability Forum (FSF) (2008), Report of the Financial Stability Forum on Enhancing Market and Institutional Resilience, 7 April.

Freixas, X. (2003), "Crisis Management in Europe", in: J. Kremers, D. Schoenmaker and P. Wierts (eds.), *Financial Supervision in Europe*, Cheltenham: Edward Elgar, pp. 102-119.

Goodhart, C.A.E. (2000), "The Organisational Structure of Banking Supervision", *FSI Occasional Papers*, No. 1.

Goodhart, C.A.E. (2004), "Some New Directions for Financial Stability?", *The Per Jacobsson Lecture*, Zurich, Switzerland, 27 June.

Goodhart, C.A.E. (2006), "A Framework for Assessing Financial Stability?", *Journal of Banking and Finance*, Vol. 30.

Goodhart, C.A.E. and Schoenmaker, D. (1995), "Should the Functions of Monetary Policy and Banking Supervision Be Separated?", *Oxford Economic Papers*, No. 47.

Goodhart, C.A.E. and Schoenmaker, D. (2006), "Burden Sharing in a Banking Crisis in Europe", *LSE Financial Markets Group Special Paper Series*, March.

Gropp, R. and J. Vesala (2004), "Deposit Insurance, Moral Hazard and Market Monitoring", *ECB Working Paper*, No. 302, February, ECB, Frankfurt.

Hadjiemmanuil, C. (2005), "Europe's Universalist Approach to Cross-Border Bank Resolution Issues", in *Systemic Financial Crisis: Resolving Large Bank Insolvencies*, edited by D. D. Evanoff and G. G. Kaufman, New Jersey: World Scientific.

Hardy, D. C. (2006), "Regulatory Capture in Banking", *IMF Working Paper*, WP/06/34, January.

Hoggarth, G. and V. Saporta (2001), "Costs of Banking System Instability: Some Empirical Evidence", *Bank of England Financial Stability Review*, Issue 10, Article 5, June.

Hüfner, F. and I. Koske (2008), "The Euro Changeover in the Slovak Republic: Implications for Inflation and Interest Rates", *OECD Economics Department Working Papers*, No. 632, OECD, Paris.

Hüpkes, E. (2005), "Too Big to Save – Towards a Functional Approach to Resolving Crises in Global Financial Institutions", in *Systemic Financial Crises: Resolving Large Bank Insolvencies*, ed. by D.D. Evanoff and G. G. Kaufman, New Jersey: World Scientific, pp. 193-216.

IIF (2008), Interim Report of the IIF Committee on Market Best Practices, April.

IMF (2008), "Global Financial Stability Report. Containing Systemic Risks and Restoring Financial Soundness", *Word Economic and Financial Surveys*, April, IMF, Washington DC.

Jokipii, T. and A. Milne (2006), "The Cyclical Behaviour of European Bank Capital Buffers", *Bank of Finland Research Discussion Papers*, No. 17.2006.

Kager, M. (2006), "The Perspective of a Practising Banker", in *Cahier Comte Boël*, No. 12, European League For Economic Co-operation.

Kayshap, A.K., R.G. Rajan and J.C. Stein (2008), "Rethinking Capital Regulation", Federal Reserve Bank of Kansas 2008 Symposium: Managing Stability in a Changing Financial System.

Lannoo, K. (2007), "Banking Supervision Returns to the Forefront", *CEPS Commentary*, 21 September.

Lindquvist, K. (2004), "Banks' Buffer Capital: How Important is Risk?", *Journal of International Money and Finance*, 23(3).

Lowe, P. (2002), "Credit Risk Measurement and Procyclicality", *BIS Working Papers*, No. 116.

Maciandaro, D. (2008), "Politicians and Financial Supervision Unification outside the Central Bank: Why Do they Do it?", *American Law and Economics Association Annual Meetings*, Paper 121.

Mishkin, F. (1990), "Asymmetric Information and Financial Crises: A Historical Perspective", *NBER Working Paper*, No. 3400.

OECD (2008), "The Subprime Crisis: Size, Deleveraging and Some Policy Options", *Financial Market Trends*, Vol. 2008/1, No. 94, OECD, Paris.

Reinhart, C. and K. Rogoff (2008), "Is the 2007 US Subprime Financial Crisis so Different? An International Historical Comparison", *NBER Working Paper*, No. 13761.

Schoenmaker, D. and S. Oosterloo (2008), "Financial Supervision in Europe: A Proposal for a New Architecture", in: L. Jonung, C. Walkner and M. Watson (eds), *Building the Financial Foundations of the Euro – Experiences and Challenges*, Routledge, London.

Schüler, M. and F. Heinemann (2005), "The Costs of Supervisory Fragmentation in Europe", *ZEW Discussion Paper*, No. 05-01, Centre for European Economic Research, Mannheim.

de Serres, A. *et al.* (2006), "Regulation of Financial Systems and Economic Growth", *OECD Economics Department Working Papers*, No. 506, OECD, Paris.

Stolz, S. and M. Wedow (2005), "Banks' Regulatory Buffer and the Business Cycle: Evidence for German and Co-operative Banks", *Deutsche Bundesbank Working Paper*, 07/05.

The Banker (2008), "Top 1 000 World Banks", July.

Tieman, A, G. De Nicolò and R. Corker (2007), "Risk Profiles of Financial Institutions" in: *Integrating Europe's Financial Markets*, edited by J. Decressin, H. Faruqee and W. Fonteyne, IMF.

Tieman, A. and M. Čihák (2007) "Internationally Active Large Banking Groups", in *Integrating Europe's Financial Markets*, edited by J. Decressin, H. Faruqee and W. Fonteyne, IMF.

World Bank (2001), *Finance for Growth: Policy Choices in a Volatile World*, Washington.

World Bank (2007), "Credit Expansion in Emerging Europe: A Cause for Concern?", *World Bank EU8+2 Regular Economic Report, Part II: Special Topic*, January.

World Bank (2008), *EU10 Regular Economic Report*, June.

ISBN 978-92-64-04824-9
OECD Economic Surveys: Euro Area

Chapter 4

Fiscal policy

The budgetary position has improved in recent years against the background of buoyant revenue growth. However, revenue growth is faltering as activity eases, while durable progress towards fiscal sustainability has been limited. Moreover, some countries continue to experience large underlying deficits and rising debt. The downturn will lower revenues and there is pressure on the cost of borrowing for some countries. Some governments have used fiscal policy to cushion the economic slowdown. Fiscal sustainability should remain a priority. Moreover, by improving the quality of public finances the euro area authorities can contribute more to raising living standards. This involves a better design of tax policies and greater focus on public sector efficiency.

The fiscal position has strengthened in recent years as budget balances have improved, leading to some progress in addressing long-run fiscal sustainability through lowering debt and preparing for long-term pressures in many countries. These favourable developments were facilitated by the buoyancy of revenue relative to the economic cycle, particularly through corporate profits and in relation to the boom in asset prices. It is therefore likely that there will be a deterioration in the fiscal position in many countries in the coming years. This will be a major test of the apparent success of the revised Stability and Growth Pact (SGP). There is a risk that financial market developments could put considerable pressure on public finances.

Durable progress towards fiscal sustainability has been limited

The euro area fiscal position has improved in recent years: the government deficit shrank from 2.6% of GDP in 2005 to 0.6% in 2007. Most of this reduction reflected an apparent improvement of the underlying fiscal balance, although the cyclical position also improved and contributed to reducing government borrowing (Figure 4.1). This performance has been better than in many other major developed economies. Reflecting these developments, euro area gross government debt on the Maastricht definition fell from 70.4% to 66.5% of GDP over the same period.

The picture is mixed looking across the euro area countries. Finland, Luxembourg and Spain ran healthy surpluses in 2007 (Figure 4.2). No euro area country is currently subject to an Excessive Deficit Procedure (EDP) but most had fiscal deficits in 2007. In four countries – Greece, France, Portugal and Italy – this deficit was close to or greater than 2% of GDP. This partly reflects weak economic performance. Almost all euro area countries had a primary surplus in 2007. For some highly-indebted countries such as Belgium and Italy, the cyclically-adjusted primary surpluses have been sufficiently large to contribute to substantial reductions in indebtedness as a share of GDP. Some low debt countries such as Finland and the Netherlands have also had a primary surplus consistent with further consolidation. But France and Greece should step up their efforts to reduce their levels of outstanding debt.

The use of creative accounting and one-offs has been limited in recent years, in part reflecting strong revenue growth which has reduced the pressure on governments to resort to these measures. The OECD has developed a new measure of the underlying fiscal balance (Joumard *et al.*, 2008). This corrects both for the economic cycle, following the established OECD methodology (Girouard and André, 2005), and one-off payments defined as deviations of net capital transfers paid by the government from trend.[1] This measure excludes non-recurrent items such as securitisation of tax arrears and transfers related to pension schemes. While these operations were frequent in the past in countries such as Belgium, Italy and Portugal and often exceeded 1% of GDP (Koen and van den Noord, 2005), one-offs have had little impact on the fiscal balance since 2005 except for Greece where, however, they have been diminishing in size.

Figure 4.1. **Fiscal balances**

In per cent of GDP/potential GDP

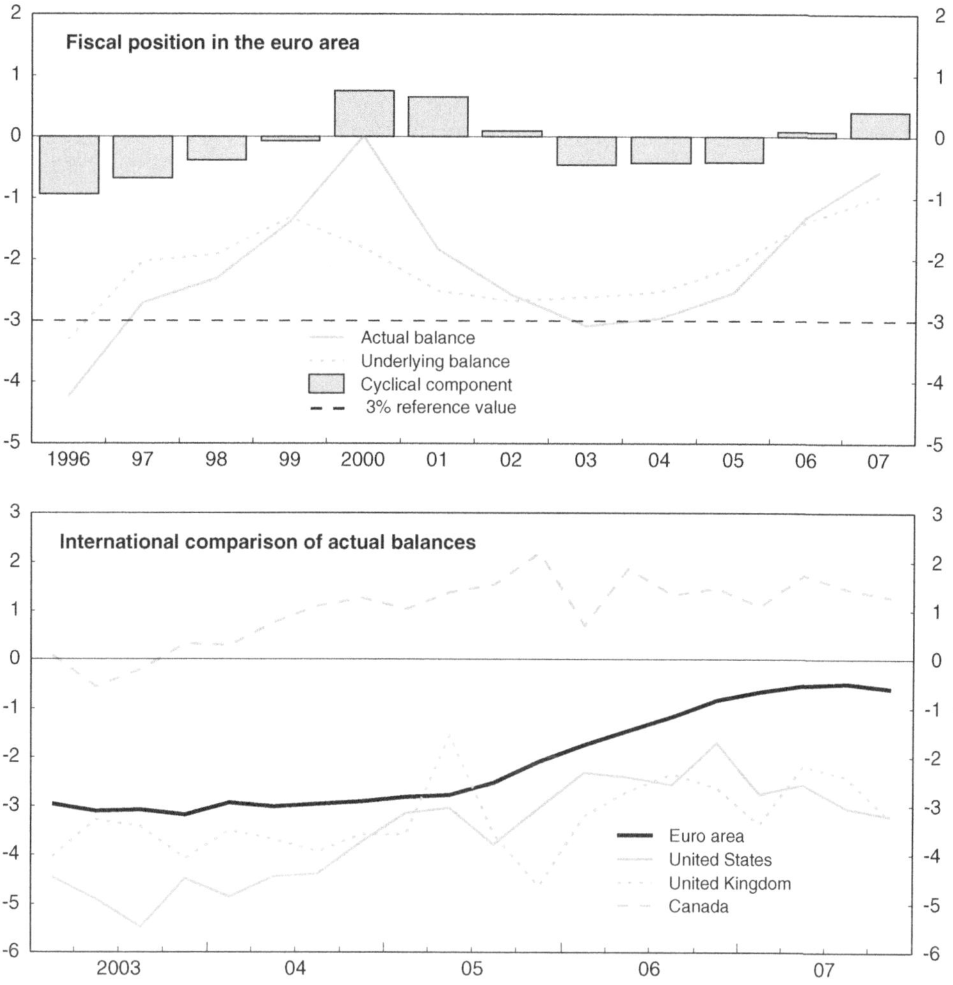

Source: OECD, *OECD Economic Outlook 84 database.*

StatLink http://dx.doi.org/10.1787/518754007866

The improvement in the euro area fiscal position over recent years has largely been driven by stronger revenue. Some of this strength was consistent with the operation of the automatic stabilisers. However, revenue growth between 2005 and 2007 was particularly buoyant even taking into account the standard cyclical factors so that underlying revenues appeared to increase as a share of potential GDP (Figure 4.3). The measured improvement in underlying revenues was in large measure due to unexpectedly strong receipts from corporation tax and taxes related to capital gains and property (Joumard and André, 2008). Conventional measures of underlying balances do not take these factors into account when adjusting for the economic cycle, focussing more on how wages and employment evolve over the cycle and what impact this has on government revenues. Although there is also considerable uncertainty about the output and unemployment gaps, evidence suggests that for most euro area countries the uncertainty about the relationship between tax revenues and output is greater; uncertainty about unemployment and output gaps is of "minor importance" for all countries except Germany and Italy (Koske and Pain, 2008).

Figure 4.2. **Fiscal balances and government gross debt**

In per cent of GDP/potential GDP, 2007

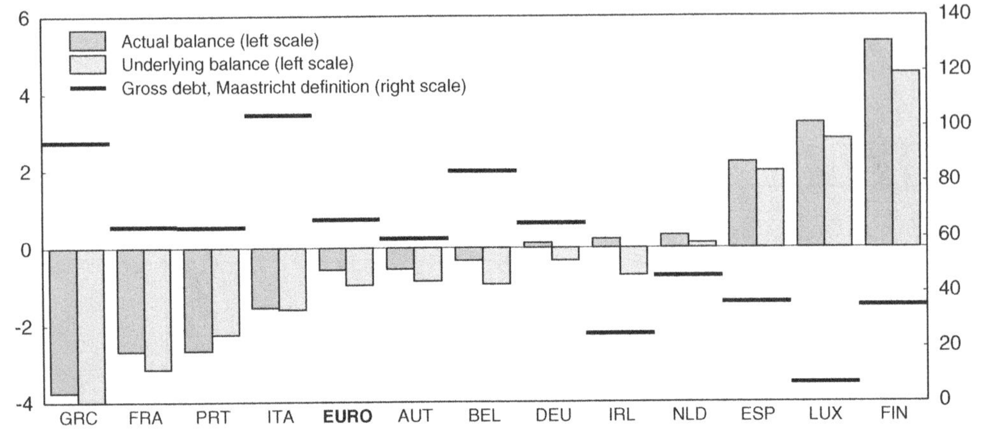

Source: OECD, *OECD Economic Outlook 84 database.*

StatLink http://dx.doi.org/10.1787/518764171068

Figure 4.3. **Revenue growth has improved the underlying fiscal position**

Annual change, in per cent of potential GDP

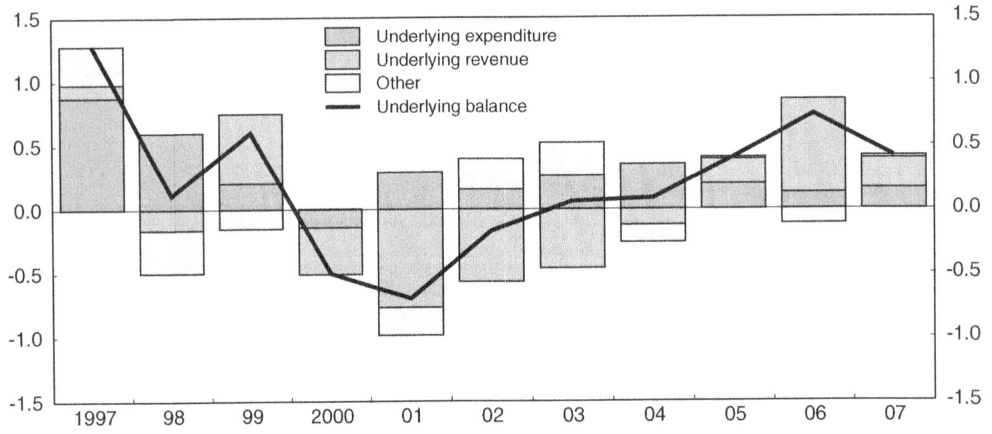

Source: OECD, *OECD Economic Outlook 84 database.*

StatLink http://dx.doi.org/10.1787/518814188486

These developments also underline the importance of asset price cycles that may last longer than one business cycle or, for some economies, rises in asset prices and construction booms that relate to prolonged one-off catch-up growth. In these cases, revenue buoyancy may be structural or long-lasting but not permanent. Such outcomes are more likely within a monetary union where the absence of national monetary policy could make prolonged periods of booming or sluggish performance more frequent at the country level.

The improved fiscal performance has provided some room to lower tax rates (Figure 4.4). Although these do not provide a complete picture of how revenue is raised because tax bases may also be affected by policy changes, tax rates have generally fallen for corporation tax and to some degree for income taxes. VAT rates have increased in Germany, Greece, the Netherlands and Portugal. The reduction in corporation tax rates is

Figure 4.4. **Tax rates**

In per cent

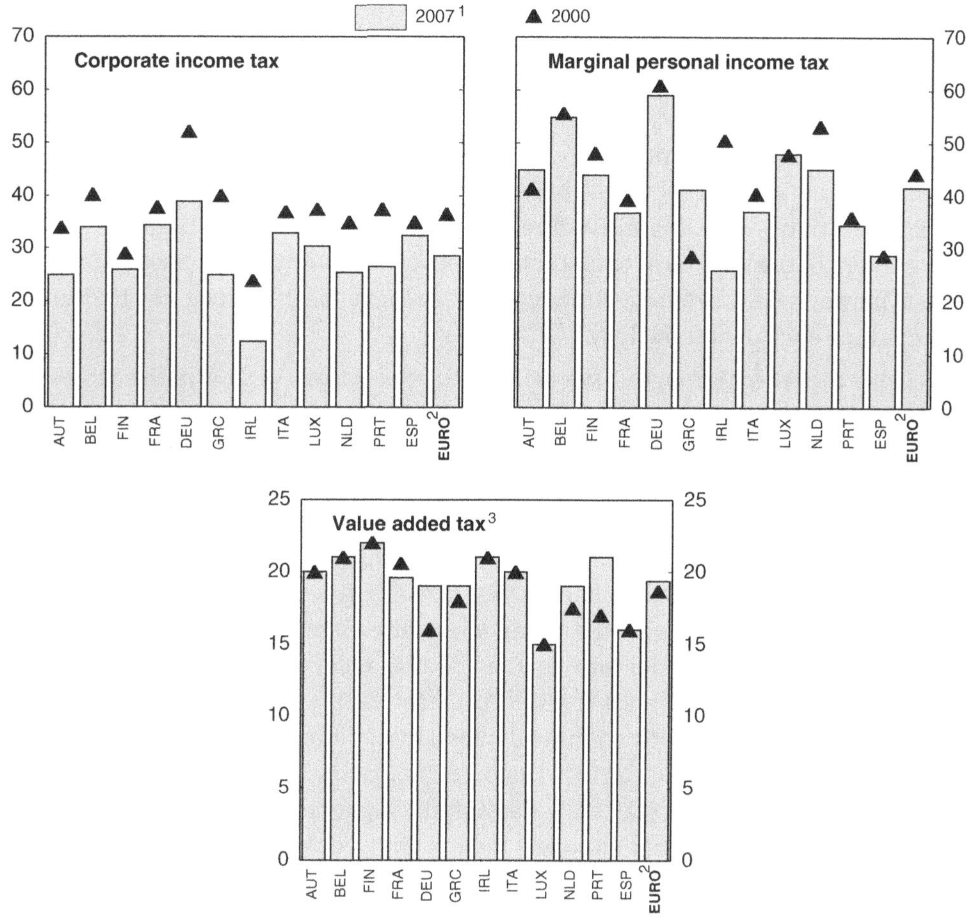

1. 2006 for the marginal income tax rates.
2. Unweighted average.
3. The standard VAT rate was lowered in Portugal by 1 percentage point in July 2008.

Source: OECD, *Tax database*.

StatLink http://dx.doi.org/10.1787/518826478234

likely to reflect in some part tax competition and the shift towards less mobile tax bases, such as VAT, in response to globalisation. This requires a shift in how taxes are raised. This may have been obscured over recent years by the buoyancy of other sources of revenue but pressures from globalisation are a challenge for the future.

The impact of the recent buoyancy of revenues explains much of the measured improvement in the underlying fiscal position in 2007 and may lead to a sharp turnaround. This implies that to ensure that the EDP is not triggered under adverse cyclical circumstances, either the measurement of structural fiscal balances should be improved to take these considerations into account during good times, or that a higher fiscal balance should be targeted on average to take account of the wider cyclical variation. Estimates suggest that taking these factors into account requires an additional margin on the structural deficit of around 0.2% of GDP on average for the euro area to meet the same lower bound constraint on the actual deficit (Morris and Schuknecht, 2007). Although the Commission's assessment of Stability and Convergence Programmes already takes into account a wide range of factors and there is some virtue in the accepted and simple measures of cyclical adjustment that are already embedded in the process, there is a strong case for giving greater weight to other indicators of the structural position and adopting a fiscal strategy that is more robust with respect to shocks emanating from asset price developments. A possible approach would be to adopt a method similar to that employed by the European System of Central Banks (Bouthevillain *et al.*, 2001), which forecasts the fiscal position based on a more disaggregated approach that looks at different revenue streams separately. Such methods, however, remain imperfect as they do not allow for cyclical variation in the tax elasticities and do not address the issue of the correct measurement of the long-term equilibrium level of the underlying tax bases. More detailed analysis may still be warranted, although there are substantial difficulties to overcome in implementing such a methodology.

Despite the recent strength, revenue growth is now likely to slow both as the economy weakens and as receipts from corporation tax and taxes related to property and capital gains come under pressure. The fiscal position in recent years has further been strengthened by falling expenditure as a share of GDP: the cyclically-adjusted share has fallen by one percentage point to 44% since 2003. This, however, reflects to a great extent the substantial spending restraint in Germany: the corresponding reduction in the cyclically-adjusted expenditure share is just 0.2% for the euro area excluding Germany. This compares favourably with the rising share of expenditure in the United Kingdom, although less so with countries such as Canada that reduced the share of spending more rapidly despite starting from a lower level. Furthermore, there are signs that expenditure is not firmly under control with continued substantial slippage in expenditure compared with announced plans (EC, 2008). Despite the favourable economic background, government spending in the euro area is around 1% higher in 2007 than suggested by plans made two years earlier. This slippage means that countries are entering a cyclical slowdown with weaker fiscal positions than would otherwise have been the case.

The actual euro area budget deficit is expected in OECD projections to increase from 0.6% to 1.4% of GDP in 2008 as the economy slows and revenues become less buoyant, with a further weakening in the fiscal position in 2009 and 2010. The anticipated deterioration in the fiscal balance is greater than the economic cycle alone would predict and is likely to be particularly severe in countries such as Ireland and Spain. These trends are largely driven by a deceleration in revenues, although it is likely that spending growth will be somewhat muted in the coming years. Some small positive revenue impact on the fiscal balance from higher oil prices is likely (Box 4.1).

Debt sustainability

The government debt to GDP ratio provides an indicator of long-run fiscal sustainability, alongside the current fiscal stance, although contingent liabilities under current policies also need to be factored in to give a complete overview. Over the period 2002 to 2007, most euro area countries reduced the level of debt relative to national income (Table 4.1). In most but not all euro area countries, the rate of GDP growth exceeded the implicit interest rate on government borrowing and therefore more than met the basic condition for solvency. Healthy primary surpluses were an important part of consolidation in a number of countries where debt was reduced substantially. The potential for GDP growth to contribute much to reducing debt is generally limited for euro area countries.

Box 4.1. **Oil prices and tax revenues**

Higher oil prices increase tax revenues through a number of channels. Firstly, oil and particularly motor fuels are heavily taxed. At current prices, around half of the cost of petrol in most countries is accounted for by excise duty. VAT is around 16% on average and is paid on the price including duties. The high level of excise duties, which are related to the volume and not the value of fuel, implies that the post-tax price of petrol rises far less than proportionally with the value of the underlying product, although relatively high rates of VAT mean that the absolute change is greater than it would otherwise be. Heating fuels typically attract lower rates of excise duty and either the same or slightly lower rates of VAT. The effect on revenue may be mitigated as higher prices reduce the amount of hydrocarbons consumed. In addition, the impact of higher oil prices on real incomes is slowing the economy and depresses tax receipts more widely.

Figure 4.5. **Taxation of petrol**[1]

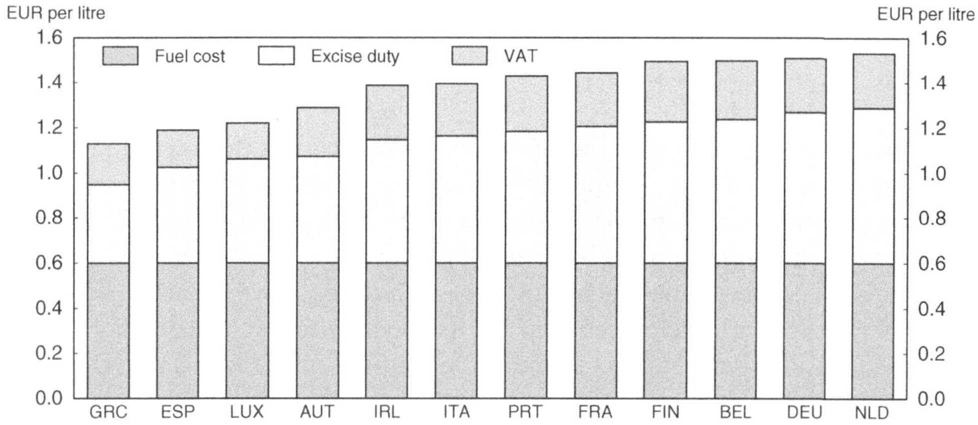

1. Calculations assume a pre-tax petrol price of EUR 0.60 per litre.

Source: European Commission (2008), *Excise Duty Tables – Part II Energy Products and Electricity* and OECD calculations.

StatLink http://dx.doi.org/10.1787/518833725600

Secondly, revenues can increase due to the greater value of oil production. Among euro area countries, only the Netherlands receives substantial royalty revenues from oil and gas extraction. However, oil companies are substantial payers of corporate taxes in many countries and their profits have been boosted by the rise in oil prices. In addition, two countries have adopted "windfall" taxes on oil companies: corporation tax rates for oil companies in Italy have been raised conditional on economic circumstances and oil prices, and Portugal has imposed an extraordinary tax on oil companies' reserves. Overall, the impact of energy prices on revenues should be closely monitored and any recent buoyancy of revenues from this source should not be locked into further spending commitments.

The high oil price raises other policy issues. Some have argued that taxes on fuel should be lowered to offset the higher cost of oil. The 2005 Manchester Agreement commits EU member states to avoiding measures that artificially boost oil demand when prices are high by blunting the price signal and thus avoiding the necessary adjustment. The Agreement, however, does allow short-term targeted action to alleviate the impact of high energy prices on vulnerable households through lump-sum payments or increases in social transfers. Some countries have announced increases in certain social benefits to help with higher fuel costs. These measures should be used sparingly and carefully targeted at the most vulnerable.

Table 4.1. **Debt sustainability**

Contribution to change from 2002 to 2007, annualised as % of GDP

	Primary surplus	Net interest	Growth	Other[1]	Overall change in net debt
Austria	–0.2	2.0	–1.4	–1.6	–1.3
Belgium	–3.3	3.9	–3.4	–1.2	–4.0
Finland	–2.8	–0.2	2.2	–7.1	–7.9
France	0.6	2.2	–1.5	–2.8	–1.5
Germany	0.0	2.3	–1.1	–0.4	0.7
Greece	0.5	3.8	–5.4	–4.0	–5.1
Ireland	–1.2	0.0	–0.5	–1.1	–2.8
Italy	–0.9	4.0	–2.9	–1.8	–1.6
Luxembourg	–0.1	–0.6	3.5	–0.6	2.1
Netherlands	–0.9	1.6	–1.3	–0.5	–1.0
Portugal	1.0	2.5	–1.4	–0.3	1.8
Spain	–2.2	1.3	–2.0	–1.3	–4.2
Euro area	**–0.5**	**2.4**	**–1.9**	**–1.1**	**–1.1**

1. Statistical discrepancy and approximation error.

Source: OECD, *OECD Economic Outlook 84 database.*

The sustainability of a given level of debt depends in part on the interest rate at which the private sector is willing to lend to the government. Since the financial market turmoil began, long-term interest rates on government debt have increased for many euro area countries with interest rates rising by more than 50 basis points in several cases relative to the rate on German government debt (Figure 4.6), which may have benefited from a "flight to quality" effect. These developments may be a temporary consequence of market turmoil and reflect liquidity effects more than a permanent shift in market views of the sustainability of different fiscal positions: the initial increase in Ireland was relatively large despite the fact that net government debt is a lower share of income than in most other euro area countries. However, this could also mark a reassessment of market views and the return of a permanent differentiation of European government debt. For a country that experiences a permanent increase of 50 basis points in the cost of borrowing, the steady-

Figure 4.6. **Spread on government debt**

Long-term interest rates relative to the German rate

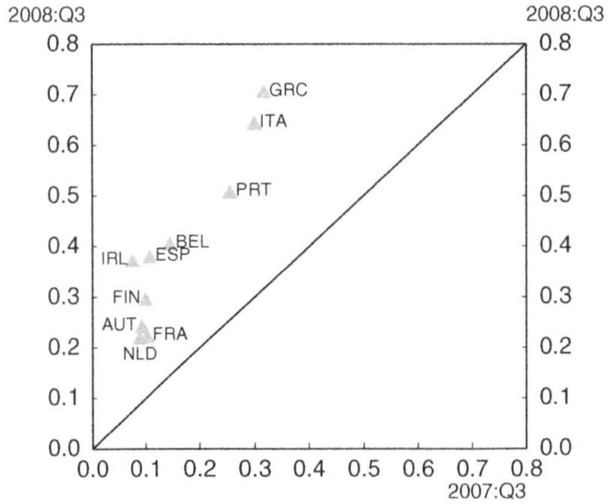

Source: OECD, *OECD Economic Outlook database.*

StatLink http://dx.doi.org/10.1787/518865881358

state impact on public finances would be substantial if it is heavily-indebted. Furthermore, much of public debt is for relatively long maturities so that the impact of a change in the current cost of borrowing only affects public finances at the margin. However, debt with maturity of less than one year at issue represents over 15% of GDP in Italy and Portugal so the overall fiscal position is sensitive to short-term interest rates in those countries.[2] The current episode is a reminder of the dangers of assuming that borrowing conditions will never deteriorate.

The major challenge for long-run fiscal sustainability, however, comes from the effects of demographic ageing and rising health spending on government expenditure rather than the stock of government debt currently on the balance sheet; the present discounted value of the ageing-related increase in spending for the euro area between now and 2050 is greater than the current stock of outstanding debt. New projections of the fiscal situation to 2050 under existing policies have updated the estimates published in 2006 with the latest fiscal data (EC, 2008).[3] For the euro area as a whole, age-related expenditure is projected to rise by 2.5% of GDP from 2010 to 2030 and then to reach 4.4% above its 2010 level as a share of GDP by 2050. Current estimates of the cost increases are broadly in line with those in 2006, although pension reform in Portugal has had a substantial impact on reducing future liabilities. There is great uncertainty about these long-run estimates and earlier analysis by the OECD suggested a change in the burden from health and long-term care more than 3% of GDP higher than those made by the Commission (OECD, 2006a).

One notable feature of preparations for demographic ageing is the limited use of pre-funding of future public obligations among euro area countries, along the lines of building pension reserves or sovereign wealth funds. Only Finland, France, Ireland, Portugal and Spain have such arrangements and the accumulated assets in most but not all of these countries are small in relation to GDP compared with other OECD countries with similar funds (OECD, 2008a). Although contributing to these funds is similar to paying down public debt, there is a possible role for investment in higher yielding assets than government bonds even if this implies a higher level of risk. Furthermore, this can be a useful communication tool to explain the issues surrounding the rising future burden of pension costs and a good way of committing to meaningful long-term fiscal consolidation. Pre-funding may be a useful instrument in achieving long-run fiscal sustainability alongside undertaking further necessary pension and structural reforms that would reduce future pension costs and may raise national incomes.

The real test of the revised Stability and Growth Pact is yet to come

A substantial revision to the Stability and Growth Pact (SGP) was approved by the Economic and Financial Affairs Council (ECOFIN) of finance ministers in March 2005. The SGP intends to achieve three objectives: the long-run sustainability of public debt positions, the avoidance of a deficit bias at national level for countries inside the monetary union, and "fiscal neutrality" such that the cyclical role of fiscal policy in ordinary times is limited to the automatic stabilisers. At face value, the revision has been successful as fiscal positions have improved and the remaining excessive deficit procedures against euro area countries have been abrogated. A broader assessment suggests that the revised SGP has led to some improvements in fiscal sustainability, while some weaknesses remain, and this progress is consistent with the idea that improved national ownership of the revised process has worked as intended.

No euro area country was subject to an excessive deficit procedure (EDP) as of October 2008, although it applied to Hungary and the United Kingdom. Portugal and Italy were subject to EDPs from 2005 to 2008. France, Germany and Greece had been in the EDP for a number of years until 2007. Although the revised Pact made criteria for the identification of excessive deficits somewhat more flexible by softening the definition of a "severe economic downturn" and making explicit a number of factors to be considered before placing a country in excessive deficit,[4] the double condition that a deficit must remain close to the 3% of GDP threshold and that the excess over it must be temporary before such factors can be taken into account greatly limits the scope to use the greater flexibility to escape the discipline of the Pact: countries were placed in excessive deficit in all the cases where the deficit exceeded 3% of GDP. This is an encouraging sign that the revised conditions have not reduced the force of the Pact, although it may also be a reflection of the relatively favourable economic circumstances. Given that the 3% deficit limit is defined in actual rather than structural terms, the real test of the revised SGP will come as the economy slows.

The 2005 revision developed the role of the "preventive arm" of the SGP by increasing the focus on long-run sustainability. This complements the "dissuasive arm" by introducing a greater degree of economic judgement into the rules-based system. Each country has a specific medium-term objective (MTO) for the structural fiscal balance, which is either a surplus, balance or a deficit that should not exceed 1% of GDP. The MTO is intended to give countries a sufficiently strong structural position to avoid actual deficits greater than 3% of GDP, which would trigger the EDP, and to provide some room for budgetary manoeuvre in the medium term. In addition, it is intended to give a richer picture of longer run fiscal sustainability. For those countries that have not achieved their MTO, there is an expectation that the structural fiscal balance will improve by 0.5 percentage points as a benchmark each year along the adjustment path. There is some leeway in bad times to make a lesser adjustment but faster progress than the 0.5 percentage points should be made when the economy is growing strongly. The enhanced "preventive arm" of the Pact has had mixed success. In 2007, half of the euro area countries had not met their MTOs (Figure 4.7). But, Italy and Portugal, countries still well away from their MTOs, improved their structural fiscal balances by 1% or more of GDP in 2007 and Germany also made substantial progress. By contrast, Austria, Belgium and Greece only met the benchmark standard at around 0.5% of GDP. There was no improvement in the structural balance in France and there has been some slippage in performance among those countries that have already achieved the MTO, such as Ireland. Even this picture may be overly positive given the impact of buoyant revenues on measured structural balances in recent years. The Pact calls for more consolidation in good times but, taking into account the transitory nature of the improvement on the revenue side, has actually delivered less because most countries only just met the minimum standard despite the buoyant revenue. The effectiveness of the approach is weakened by the absence of a clear operational definition of "good times" and how much additional progress in improving structural fiscal positions would be desirable. The position of the economy is primarily judged against the level and change in the output gap (EC, 2006), although it also takes into account complementary indicators such as the rate of capacity utilisation. Although the cyclical position of the economy is inherently difficult to measure, an agreed view of each economy's position would make clearer what each country should achieve. In April 2007, the Eurogroup, the informal grouping of euro area finance ministers, met in Berlin and committed to meet their MTOs by 2010 at the

Figure 4.7. **Progress towards medium-term budgetary objectives (MTOs)**

Structural balance in per cent of GDP

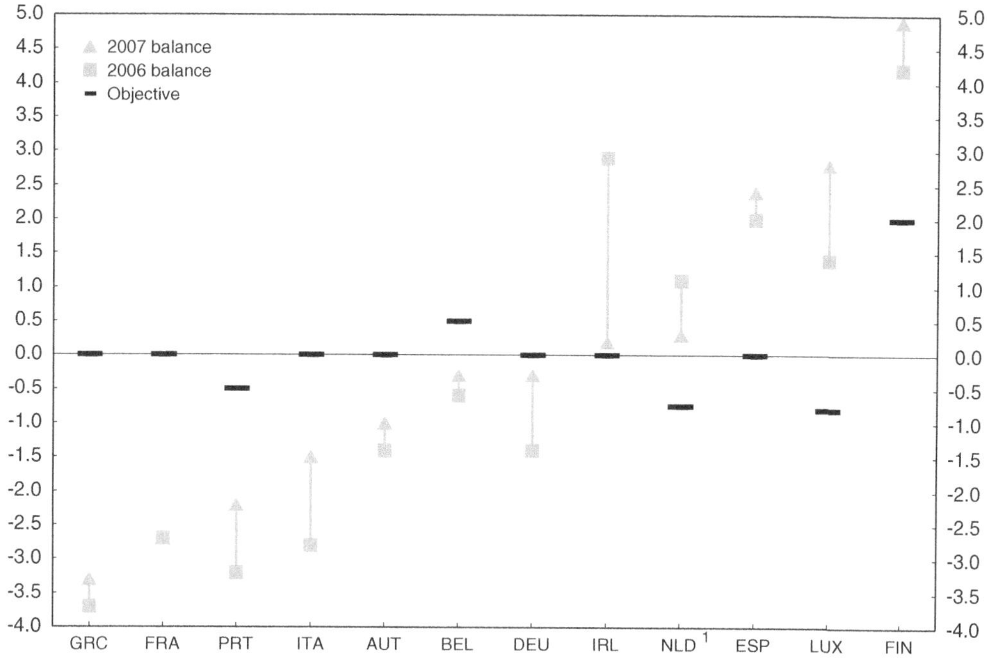

1. Netherlands MTO is shown as the mid-point of the range –0.5 to –1.0.

Source: European Commission (2008), "Public Finances in EMU – 2008", *European Economy*, Vol. 2008, No. 4, Brussels.

StatLink http://dx.doi.org/10.1787/518885846552

latest, cyclical conditions permitting (Eurogroup, 2007). In May 2008 and against an uncertain economic outlook, the Eurogroup ministers committed to maintain sound structural positions and continue progress towards their MTOs where appropriate. Greater flexibility was signalled by the Eurogroup in October 2008 as the outlook again weakened.

There is some additional evidence of improved national ownership, which strengthens the fiscal framework. For example, there is increased acceptance of the Commission's forecasts for setting targets, even if some member states have preferred to plan their commitments on the basis of their own more optimistic forecasts. The use of one-offs has also fallen: this is likely to reflect the reduced incentive to resort to such gimmicks because the MTOs are based on the structural position excluding such measures. However, back-loading of fiscal adjustment remains widespread with countries planning to do more in three to four years ahead than in the coming years (EC, 2008). In May 2008, the Commission issued to France its first ever public "policy advice" under the so-called Code of Conduct, endorsed by ECOFIN in 2005, on the grounds of weak structural macroeconomic performance and stalling budget consolidation. It remains to be seen how effective such advice will be.

A feature of the "preventive" arm of the fiscal framework has been that countries were able to set their own country-specific MTOs, without explicitly taking into account long-term sustainability pressures. Most euro area countries set fiscal balance as their MTO. Finland raised its objective from a 1.5% to a 2% of GDP surplus in 2006 and Belgium, which still has relatively high public debt, targets a surplus of 0.5% of GDP. The Netherlands,

Luxembourg and Portugal have a deficit as an MTO. This configuration of objectives does not correspond closely to the variation in needs across different countries with Italy and Greece both targeting balance despite high levels of debt and, especially for the latter, ageing pressures, as compared with Ireland aiming for balance despite low debt and a massive public investment programme. The variation in MTOs across high debt countries is a particular concern. It is therefore welcome that, following the ECOFIN Council Conclusions of 9 October 2007, new MTOs taking account of implicit liabilities will be set from 2009 using a common methodology to be agreed by spring 2009. For some countries, this is likely to imply a significant but necessary change in their medium-term fiscal strategy, including changes to the adjustment path in the short run. Given the fiscal challenges that exist in the euro area, the new methodology should not imply an overall relaxation of standards.

The role of fiscal policy in the economic cycle

The cyclical role of fiscal policy has continued to vary across countries (Figure 4.8). Policy tightened in Finland and Germany as the economy strengthened. By contrast, Greece and France should have run tighter fiscal policies during the upswing. Italy and Portugal were faced with having to tighten fiscal policy while the economy was weak. These measures, however, ignore the particular buoyancy of revenue in recent years without which many countries would have had to tighten the fiscal belt and hence, in some cases, run a policy that would have been more pro-cyclical. The *ex post* result of fiscal policy may also understate the extent to which policy aimed to be counter-cyclical as there is a tendency for outcomes to be more pro-cyclical than was intended on the basis of information available in real time (Cimadomo, 2008).

Figure 4.8. **Cyclicality of fiscal policy**

2007

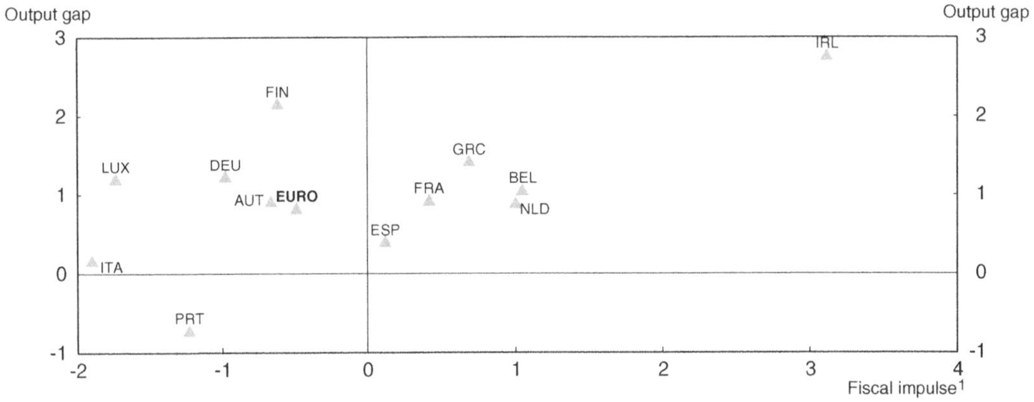

1. Change in the cyclically-adjusted primary deficit.

Source: OECD, *OECD Economic Outlook 84 database.*

StatLink http://dx.doi.org/10.1787/518886277710

There is no strong case in general for a discretionary fiscal policy response in most euro area countries when economies slow. The automatic stabilisers in the euro area are already larger than in most other OECD economies due to the bigger size of the government, higher marginal tax rates, and more generous social and unemployment benefits. Furthermore, where economies experience both negative supply and demand shocks, it is inappropriate to seek to boost aggregate demand through fiscal policy beyond the reduced level of potential output. For smaller countries, the impact of fiscal policy is likely to be limited in any case as the multiplier will be lower due to the high propensity to import (Hoeller *et al.*, 2002). In the medium run, most euro area economies continue to face substantial challenges to maintain or achieve fiscal sustainability and this limits the room for manoeuvre in cyclical downturns. The revised SGP intends to provide such room when countries have reached their MTOs but few countries are in this situation. However, with the current financial crisis aggravating the economic slowdown, the case for fiscal measures supporting demand may be stronger than in normal times due to the exceptional nature of financial events. Any such policy should be timely, temporary and targeted. It should concentrate on measures that can be implemented rapidly and will provide immediate support to the economy. Additional resources should be focussed where they can be used effectively to support structural reforms, apart from providing income support to poorer households. Given weaknesses in medium-run fiscal sustainability, fiscal measures should be temporary and set in the context of a policy orientation that will deliver sustainability in the future. The appropriate policy will depend on the economic and financial pressures a country faces, the starting position in terms of medium-run sustainability, the fiscal impact of measures to support the financial system directly and the effect of higher debt financing costs.

Fiscal aspects of financial instability

The financial turmoil since August 2007 had relatively little impact on euro area fiscal positions until October 2008 but these pressures have since intensified due to the costs of emergency actions taken by governments to stabilise financial markets and the weakening of the economic outlook due to financial developments. Financial instability can have an impact on the fiscal position in three ways. Firstly, there is an immediate impact on tax revenue from reduced financial market activity such as lower capital gains tax as a result of fewer transactions or falls in asset prices. Secondly, the government can use its balance sheet to support the financial system. This can arise both where the central bank provides emergency liquidity assistance (ELA) and more generally if banks are recapitalised or assisted in other ways. Such intervention can either be the result of explicit public guarantees, such as backing for a deposit insurance scheme, or the result of discretionary intervention to support the financial system. Thirdly, financial instability weakens wider economic activity giving rise to both higher expenditure and lower revenue as the automatic stabilisers come into play. Box 4.2 reviews recent and historical experience of the cost of financial instability. The potential fiscal impact of financial instability is an important motivation for ensuring that financial activities are effectively regulated (Chapter 3).

The possibility of financial crises does not have an explicit role in the European Union's fiscal policy framework and it is not directly mentioned in the "exceptional circumstances" under which the fiscal rules can be temporarily breached, although such an event might naturally be regarded as being beyond the government's control. Furthermore, a financial crisis could eventually impair the normal functioning of monetary policy, either if interest rates were to reach their zero lower bound or if monetary policy transmission were to become ineffective due to stress in financial markets. If this were to happen, unorthodox monetary policy operations could be used, but area-wide fiscal policy expansion might also be warranted as a last resort. Such circumstances would be exceptional and might require

Box 4.2. **The costs of financial instability**

The fiscal impact of the current financial crisis has risen sharply since pressures intensified in financial markets in mid-September. Many countries in the euro area and internationally have made substantial public funding available to support the stability of the financial system (see Chapter 3). The minimum ceiling for deposit insurance in the European Union has been raised to EUR 50 000 and further in some countries. Austria, Germany and Greece have explicitly guaranteed all retail deposits. These measures add substantially to the implicit liabilities as total retail deposits in most euro area countries are around 60% of GDP.[1] Greece, Ireland, Portugal and Spain have extended guarantees to some other bank liabilities, which may add substantially more to implicit liabilities. Furthermore, some governments have recapitalised or taken over financial institutions. These have been non-negligible in three euro area countries associated with the rescues of the Fortis and Dexia banks: Belgium (2.2% of GDP), Luxembourg (7.6%) and the Netherlands (3.5%). In addition, Austria, Germany, France and Spain have established funds to purchase or capitalise financial institutions or to purchase other assets to stabilise the financial system. These have yet to be disbursed but for those countries that have adopted them, the funds typically represent 2-5% of GDP. These transactions would in principle add both to gross liabilities and assets and may have no impact on net public liabilities.[2] For the euro area as whole, around 2% of GDP has been allocated to funds to support the financial system through direct interventions and guarantees worth around 15% of GDP have been extended, in addition to the extension of deposit guarantees.

The evolution of these costs will depend on how the financial crisis develops as well as the policy response. Past episodes of financial failures and instability can provide some guidance about possible outcomes: the budgetary costs of government intervention in banking crises may be very large, even among OECD countries with well-developed financial markets. Honohan and Klingebiel (2003) estimate the direct fiscal costs of banking crises up to 2003 (Table 4.2). This direct measure includes the immediate costs of defaults on loans from the central bank, capital injections to insolvent or weak banks, the capitalised value of lending to insolvent banks or borrowers, and the cost of payouts to depositors and other creditors. In OECD countries, most of the costs have related to recapitalisations. This measure may overstate the direct costs in the medium run as it gives the net present value of current supports if they are continued, and governments may be able to recover some of their outlays by selling interests they acquired in troubled institutions when the banks and markets recover. The direct costs depend in part on how the authorities chose to respond. In terms of this narrow measure of budgetary costs, a strict approach is preferable to an accommodative approach as it is both less costly in the short run and reduces moral hazard and hence the likelihood of future claims. But, these considerations need to be weighed against the overall costs to the public finances and the economic impact of stress on financial institutions.

Table 4.2 also shows estimates of the fiscal costs associated with lost output in past episodes. In some cases, the failure of an institution has no costs in this sense because there is no substantial impact on the wider economy. However, these costs can also be large and there is a trade-off between the direct support to banks and the likely impact on the wider economy.

Box 4.2. **The costs of financial instability** *(cont.)*

Table 4.2. **Fiscal costs of past banking crises**

In per cent of GDP

	Episode	Direct fiscal cost	Fiscal cost of lost output[1]	Total
Australia	1989-1992	1.9	0.0	1.9
Finland	1991-1994	11.0	11.1	22.1
France	1994-1995	0.7	0.0	0.7
Japan	1992-[2]	n.a.	9.1	n.a.
New Zealand	1987-1990	1.0	6.8	7.8
Norway	1987-1993	8.0	10.4	18.4
Korea	1997-[2]	n.a.	3.6	n.a.
Sweden	1991-1994	4.0	3.6	7.6
United States	1981-1991	3.2	1.8	5.0

1. Based on estimated output growth from Table 7 of Honohan and Klingebiel (2003) and elasticity of budget balance to GDP from Table 9 of Girouard and André (2005). Alternative estimates of the costs of some of these episodes are made in Laeven and Valencia (2008)
2. Episode on-going at time of original analysis. The direct fiscal costs are not shown for ease of comparison as these partly depend on how much of the initial cost can be recovered as the crisis is resolved.

Source: Honohan and Klingebiel (2003) and Girouard and André (2005).

The current market turmoil has highlighted the role of central banks providing liquidity to financial markets and institutions (Chapter 1). This exposes the public sector balance sheet to counterparty risk through monetary operations. Although the scale of lending to the private sector by the ECB has not increased substantially, the riskiness of the central bank's position may have worsened as individual borrowing institutions are weaker and as the quality of assets posted as collateral has fallen, both as particular types of assets have become more risky and as the composition of collateral has changed. In principle, higher valuation margins should offset this risk but it is also possible that this risk has increased. In 2007, the ECB had capital of around 5% of its assets, of which around 15% was accounted for by the stock of refinancing, so it has some capacity to withstand losses.

1. This figure refers to total deposits of households and non-profit institutions serving households in 2006. This does not necessarily coincide with the amount covered by deposit guarantee schemes or implicit guarantees nor does it reflect funds intended to finance payouts under these schemes.
2. The impact on the net fiscal position will depend on how the value of the assets purchased evolve and whether the initial purchase price represents fair value as defined by Eurostat.

an *ad hoc* response to the particular situation, but it would nevertheless be useful to reflect on the framework for addressing such severe events.

The international financial market crisis raises the issue of what fiscal policy measures can be used for stabilisation purposes. While changing the overall fiscal stance is likely to be a blunt instrument to dampen the credit cycle, it may be possible to use particular fiscal instruments to enhance financial stability. There are useful mechanisms that provide a degree of automatic stabilisation. In particular, capital gains taxes reduce the incentive to speculate. Well-designed property taxes dampen the net gains of higher valuation of houses. The case for taxing housing appropriately is particularly strong from this perspective: there is clear evidence that generous tax treatment of housing increases the volatility of housing markets (van den Noord, 2005). Property taxes are very low in the euro area and valuations lag market prices. For other assets, loss carryover provisions for corporate taxes may also shape risk-taking behaviour by influencing the post-tax pay off of losses on risky investments. In addition to structural features of the tax system, discretionary measures could be applied more widely to deal with credit and asset-price cycles. This kind of policy would be subject to some of the same considerations as using monetary or regulatory policy in the same way, but it is clear that unexpected and substantial changes in, for example, transactions taxes on houses can have an impact on the housing market. This is subject to some of the same difficulties to be experienced with other types of fiscal activism in terms of appropriate timing, although it may be simpler in this case as the objective is to react against a persistent asset price boom rather than to time correctly the response to a crash. Experience suggests it may be difficult to commit to such policies at a time of economic expansion as it is politically difficult to set policies that reduce perceived gains from asset booms.[5] This would argue for greater reliance on automatic than discretionary policy. Although there is little experience of either employing fiscal instruments to lean against the wind or at times where monetary policy could become ineffective, consideration should be given in the medium term to the design of such policies and attention paid to the effects of fiscal policy design on credit cycles and asset price booms.

Taxes and spending should be better designed to promote growth

The efficiency of government intervention in the economy is an important lever through which policy can contribute to good economic outcomes in the longer term, together with levels of taxation consistent with national preferences for the level of spending. Given the pressures from ageing-related spending and the fiscal discipline required to achieve fiscal sustainability, raising public-sector efficiency is necessary to provide high-quality public services in the future. As such, it has an important role to play in achieving the objectives of the Lisbon Strategy.

Efforts have been made to develop the analysis and surveillance of the quality of public finances under the SGP (EC, 2008). This is organised around six aspects of fiscal policy which can have an impact on growth:

- The size of government.
- The level and sustainability of fiscal positions.
- The composition and efficiency of expenditure.
- The structure and efficiency of revenue systems.
- The fiscal rules and institutions that can influence the four channels listed above.
- The interaction of non-budgetary items, such as product market and employment protection regulation and administrative burdens, with fiscal policies.

As the Commission acknowledges (EC, 2008), the relationship between fiscal policy and economic and social well-being is hard to evaluate. The quality of public finances therefore cannot be treated in exactly the same way as enforcement of the Treaty terms through the Pact. However, given the large size of euro area governments in their national economies, the public sector plays a very important role in shaping overall performance. It is also necessary that the objectives around the Pact to achieve sustainability are matched by the most appropriate policies in other areas, both to maximise the benefits of the Pact and to ensure strong underlying public support.

Public spending accounts for around 45% of GDP on average in the euro area, well above the OECD average. Although spending is somewhat lower in Ireland, Luxembourg and Spain, most euro area countries have relatively large governments. This is partly a matter of social choice about what goods and services are provided and by what means, and also how far direct spending is used to achieve social objectives rather than incentives under the tax system.[6] It may, however, also reflect to some degree inadequate control of public finances with a tendency to increase spending rather than improve services by greater efficiency. It is hard to find robust evidence about the optimal size of government and the impact on growth (EC, 2008), reflecting the difficulty of untangling the effects of size and other features of state intervention.

The composition of expenditure varies widely across euro area countries (Figure 4.9). Different types of expenditure can be more conducive to economic growth than others, although it is also possible to spend money badly on useful categories of spending. Investment in infrastructure and human capital, through education, should yield future returns. High unemployment rates and generous benefits are costly and essentially reflect the costs associated with poor labour market performance.

Figure 4.9. **Total general government expenditure by function**

In per cent of GDP, 2006

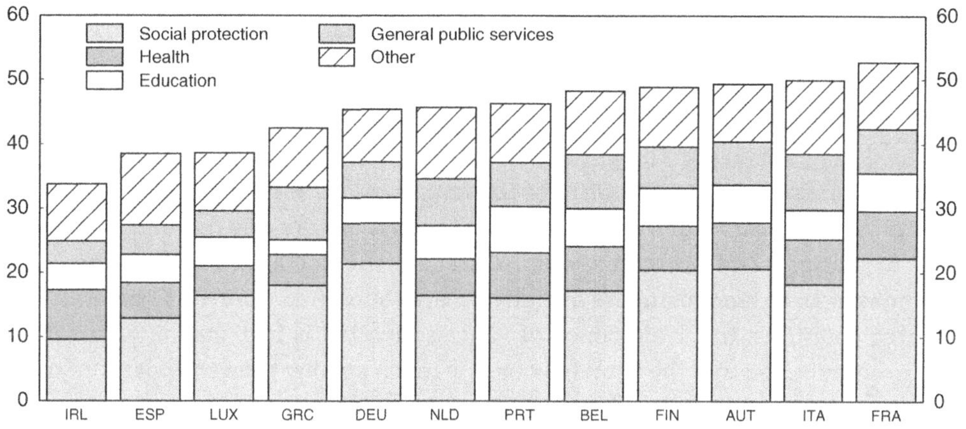

Source: OECD (2008), *National Accounts database*, November.

StatLink http://dx.doi.org/10.1787/520018525255

Infrastructure investment is a small component of overall government spending in euro area countries and is generally a much smaller share of output than in the 1960s and 1970s. The impact of infrastructure on growth is hard to evaluate, not least as the stock of infrastructure tends to rise as societies become richer. A recent review of the literature suggests that there is a positive effect but that this is weaker than early studies suggested and depends on the exact circumstances (Romp and de Haan, 2007). This is confirmed by preliminary empirical work by the OECD suggesting a positive impact in some countries and sectors, although weaker where there is already a high stock of public capital. However, it is not just the amount of spending on infrastructure that is important but how effectively it is designed and used. Public ownership can hinder the efficient use of infrastructure capital, and effective regulation of private sector infrastructure owners and measures such as congestion charges are useful ways of making the most of capital resources.

The efficiency of public spending also depends on the volume of output produced in each area for the amount of resources used as inputs. It is inherently difficult to evaluate the volume of outputs given that most government services are not traded in competitive markets and do not have an explicit price (Atkinson, 2005). For education, indicators of school performance suggest that it is possible to make robust inferences about *relative* productivity in different education systems based on data envelopment analysis (DEA) techniques although there is substantial uncertainty around the estimates (Sutherland *et al.*, 2007). On these measures, a number of euro area countries perform consistently poorly. Belgium, Greece, Italy and Spain could each raise their PISA scores by at least 10%, without increasing resources, if they were to move closer to the efficiency frontier (or they could achieve the same performance at substantially lower cost).[7] There is considerable scope to raise overall performance by bringing more schools towards best practice within their own countries. Greater decision-making autonomy at the school-level and benchmarking between schools is associated with higher levels of efficiency (Sutherland and Price, 2007). Regular monitoring of students tends to raise efficiency, while small school sizes and residence-based selection are linked to weaker efficiency. Increased flexibility and accountability could raise the graduation rates of universities substantially in a number of euro area countries and the absence of fees weakens incentives for institutions to be responsive to their students and for students to optimise their studies (Oliveira Martins *et al.*, 2007), in addition to raising the cost to the tax payer and contributing to underfunding of higher education. The analysis of the efficiency of health care spending is more difficult, in part because there is less agreement about appropriate measures of performance (Häkkinen and Joumard, 2007).

The design of taxation to raise a given level of revenue has an impact on growth and welfare (Johansson *et al.*, 2008). Taxing consumption has less of an effect on economic performance than personal income taxes, although these are less harmful than corporate taxes. The appropriate mix depends in part on the social preference for equity as consumption taxes tend to impose a relatively large burden on poorer households. In many euro area countries, the C-efficiency of value-added tax is low, meaning that there are many exemptions so that the actual tax base is much smaller than the potential tax base.[8] The low C-efficiency implies that there may be gains not only in terms of economic efficiency but also equality by broadening the tax base for VAT. Well-designed property taxes have the potential to raise revenue with a less distortionary impact on the economy even than consumption taxes. In many euro area countries, however, the design of property taxes is poor and the tax take is also low. There is therefore a strong case in these countries, both in terms of economic efficiency and avoiding financial instability, to reform these taxes.

The role of fiscal policy is particularly important given that many other policy settings in the euro area do not encourage strong economic performance (Chapter 1). In particular, product market regulation hinders competition in many countries and labour market regulation is tight (Figure 4.10). Furthermore, the combined impact of tax and benefit systems on labour can be detrimental to employment (Bassanini and Duval, 2006). High tax wedges can also raise unemployment where minimum labour costs are high by reducing the scope for shifting the burden onto labour. Hence, there is scope for well-designed tax and expenditure reforms to raise economic performance. The main recommendations on fiscal policy in this chapter are summarised in Box 4.3.

Figure 4.10. **Structural policies are less market-orientated**

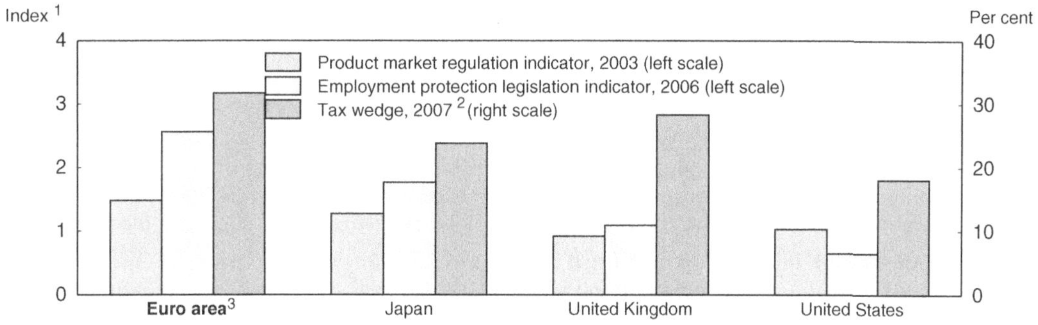

1. Scale from 0 to 6, from least to most restrictive.
2. Income tax plus employee and employer contributions less cash benefits as a per cent of labour costs for a one-earner married couple with two children at 100% of average earnings.
3. Unweighted average.

Source: OECD (2007), *Going for Growth, Economic Policy Reforms*; OECD (2008), *Taxing Wages 2006/2007*; Conway, P., V. Janod and G. Nicoletti (2005), "Product Market Regulation in OECD Countries: 1998 to 2003", *OECD Economics Department Working Papers*, No. 419, OECD, Paris.

StatLink http://dx.doi.org/10.1787/520022448454

Box 4.3. **Main recommendations on fiscal policy**

- The relatively large automatic stabilisers in the EU can help cushion the slowdown, while respecting the 3% of the GDP deficit threshold. In countries facing a more severe slowdown and where room for manoeuvre exists, temporary and targeted measures may be taken.
- Under the revised Pact, the application of the "exceptional and temporary factors" introduced by the revised SGP allowing small and temporary breaches of the 3% rule should be used sparingly, in order not to weaken its dissuasive effect.
- The assessment of structural fiscal balances and the underlying fiscal position should give more weight to information from a dis-aggregated analysis of revenues and to the variability of tax elasticities in order to obtain a clearer picture of the role of asset prices and other economic developments.
- The methodology for setting Medium Term Objectives (MTOs) under the Pact should take implicit liabilities related to ageing more rigorously into account and should allow better national ownership of MTOs. Consideration should also be given to more extensive pre-funding of the fiscal costs of ageing alongside pension and structural reforms.
- Greater progress should be made towards sustainable achievement of the MTOs with clearer and more objective assessment of when it is appropriate to make greater than the minimum required degree of progress.
- Efforts should be made to enhance the contribution of fiscal policy to raising living standards. Euro area countries could benefit from measures to obtain better value for money from education and health spending. A further shift in the composition of taxation should be considered, although this is a decision for individual countries. Strong fiscal governance frameworks could also contribute to ensuring sustainability of social spending and improve the efficiency of expenditure.

Notes

1. The measure can be adjusted in a discretionary way for any exceptional items that are not captured in net capital transfers.
2. Eurostat does not publish cross-country data on whether debt is at fixed or variable interest rates but any country with a high proportion of floating-rate debt may be similarly affected.
3. The new projections only update ageing expenditure in those countries with sizeable pension reforms. The estimates have also been extended to include net property income of the government, which is a fairly minor detail in almost all cases and small relative to the uncertainty surrounding such projections. The 2009 updates will be based on revised demographic projections.
4. "Exceptional circumstances" are defined as an unusual event outside the government's control which has a major impact on the fiscal balance or a severe economic downturn with either an annual fall in GDP or a cumulative shortfall in output over a prolonged period due to weak growth. The new grounds introduced by the revised Pact are: *i)* implementation of structural reform, *ii)* expenditure to foster innovation and R&D, *iii)* past fiscal consolidation during periods of strong economic growth, *iv)* the debt sustainability position, *v)* the quality of public finances, and *vi)* financial contributions to fostering international solidarity and achieving European Union goals.
5. See, for example, Box 7.1. "Tax breaks for housing and policy flip-flops" of OECD (2006b).
6. See Box 3.1, "How large is the welfare state?" of OECD (2008b).
7. Moving the efficiency level to at least the 95 percentile level. See Figure 12 of Sutherland *et al.* (2007).
8. C-efficiency is defined as the ratio of actual VAT revenue to consumption, divided by the standard VAT rate.

Bibliography

Anderson, B. and J. Minarik (2006), "Design Choices for Fiscal Policy Rules", *OECD Journal on Budgeting*, Volume 5, Number 4.

Arpaia, A. and A. Turrini (2008), "Government Expenditures and Economic Growth in the EU: Long-run Tendencies and Short-term Adjustment", *European Commission Economic Papers*, No. 300, February.

Atkinson, A. B. (2005), *The Atkinson Review: Final Report – Measurement of Government Output and Productivity for the National Accounts*, Palgrave MacMillan, London.

Bassanini, A. and R. Duval (2006), "Employment Patterns in OECD Countries: Reassessing the Role of Policies and Institutions", *OECD Social, Employment and Migration Working Papers*, No. 37, OECD, Paris.

Bouthevillain, C. *et al.*, (2001), "Cyclically Adjusted Budget Balances: an Alternative Approach", *ECB Working Paper Series*, No. 77, ECB, Frankfurt.

Briotti, M. G. (2005), "Economic Reactions to Public Finance Consolidation: a Survey of the Literature", *ECB Occasional Paper Series*, No. 38, ECB, Frankfurt.

Cimadomo, J. (2008), "Fiscal Policy in Real Time", *ECB Working Paper Series*, No. 919, Frankfurt.

Cournède, B. (2007), "The Political Economy of Delaying Fiscal Consolidation", *OECD Economics Department Working Papers*, No. 548, OECD, Paris.

Cournède, B. and F. Gonand (2006), "Restoring Fiscal Sustainability in the Euro Area: Raise Taxes or Curb Spending?", *OECD Economics Department Working Papers*, No. 520, OECD, Paris.

Curristine, T., Z. Lonti and I. Joumard (2007), "Improving Public Sector Efficiency: Challenges and Opportunities", *OECD Journal on Budgeting*, Volume 7, Issue 1.

EC (2006), "Public Finances in EMU 2006", *European Economy*, Vol. 2006, No. 3, Brussels.

EC (2008), "Public Finances in EMU 2008", *European Economy*, Vol. 2008, No. 4, Brussels.

Eurogroup (2007), Statement on Spring Orientation Debate on Budgetary Policies: Orientations for Fiscal Policies in Euro Area Member States, 20 April, Berlin. *www.gouvernement.lu/salle_presse/actualite/2007/04/20pm_krecke_berlin/MTBR_EG_conclusions-finalCLEAN.rtf*

Eurostat (2008), Taxation Trends in the European Union: Data for the EU Member States and Norway, Eurostat, Luxembourg.

Girouard, N. and C. André (2005), "Measuring Cyclically-adjusted Budget Balances for OECD Countries", *OECD Economics Department Working Papers*, No. 434, OECD, Paris.

Guichard, S. *et al.* (2007), "What Promotes Fiscal Consolidation: OECD Country Experiences", *OECD Economics Department Working Papers*, No. 535, OECD, Paris.

Häkkinen, U. and I. Joumard (2007), "Cross-country Analysis of Efficiency in OECD Health Care Sectors: Options for Research", *OECD Economics Department Working Papers*, No. 554, OECD, Paris.

Hauptmeier, S., M. Heipertz and L. Schuknecht (2006), "Expenditure Reform in Industrialised Countries: a Case Study Approach", *ECB Working Paper Series*, No. 634, May, ECB, Frankfurt.

Henrkisson, J. (2007), "Ten Lessons about Budget Consolidation", *Bruegel Essay and Lecture Series*, Brussels.

Hoeller, P., C. Giorno and C. de la Maisonneuve (2002), "Overheating in Small Euro Area Economies: Should Fiscal Policy React?", *OECD Economics Department Working Papers*, No. 323, OECD, Paris.

Hoeller, P. and C. Giorno (2006), "Nothing Ventured, Nothing Gained: the Long-Run Fiscal Reward of Structural Reforms", *OECD Economics Department Working Papers*, No. 493, OECD, Paris.

Honohan, P. and D. Klingebiel (2003), "The Fiscal Cost Implications of an Accommodating Approach to Banking Crises", *Journal of Banking and Finance*, No. 27.

Jamet, S. (2007), "Meeting the Challenges of Decentralisation in France", *OECD Economics Department Working Papers*, No. 571, OECD, Paris.

Johansson, Å. *et al.* (2008), "Taxation and Economic Growth", *OECD Economics Department Working Papers*, No. 620, OECD, Paris.

Joumard, I. *et al.* (2004), "Enhancing the Effectiveness of Public Spending: Experience in OECD Countries", *OECD Economics Department Working Papers*, No. 380, OECD, Paris.

Joumard, I. and C. André (2008), "Revenue Buoyancy and its Fiscal Policy Implications", *OECD Economics Department Working Papers*, No. 598, OECD, Paris.

Joumard, I. *et al.* (2008), "Accounting for One-Off Factors When Assessing Fiscal Positions: Proposals for a Revised Methodology", *OECD Economics Department Working Papers*, No. 642, OECD, Paris.

Koen, V. and P. van den Noord (2005), "Fiscal Gimmickry in Europe: One-off Measures and Creative Accounting", *OECD Economics Department Working Papers*, No. 417, OECD, Paris.

Koske, I. and N. Pain (2008), "The Usefulness of Output Gaps for Policy Analysis", *OECD Economics Department Working Papers*, No. 621, OECD, Paris.

Laeven, L. and F. Valencia (2008), "Systemic Banking Crises: A New Database", *IMF Papers*, No. 224, February.

Mandl, U., A. Dierx and F. Ilzkovitz (2008), "The Effectiveness and Efficiency of Public Spending", *European Commission Economic Papers*, No. 301, February.

Morris, R., H. Ongena and L. Schuknecht (2006), "The Reform and Implementation of the Stability and Growth Pact", *ECB Occasional Paper Series*, No. 47, June, Frankfurt.

Morris, R. and L. Schuknecht (2007), "Structural Balances and Revenue Windfalls: The Role of Asset Prices Revisited", *ECB Working Paper*, No. 737, ECB, Frankfurt.

van den Noord, P. (2005), "Tax Incentives and House Price Volatility in the Euro Area: Theory and Evidence", *Économie Internationale*, No. 101, Issue 1.

OECD (2006a), "Projecting OECD Health and Long-term Care Expenditures: What Are the Main Drivers?", *OECD Economics Department Working Papers*, No. 477, OECD, Paris.

OECD (2006b), *OECD Economic Surveys: Ireland*, OECD, Paris.

OECD (2007), *OECDEconomic Surveys: Euro Area*, OECD, Paris.

OECD (2008a), *Financial Market Trends*, No. 94, Volume 2008/1, OECD, Paris.

OECD (2008b), *OECD Economic Surveys: Finland*, OECD, Paris.

Oliveira Martins, J. *et al.* (2007), "The Policy Determinants of Investment in Tertiary Education", *OECD Economics Department Working Papers*, No. 576, OECD, Paris.

Romp, W. and J. de Haan (2007), "Public Capital and Economic Growth: A Critical Survey", *Perspektiven der Wirtschaftspolitik*, 2007:8 (Special Issue).

Schuknecht, L. and V. Tanzi (2005), "Reforming Public Expenditure in Industrialised Countries: Are There Trade-Offs?", *ECB Working Paper Series*, No. 435, ECB, Frankfurt.

Sutherland, D. and R. Price (2007), "Linkages between Performance and Institutions in the Primary and Secondary Education Sector", *OECD Economics Department Working Papers*, No. 558, OECD, Paris.

Sutherland, D. *et al.* (2007), "Performance Indicators for Spending Efficiency in Primary and Secondary Education", *OECD Economics Department Working Papers*, No. 546, OECD, Paris.

Sutherland, D., R. Price and F. Gonand (2008), "Public Spending Efficiency in the Primary and Secondary Education Sector", *OECD Economic Studies*, forthcoming, OECD, Paris.

ISBN 978-92-64-04824-9
OECD Economic Surveys: Euro Area

Acronyms and abbreviations

BCBS	Basel Committee on Banking Supervision
BIS	Bank for International Settlements
BLS	Bureau of Labour Statistics
BSC	Banking Supervision Committee
CDO	Collateralised debt obligations
CEBS	Committee of European Banking Supervisors
CEIOPS	Committee of European Insurance and Occupational Pensions Supervisors
CESR	Committee of European Securities Regulators
CPI	Consumer price index
CRA	Credit rating agencies
CRD	Capital Requirements Directive
DEA	Data Envelopment Analysis
DGS	Deposit guarantee scheme
EBC	European Banking Committee
ECB	European Central Bank
EDP	Excessive Deficit Procedure
EFC	Economic and Financial Committee
EIOPC	European Insurance and Operational Pensions Committee
ELA	Emergency liquidity assistance
EMU	Economic and Monetary Union
ESC	European Securities Committee
ESCB	European System of Central Banks
FCD	Financial Conglomerates Directive
FSAP	Financial Services Action Plan
FSC	Financial Services Committee
FSF	Financial Stability Forum
FST	Financial Stability Table
GDP	Gross Domestic Product
IASB	International Accounting Standards Board
IOSCO	International Organisation of Securities Commissions
IFRS	International Financial Reporting Standards
IMF	International Monetary Fund
LCFI	Large, cross-border financial institutions
MiFID	Markets in Financial Instruments Directive
MFI	Monetary and Financial Institutions
MPTN	Monetary Policy Transmission Network
MTF	Multilateral Trade Facilities
MTO	Medium-term objective

NCB	National Central Bank
PRA	Purchase and resale agreement
RMSE	Root mean square of errors
SEPA	Single European Payments Area
SGP	Stability and Growth Pact
UCITS	Undertaking for Collective Investment in Transferable Securities

OECD ECONOMIC SURVEYS: EURO AREA – ISBN 978-92-64-04824-9 – © OECD 2

OECD PUBLISHING, 2, rue André-Pascal, 75775 PARIS CEDEX 16
PRINTED IN FRANCE
(10 2009 01 1 P) ISBN 978-92-64-04824-9 – No. 56519 2009

Made in the USA
Las Vegas, NV
13 October 2024

96763478R00083